SEX AND SENSIBILITY

SEX AND SENSIBILITY

Stories of a Lesbian Generation

ARLENE STEIN

UNIVERSITY OF CALIFORNIA PRESS
BERKELEY   LOS ANGELES   LONDON

University of California Press
Berkeley and Los Angeles, California

University of California Press, Ltd.
London, England

© 1997 by The Regents of the University of California

Library of Congress Cataloging-in-Publication Data

Stein, Arlene.
  Sex and Sensibility : stories of a lesbian generation / Arlene
Stein.
      p.   cm.
  Includes bibliographical references and index.
  ISBN 0-520-20257-0 (alk. paper).—ISBN 0-520-20674-6 (pbk. :
alk. paper)
      1. Lesbianism.   2. Lesbians.   3. Identity (Psychology)   4. Lesbian
feminism.   I. Title.
HQ75.5 .S75   1997
306.76'63—dc20   96-12500
                                                                        CIP

Printed in the United States of America

08   07   06   05   04   03   02   01
9   8   7   6   5   4   3

The paper used in this publication meets the minimum requirements of
ANSI/NISO Z39.48-1992 (R 1997) (*Permanence of Paper*). ∞

For my mother, and in memory of my father

Contents

Acknowledgments

The roots of this book lie in the lesbian/gay community of San Francisco, as well as in the emerging international community of lesbian/gay scholars. As I began the research, I was fortunate to be associated with *Out/Look* magazine and the San Francisco Gay and Lesbian History Project, which provided a lively forum for discussing lesbian/gay history and sexual politics.

Nancy Chodorow encouraged me to pursue a study of lesbian identities, helped me to hear women's voices more clearly, and provided incisive feedback along the way. Her intellectual challenges strengthened this project in numerous ways. Anita Garey and Karla Hackstaff provided valuable support and direction during the writing process. Steve Epstein helped clarify my thoughts about many things.

The Lesbian Herstory Archives in New York and the archives of the Gay and Lesbian Historical Society of Northern California gave me access to many original source materials. At various points, Robert Bellah, E. G. Crichton, Josh Gamson, Deborah Gerson, Alexis Jetter, Miriam Johnson, Liz Kotz, Susan Krieger, Louise Lamphere, Kristin Luker, Ruth Mahaney, Annelise Orleck, Rachel Pfeffer, Steven Seidman, Terry Strathman, and Carla Trujillo offered contacts, helpful suggestions, or critical comments that proved valuable. Vera Whisman shared with me her related work in progress. Audiences at the University of California at Santa Cruz, at Dartmouth College, at lesbian/gay/bisexual studies conferences at Rutgers University, and at the University of Amsterdam challenged me to rethink parts of my analysis.

Jeffrey Escoffier, who first introduced me to the study of sexual identities in a course he taught at Berkeley, read and commented on the manuscript as it was nearing completion, as did Deborah Gerson, Sabine Hark, Elizabeth Lapovsky Kennedy, Ellen Lewin, and Ann Weinstone. Naomi Schneider, Will Murphy, and Nina D'Andrade at the University of California Press ably guided me through the process of preparing the manuscript for publication. I am indebted to them all.

The Woodrow Wilson Foundation provided initial financial support for my research, as did a fellowship at the Doreen B. Townsend Center for the Humanities at the University of California, Berkeley. For nearly two years, the Department of Sociology at the University of Essex, England, provided good company and challenging students. At Essex I was fortunate to have worked with and alongside Ken Plummer and Mary McIntosh, whose pioneering work on the sociology of homosexuality inspired my own modest contribution. During the last two years, the Department of Sociology at the University of Oregon has been a stimulating home. A faculty research grant from the University of Oregon aided the completion of this manuscript.

Nancy Solomon kept a roof over my head and food on my plate, gave me periodic pep talks, provided a sounding board for my ideas, and read and commented on the manuscript in its final stages. Without her, this book would never have seen the light of day.

Finally, I am very grateful to the women whose voices appear in these pages, who gave me their time for little in return. I hope that I have done justice to their stories.

An earlier version of the chapter "Difference, Desire, and the Self: Three Stories," was published in *Women Creating Lives: Identities, Resilience, and Resistance,* ed. Carol Franz and Abigail Stewart (Boulder: Westview, 1994). Portions of this book also previously appeared in "Sisters and Queers: The Decentering of Lesbian Feminism," *Socialist Review* 22, no. 1 (1992): 33–55.

Introduction

Questions of Identity

These are the stories of women who imagined new forms of gender and sexuality that centered on women—and how their imaginations sometimes ran ahead of their capacities to change themselves and their world. Members of the postwar baby boom generation, some seventy-five million strong, lived their formative years during a period of tremendous change. The civil rights, anti–Vietnam War, and feminist movements, events that were radically at odds with their childhood and early adolescent experience during the staid and settled 1950s, challenged many of their assumptions about how America was organized.

Through their activities in the feminist movement, some members of this generational cohort became, in the early 1970s, among the first to boldly declare themselves lesbian. They marched in the streets, encouraging others to come out and join them and affirming that which had been forbidden. They created a culture that proclaimed lesbianism as a viable sexual and lifestyle choice. They promised to transform identities and give women a new sense of self. Lesbian feminism, and the social and cultural challenges it posed, irrevocably changed the American sexual landscape.

Today, twenty-five years later, the legacy of this period and of the generation that shaped it most, the baby boomers, has become a highly contested subject. As the vision of a Lesbian Nation that would stand apart from the dominant culture, a haven in a heartless (male and heterosexual) world, recedes, the collective memory of lesbian feminism has become a symbolic battleground.

On one side are those who wish to complete the unfinished lesbian feminist project. "We used to talk a lot about lesbianism as a political movement," philosopher Janice Raymond lamented, "back in the days when lesbianism and feminism went together, and one heard the phrase 'lesbian feminism.' Today we hear more about lesbian sadomasochism, lesbians having babies, and everything lesbians need to know about sex."[1] She and others wish to reinvigorate a collective sense of lesbian selfhood, which they view as a bulwark against male domination and compulsory heterosexuality. Strong believers in a politics of identity organized around a collective definition of lesbianism, they consider the current diversification and fragmentation of lesbian communities to be frightening developments, fostering lesbian invisibility and silence and threatening individual selfhood.

On the opposing side are those who cast lesbian feminists and the "lesbian community" as the repressive mother who stands in the way of sexual pleasure and imposes uniformity on the diversity of desires, identities, and practices. As one woman, writing to the editor of a lesbian/gay journal, suggests: "Lesbians are doing and talking about things we have never done or talked about before . . . that the self-righteous atmosphere of political correctitude and erotophobia we called lesbian-feminism kept us from uttering."[2] She suggests that the label *lesbian* is a fiction, a means of social control that has been foisted upon certain women by the medical establishment, and one that many lesbians, particularly lesbian feminists, have accepted unquestioningly. In response, she and others call into question all settled notions of homosexuality, emphasizing the differences, discontinuities, and flux within the group of women who call themselves "lesbian."

At the risk of oversimplification, one might see the contemporary clash over the legacy of lesbian feminism as a conflict between two different understandings of the political uses of sexual identity. There are those who understand lesbianism to be a settled, stable source of identification and a base for political action against male domination and compulsory heterosexuality. They see "lesbians" as roughly analogous to an ethnic group, who share a collective "one true self," a bounded group with a common history that is distinct from the dominant patriarchal, heterosexual society. Others, however, who understand sexuality as inherently unsettled and ambiguous, see efforts to form a collective sexual identity as fraught with potential contradictions. Rather than embrace marginalized identities such as "lesbian," they contend that the true radical act is to refuse such identity; that the dichotomous categories homosexual/heterosexual are inherently limiting; and that the relationship among sexuality, identity, and politics is necessarily inconsistent, transient, and shifting.

Born at the tail end of the baby boom, I came of age in the early 1980s, ten years after the second wave of feminism began. Partly as a consequence, I have one foot planted in the collectivist 1970s and the other in the 1980s, when feminist efforts came under growing scrutiny from "sex radicals," women of color, and others who posed a powerful critique of the belief that women constitute a cohesive collectivity. Similarly, I often find myself torn between the conviction that the development of lesbian culture and identity is of utmost importance and the fear that categorization can easily become a prison, between the pressures to make my sexuality a primary identity that would always set me apart and the hope that at some point it may not be so significant.

My previous writings on sexual politics reflect this ambivalence. Through my work as an editor of the short-lived but influential lesbian/gay journal *Out/Look,* I took part in a public discussion about lesbian/gay culture, politics, and sexuality; I subsequently edited an anthology called *Sisters, Sexperts, Queers: Beyond the Lesbian Nation.* I wanted to provide a forum for writing on lesbian culture and politics that reflected the rapidly changing lesbian world of San Francisco in the 1980s and 1990s, as well as the lively debates and struggles over sex, gender, race, culture, and collective definitions of lesbianism that those developments generated.

Grounding that book was a set of assumptions, sometimes but not always explicit, about the legacy of lesbian feminism and the generation of women who constituted that diffuse movement and its culture. Many lesbian feminists, it seemed to me, had become overly preoccupied with policing the borders of lesbian communities, minimizing the messiness of difference: different desires, different sensibilities, different self-conceptions. They had tried to create a normative lesbianism that only the most dedicated few could or would live up to. As Barbara Ehrenreich pointed out, while feminists spoke of "universal sisterhood," they were often "horrified by women who wear spiked heels and call themselves girls."[3]

In the interest of building a broader, more diverse lesbian culture, the time seemed ripe to question those borders and, as the subtitle of my book suggested, go "beyond the Lesbian Nation." I was not the only one to make these sorts of arguments. In the 1980s, a series of books appeared that were highly critical of different elements of lesbian feminist theory and practice.[4] Certainly many of the complaints were well-founded. But in retrospect, my book, among others, appears overly critical of lesbian feminists' excesses and insufficiently appreciative of some of their contributions. It also tended to homogenize the legacy of lesbian feminism, which was far from seamless and monolithic. In this book, I delve in a more systematic way into the origins and legacy of lesbian feminism, focusing upon the generation of women who constructed it and were changed by it.

Studying Identities

Identity has become a much-used word.[5] We employ it to make sense of the place of the individual in the modern (and late modern) world. We speak of "finding ourselves," "healing ourselves," "constructing identities," and so forth. The term captures the American "dilemma of self," for it describes and seems to explain the contradictions of living in a society that appears to be in constant change. We live in a culture that fosters both commitment and mobility, in which the relationship of the individual to her world is rendered problematic, in which the social world "requires that we bargain with life for our identities" since there are "few bases for external imposition of continuities."[6] The dilemmas of contemporary American life—of finding a sense of belonging and membership in a community that is continually changing, of maintaining stability amid rapid social transformation—are the dilemmas of the late modern world.

For many of us living in the affluent West today, self-identity is a reflexive project, an achievement rather than a given. As Anthony

Giddens suggests, most aspects of social activity undergo chronic re-
vision in light of new information or knowledge. All existence is contingent and is a problem, a project to be worked on.[7] Witness the
expanding role of therapeutic culture in the United States, in the
form of self-help groups, psychological literature, and the prolifera-
tion of television talk shows that probe the intimacies of private life.

While questions of identity—and the search for self, belonging,
and meaning that they provoke—are not limited to lesbians and gay
men, as a group we seem to be acutely aware of their existence and
heavily invested in debating their consequences. Sexual "minority"
communities are today among the most self-conscious and well-organized groups in America, having mobilized in opposition to one of
the most powerful and persistent forms of stigma in modern Western
cultures. As outsiders in many respects, we tend to be highly self-
reflexive about our status in society and about society's foibles. Perhaps nowhere is this more evident than among the young women
who came of age in the 1970s, who had been touched by the feminist
and lesbian movements. Often highly analytical, they took critiques
of gender and sexuality very seriously. They believed that they could
resocialize themselves to love women and, by implication, love themselves.

The generation of women who had come out as lesbians in the
context of feminism turned the dominant narrative of sexual development on its head, contending that progress from heterosexuality to
homosexuality is healthy and that lesbianism is a mature developmental achievement. Some went so far as to suggest that any woman
was a potential lesbian—she simply had to declare herself one and
go through the process of "coming out." These were radical, even
revolutionary, ideas, ideas that changed numerous lives. Twenty years
later, and in a very different cultural context, what had become of
these women and their ideas? Was the lesbian feminist "experiment"
a success? These were the broad questions that initially motivated
my interest in this project.

In 1990 I interviewed forty-one lesbian-identified women and
asked them about their lives and loves. I chose thirty-one subjects
who were born between the years 1945 and 1961, during the postwar baby boom, from a range of different class, racial, and ethnic

backgrounds. They came to identify as lesbians between the late 1960s and the late 1970s, when definitions of gender and sexuality were being reshaped by the feminist and gay liberation movements. At the time of the interviews, their mean age was forty-two. For comparative purposes I also interviewed ten women from a later cohort, who were born between 1961 and 1971 and were between the ages of nineteen and twenty-nine when interviewed. The study is based largely upon this interview data.

I decided to interview only women who assumed the label "lesbian" (a much smaller grouping than the universe of women who have homosexual desires or who engage in homosexual activity) and purposely excluded women who engaged in lesbian practices without embracing a lesbian identity. Having lived in the San Francisco Bay Area for over ten years, I found most of my interviewees by using a snowball method of sampling; I began with a series of personal contacts, using it to branch out to networks previously unfamiliar to me. Rather than focus on the experiences of the most self-conscious activists, I sought out women who were not necessarily "joiners" in a political sense—though in the context of a moment in which politics was often expressed through the routines of daily life, it is difficult to draw clear distinctions between activist and nonactivist women. Many—but certainly not all—of the women of the baby boom are feminists. Likewise, many—but not all—feminists are baby boomers.

I would not claim that my sample is representative of lesbians, or even of lesbians of a particular age cohort. Representative samples of stigmatized populations are impossible to obtain; this is perhaps doubly true for groups such as lesbians whose statistical contours are unclear and who do not agree among themselves on the criteria for membership.[8] Like other studies of lesbians, which have tended to focus on major urban areas, mine favors women for whom sexual identity is highly salient, who are more likely to be white, middle class, and well educated. It underrepresents women of color and working-class women, whose numbers in the population we call "lesbian" are probably much more numerous than anyone has yet documented in this country, as well as others for whom lesbianism is less salient. Yet my interview sample is more diverse than that of other comparable studies. Twenty percent of my interviewees consider themselves to be people of color and 40 percent come from working-class backgrounds. I was interested in these categories to the extent that they were meaningful to the individuals I spoke with. To treat each individual as a representative of her race, for example, would gloss over the differences of class, age, religion, and other variables that crosscut race and ethnicity.[9]

Through my interviews I sought to understand how individual women who share a marginalized identity make sense of their lives in a particular historical context. Toward this end, I interviewed two groups of women, belonging to two different "gay generations." Some have suggested that membership in a gay generation is determined by when one comes out, or identifies as lesbian or gay.[10] Yet early homosexual desires sometimes create an inchoate sense of lesbian identity even if someone does not consciously and publicly identify as lesbian until later in life. Moreover, coming out is often a lifelong process. Allowing both for this process and for the wide range of ages at which people come out, I designated my cohorts by year of birth.

I gathered what might be called *self stories*. A self story is literally a story of and about the self in relation to an experience, in this case the development of a lesbian identity, that positions the self of the teller centrally in the narrative that is given. Although I probed to gain a sense of the "whole" person, my questions were focused—for reasons of time as well as interest—upon the aspect of identity that hinged upon lesbianism.[11] I allowed my interviewees to define what they saw as the salient issues concerning lesbian identity.

The interviews I conducted, which lasted from ninety minutes to three and a half hours each, were open-ended and focused mainly upon the respondent's account of the formation of her sexual identity. Typically, I began by asking how individuals describe their sexual identity; I then probed to obtain an understanding of the meaning(s) this held for her. My interviews draw upon retrospective accounts, so we cannot be certain that interviewees describe how they really felt at the time. When people talk about their lives, they actively frame their experience to suit their own needs, filtering their descriptions of actual events and behaviors through narrative devices, such as the "coming out" story. However, I assumed that interviewees' accounts reflect how they in fact feel and felt.

I wanted my subjects to talk spontaneously and freely, revealing the flux and contradictions of everyday subjective reality, pursuing other areas that they deemed central or important—such as family, career, and health considerations—as they came up. Interested in how women ordered their subjective reality—what defining events, contexts, or ideas gave symbolic order to their life transitions—I gave them a chance to frame their stories as they wished. But I also probed and asked questions: to find out how women identified themselves; to determine the chronology of their identities; to learn the meanings of lesbianism; to comprehend the ways in which an individual affiliated with the social category "lesbian" and with the community; to understand the conditions, circumstances, and experiences that led to adoption of a lesbian identity; and to note changes in that experience and its meaning over time. I followed, very roughly, the interview schedule given at the end of the appendix, deleting questions that seemed inappropriate and adding others as they seemed important. After transcribing the interviews, I coded them, noting recurrent themes that seemed to crop up repeatedly. I then analyzed the interview data, looking for similarities and differences among the members of the baby boom cohort. I followed the same procedure for analyzing the interviews of the "post–baby boom" cohort. The interviewees are named in these pages by pseudonyms and are further described in the appendix.

To understand the texture of individual lives, I needed to obtain biographical information. But I also wanted to situate these self narratives in history. Therefore I needed to understand the context from which they emerged. To fully grasp a life, and the personal experiences and self stories that represent and shape that life, one must penetrate and comprehend the larger structures that provide the languages, emotions, ideologies, taken-for-granted understandings, and shared experiences from which the stories flow. "No self or personal experience story is ever an individual production," Norman Denzin notes. "It derives from larger group, cultural, ideological, and historical contexts."[12] Coming out stories, for example, have a form that

reflects particular historical and cultural understandings about lesbianism (and by implication about male homosexuality and sexuality in
general) much more than they reveal any "natural" regularities in
psychological development.

To achieve this larger view, I tracked several significant lesbian
feminist publications, focusing particularly on two from 1970 to 1984:
Lesbian Tide, an outgrowth of the Los Angeles chapter of the Daughter of Bilitis, the first national lesbian organization; and *Lesbian Connection,* published in East Lansing, Michigan, a grassroots journal
that is composed entirely of readers' letters and is the longest continuously running lesbian periodical in existence today. I also scanned
back issues of *The Ladder,* the original journal of the Daughters of
Bilitis, and a number of local lesbian publications, including *Lavender Woman* (Chicago), *Lesbian Voices* (San Jose, California), and *The
Leaping Lesbian* (Ann Arbor, Michigan). In reading these journals,
I paid particular attention to debates about the meaning of lesbian
identity and to shifts in the definition of lesbianism over time. While
the relationship among texts, the ideologies they embody, and lived
experience is complex, this archival material permitted me to situate
my informants' lives more concretely in historical context.

Culture, History, Generation

The questions of identity formation and cultural change that frame
this book could only be posed in an era when gender and sexuality
have increasingly become regarded as "social constructions." The traditional, and still dominant, "essentialist" position views sex as an
overpowering, instinctual drive, a "basic biological mandate" that
must be kept in check by society.[13] Proponents of "essentialism"
speak of "discovering" or "denying" one's "true sexuality"; in their
view, someone "is a homosexual." For example, a recent issue of
Newsweek proclaims, "Science and psychiatry are struggling to make
sense of new research that suggests that homosexuality may be a
matter of genetics, not parenting." Homosexuality, in this perspective, requires an explanation, a cause.[14]

Essentialist research on homosexuality began in the nineteenth
century, as early sexologists attempted to find, describe, and classify

"the homosexual." Researchers believed that homosexual preference was the surface manifestation of an underlying homosexual orientation, that homosexuality was an essence, a fixed characteristic that determines emotions, desires, behaviors—whether the individual is conscious of "being homosexual" or not. The earliest sociological work influenced by this perspective tried to uncover the universal underlying properties of homosexual experience. From the 1960s onward, investigations extended to every facet of lesbian and gay life: bars, communities, individual identities, and the like. An extensive literature focused upon the process of "coming out," documenting in fine detail the highly patterned and supposedly stable sequence of stages in which individuals come to identify with social sexual categories.[15]

While building a useful body of empirical literature that documents diverse aspects of lesbian/gay experience, research deriving from this paradigm has tended to downplay the differences between lesbians and gay men, subsuming the former under the latter. It has also generally not reflected on the character of sexuality as a social category. For example, studies of sexual identity formation have tended to describe the process of "coming out" or homosexual identity formation as uniform, ahistorical, and stage driven. They tend to obscure the extent to which this model may have helped to construct the behaviors that it has purported to describe.

In response to the weaknesses of this earlier sociological approach, a strand of sociological studies began to problematize the categories "homosexual" and "lesbian." This body of work, which is loosely called "social constructionism," describes the intersections between lesbian/gay identity and experience and other social or cultural domains, emphasizing the shifting, contingent character of sexualities. It is rooted in Sigmund Freud's and in Albert Kinsey's insights into the variability of sexual behavior. Social constructionists point out that while sexuality may be grounded in biological drives, these drives are extremely plastic. Humans are driven by their biological constitution to seek sexual release and food, but their "biological constitution does not tell [them] where they should seek sexual release and what they should eat."[16] As anthropological and historical evidence shows, individuals' experiences vary widely, and they construct different types of lesbian/gay identities depending upon the particular cultural context of their coming out. These types change over time, since individuals construct identities in relation to conceptions of homosexuality that are historically contingent.[17]

In the 1950s, Alfred Kinsey and his associates conducted a series of surveys of the sexual behavior of Americans, examining such activities as masturbation, homosexuality, and premarital sex. Their research revealed that there is a much greater incidence of homosexual activity (particularly among men) than was popularly believed to exist. Acknowledging an enormous diversity of behavior within the United States that is at odds with the accepted social norm of procreative, heterosexual intercourse, Kinsey placed homosexuality and heterosexuality on a continuum.[18] Kinsey came to question whether individuals should be classified as heterosexual or homosexual; too many people showed a range of behaviors and desires for such a rigid categorization to be accurate. Behaviors, not persons, are homosexual.

Researchers subsequent to the original Kinsey group have continued to challenge the view that homosexuals constitute a uniform category. In an important 1968 essay, Mary McIntosh shifted attention away from the "homosexual condition," looking instead at the functions of the "homosexual role." She showed how the notion of a group called "homosexuals" acts as an instrument of social control, a boundary device separating the pure from the impure. Labeling homosexuality at once exaggerates the differences between gay and straight people and minimizes the diversity that exists within both groups.[19] The boundaries between the homosexual and heterosexual worlds are variable, but by stigmatizing and labeling certain individuals as "homosexual," dominant groups keep the homosexual population small.

The notion of homosexuality as a pathological condition found in a small number of individuals flew in the face of newly emerging evidence that same-sex interests exist in many people and that gay people show more commonality with than difference from heterosexuals.[20] These and other studies lent support to the view that "homosexuality"

is a socially constructed term with diverse meanings. Historically, for
example, there have always been women who have had sexual or emotional relationships with other women but who have not assumed the
label "lesbian." There have also been women whose actual sexual desires and practices don't fit the common social definition of lesbian—
women, for example, who identify as lesbian but who are bisexual (in
orientation, practice, or both), or married, or asexual; or women who
engage in homoerotic activity but who do not identify as lesbian.[21]

In the fertile environment of the feminist and the gay and lesbian
movements in the late 1970s and 1980s, sociologists documented
how lesbianism is socially constructed and malleable; sexual identities
do not simply spring forth from individuals but are formed in relationships, in community, in culture. Deborah Wolf's ethnography of
lesbian feminists in San Francisco, *The Lesbian Community* (1980),
described how this oppositional community was organized. Susan
Krieger's *Mirror Dance* (1983) utilized an object relations psychoanalysis perspective to analyze "the dilemmas of identity" of a lesbian
feminist community in the Midwest. And Barbara Ponse's ethnography of a southern lesbian community, *Identities in the Lesbian World*
(1978), provided a pathbreaking account of how lesbians negotiate a
sense of identity amid stigma.[22]

These and other studies marked a shift, in Krieger's words, from
"thinking about lesbianism in terms of deviance, narrowness, simple
causation, isolated occurrence, and fixed nature to thinking of it in
terms of normality, diversity, multiple influence, social context,
choice, and change."[23] The old question was "Who or what are homosexuals and how do they get that way?" This gave way to "How
does the state of being a person who self-identifies as homosexual
come about?"[24] In this context, lesbianism ceased to be a sexual or
social disease and became "a lifestyle choice linked with a sense of
personal identity,"[25] a product of multiple influences rather than a
single cause. Explanations of the "causes" of homosexuality ceased to
dominate the discussion, replaced by studies of behaviors and perceptions of experience that focused less on how lesbians differ from
the norm than on how they are similar to other women.

By the 1970s, lesbianism was viewed as a matter of total personal identity rather than as primarily a *sexual* condition; it was regarded as subject to choice and changeable in definition rather than as a given. Instead of seeing lesbian communities as closed or bounded systems, sociologists came to describe the intersections between lesbian/gay experience and other social and cultural domains. An extraordinary outpouring of studies of lesbian/gay history traced the growth and formation of lesbian and gay communities, explored the emergence of movements for gay self-determination,[26] and made important contributions to understanding the development of a distinctive lesbian identity and culture in the United States. Rather than depicting homosexuality as an unchanging, ahistorical essence, these studies have illustrated how desires and identities are reconfigured in particular ways at particular historical moments. As the historian Jonathan Katz has observed, "Homosexuality is situational, influenced and given meaning by its location in time and social space."[27]

Indeed, the lesbian/feminist culture that emerged in the 1970s, much like lesbian cultures that had existed before it, was the product of a particular historical moment. The 1960s and early 1970s presented in many respects a turning point in American history. In the wake of the Vietnam War and the intensified racial conflict that accompanied the civil rights movement, workers' struggles, which had largely been concerned with wresting material concessions from their employers, were on the wane. "Identity politics" was on the rise, giving birth to social movements such as feminism and black power. A huge cohort of young people, products of the postwar baby boom, was creating a distinctive culture that embodied antiestablishment values, fashioning itself against its parents' generation and against authority figures of all sorts.

Women coming of age at that time were shaped by these historical currents. Many of them became involved in or influenced by what became known as "radical feminism." As they fashioned a common conception of themselves as feminists, they shared a crucial experience that shaped their consciousness and their newly developing identity.[28] Of this larger group of feminist women, some became lesbians. In the context of radical feminist ideology, lesbianism became a political stance, a challenge to patriarchal domination.[29]

This generation of lesbians was in many respects very different from the one that preceded it. Lesbians now in their fifties and older, who came out during the period roughly from World War II to 1969, the year of the Stonewall riot in New York, were typically brought into a homosexual life strongly influenced by the events of the war, when gay subcultures developed in major cities in the United States. Members of this cohort experienced their homosexuality in largely negative terms; at the least, they were forced to live a double life, remaining closeted to avoid harassment, legal sanctions, and violence. In contrast, the baby boomers who succeeded them came out in great numbers as part of the activism of the "sexual revolution," the Gay Liberation Front, and radical feminism. The vast majority of women who actively participated in or who were influenced by lesbian feminism were members of the postwar cohort.

Not all lesbians of this generation became political activists, of course. Most preferred to live their lives quietly rather than to take boldly to the streets. Yet it was difficult to be a lesbian in the 1970s, particularly in a major American city, and not be touched by feminist ideas. At a time when politics was expressed through the routines of daily life, through the creation of a culture and collective identity, clear distinctions between activist and nonactivist women blurred. One might say that women of the baby boom constitute what Karl Mannheim calls a "political generation."[30] They shared formative experiences and, as a result, hold a common interpretive framework shaped by those circumstances. More than simply an age group, members of a political generation are bound together by a common set of beliefs or worldview.

Feminist lesbians created a "collective identity," a shared definition of themselves that emphasized members' common interests, experiences, and solidarity. They adopted labels for themselves, developed new interpretive frameworks, drew lines that separated insiders and outsiders, and redefined the ways their members saw the world. They shared a belief in the value of solidarity and a commitment to building a common culture that would resist male domination. In terms of the history of lesbian life in this country, lesbians of the baby boom were a "decisive generation."[31]

Identity and Difference

Inspired and influenced by feminism and gay liberation, the first wave of constructionist studies of lesbianism, published primarily in the 1970s and early 1980s, emphasized the common experiences of coming out, of building a subculture based upon gender separatism, and of developing a positive sense of identity to counter stigma. They analyzed the process of individual identity formation in relation to the development of a lesbian culture and community. But in the late 1980s, when I first encountered them, these studies seemed somewhat dated. They told the story of an earlier moment in history, a moment when the feminist movement had given rise to an extraordinary collectivization of lesbian identity—hence their uncritical and singular use of the terms women's *community,* lesbian *culture,* and so forth.

The lesbian feminist and gay liberation movements had fundamentally altered the texture of homosexual life in this country, generating the most open, vibrant, and visible lesbian culture that had ever existed. But in the 1980s and 1990s, the vision of collective identity embodied by the Lesbian Nation came under increasing scrutiny. In the wake of what came to be known as the feminist "sex wars," the critiques of the false universalism of the women's movement lodged by women of color, and the rise of the "lipstick lesbian," it became more and more difficult to speak of one "lesbian community," one "lesbian world," and indeed one "feminism."

History is much less linear, much more complex than the popular narrative of gay liberation suggests. There is no single story of lesbian life: there are many stories, many simultaneous and overlapping "conversations."[32] Stories of personal change often mirror collective identity formation and cultural transformation, but they are not one and the same. Social movements and cultural change operate at the level of concrete, observable phenomena, bringing individuals together in countless daily actions and interactions. But they also operate in more subtle ways, as people bring to their interactions a sense of self that is already partially formed. While we are shaped by our historical context, and by the sense of possibilities we inherit, individuals choose from, react to, ignore, interpret, and modify culture. They often experience themselves in opposition to the collective conceptions that groups fashion for themselves.

Acknowledging this, contemporary analysts of lesbian identity are less likely to understand lesbianism as a totalizing, "master" identity that overshadows other group affiliations. They are more likely than their predecessors to consider the enduring impact of racial, ethnic, class, gender, and other differences and to examine the "multiplicity" of identities.[33] The picture that is emerging from this "second wave" of constructionist studies of lesbianism is that there is no singular "lesbianism" or "homosexuality." Sexuality is a complex and dynamic phenomenon: there are many lesbianisms and many homosexualities, just as there are many heterosexualities. However, to say that sexual definitions and concepts are variable is not to say that they can vary infinitely. The salience of particular differences is itself dependent on circumstance and context.

Two axes of difference among women have been relatively unexplored: gender and sexual orientation. Lesbians are women, and they possess a homosexual identity in common. But within the categories "woman" and "homosexual" exists a range of gender and sexual differences. For example, recent writings suggest that lesbians may share an identification as women but may interpret gender in different ways and exhibit a range of gender identities. Some lesbian-identified women strongly identify with a series of attributes typically associated with femininity. Others reject these attributes, adopting more masculine styles of self-presentation and behavior. Joan Nestle has written eloquently of the historical importance of butch-femme roles in working-class lesbian subcultures. Recent studies also describe the resurgence of butch-femme role-playing and the persistence of gender differences among San Francisco Bay Area lesbians.[34] In other words, even though lesbians may all be women, we "do gender" in myriad different ways.

Similarly lesbians, despite sharing a common sexual identification, embody a range of different sexual preferences and orientations. Some women experience their same-sex desires as deep, enduring, and unchanging. For others, these desires may be fleeting, or experi-

enced relatively late in life. These differences may influence the
shape that lesbian identities take. Documenting a lesbian community
in the South in the 1970s, sociologist Barbara Ponse draws a distinction between *elective* lesbians, who experience a great deal of flexibility or fluidity in terms of sexual object choice, and *primary* lesbians, who see their sexual possibilities as much more restricted and
exclusively directed toward the same sex. Primary and elective lesbians, says Ponse, differ in their accounts of the causes of lesbianism,
their descriptions of the meaning of lesbian activity and lesbian feelings, and their age of entry into the lesbian community.[35]

A recent study by Beverly Burch further suggests that "primary"
lesbians begin to identify themselves as lesbians at an early age, often
by adolescence. However conflicted their struggles toward a lesbian
identity may have been, these women never developed a stable identity as heterosexual. They either had no significant sexual and emotional relationships with men or related to men only in an effort to
hide or deny their lesbianism. "Elective" lesbians, in contrast, had
significant relationships with men; some married and some had long-
term relationships with men with whom they felt that they were in
love and to whom they were sexually attracted. Often they had a clear
identity as heterosexual in their early years. Nevertheless, they later
"discovered" women as sexual and emotional partners and came to
identify as lesbians.[36]

In their history of the lesbian community of Buffalo, New York,
from the 1930s to the 1960s, Elizabeth Kennedy and Madeline Davis
point to the possibility that there may be a link between subjectively
felt differences of gender identification and differences in lesbians'
sexual orientation. Working-class lesbians in Buffalo were divided between those who saw themselves as butch and femme, divisions that
implied variations in the fixity or fluidity of sexual orientation. "Butch
identity," write Kennedy and Davis, "was deeply felt internally, something that marked the person as different." The butch was unmistak-
ably "homosexual"or "queer."[37] Masculine dress and actions provided
a marker of lesbian identity and of sexual interest in women.
Femmes, on the other hand, "did not experience themselves as basically different from heterosexual women except to the extent that

they were part of gay life." Their gayness, according to Kennedy and
Davis, was "dictated more by setting and circumstance than by a
sense of fundamental difference."[38]

This does not imply that some women are "better" or "more authentic" lesbians than others. It simply indicates that women who
share a lesbian identity may vary widely in terms of their gender self-
identification as well as their sexual orientation. They take different
paths to lesbian identity. Putting aside the question of whether these
differences are rooted in the unconscious, a question that is beyond
the scope of this study, we see that subjectively felt variations in sexual orientation or gender self-identification are relevant to understanding sexual identity, where—as some models posit—some conscious choice, interacting with social experiences, operates to develop
identity.

Indeed, differences between women who experience their sense
of lesbianism as fairly consistent over time and those who experience
their lesbianism as fluid emerged consistently in my research. Nearly
every woman I spoke with made some reference to these differences:
individuals who described themselves as "born lesbians" talked of
friends whose lesbian authenticity they questioned; women who described their sexualities in more "elective" terms often talked of being
attracted to "lifelong" lesbians; bisexuals and lesbians who "sleep with
men" were popular topics of interest, curiosity, and even anger; fears
of community disintegration were sometimes pinned on "fake" lesbians, who were seen as interlopers. How, I wondered, should we make
sense of these differences?

Social constructionists show us that sexual behavior is largely an
effect of cultural and social context and is "scripted" by others. They
have successfully challenged the essentialist understanding of sexuality as something that unfolds entirely from within, that exists inde-
pendently of society. But they have seemingly been unable to account
for the "deep" dimension of identity formation that these differences
imply.[39] Social constructionist accounts of sexuality stop with the de-
piction of social identity, on the grounds that the self is so thoroughly
socialized that there is no need to posit any other form of personal
organization. Not so, insists John Hewitt: "The human symbolic ca-

pacity creates personal as well as social projects" and inclines people to "look within as well as without as they seek order and predictability in their lives." One might say that in addition to collective identity, there is *personal identity,* which may be defined as "a sense of continuity, integration, identification, and differentiation constructed by the person not in relation to a community and its culture but in relation to the self and its projects." Personal identity often locates the person against or in contrast to specific communities and "gives more weight to differentiation than to identification."[40]

Variability is not infinite. How can we account for the fact that many people experience themselves as typecast in particular sexual scripts? Why do some people develop restrictive and rigid orientations, while others may be open and flexible, and still others may develop no orientations at all? By focusing upon the ways in which individuals are socialized into roles, social constructionists have tended to imagine selves as blank slates and have overlooked the extent to which individuals often resist the roles into which they are socialized. By focusing upon the process of "coming out," or constructing a lesbian/gay identity, they have been unable to specify the ways in which desire and sexual identities come to be structured over the course of people's lives and often change over time.

As I suggested earlier, I embarked on this book out of a desire to reexamine how lesbian feminism contributed to these questions. As my research progressed, I realized that this would require my painting a more complex portrait of lesbian identities and of sexualities in general. The essentialist/constructionist debate has opposed two stories of sexuality: homosexuality either unfolds from within or is constructed in the "external" world. This distinction may have outlived its usefulness. It appears that our next challenge is to theorize the interweaving of personal life and social worlds without falling into voluntarism or overdeterminism, on one side, or biological or psychological reductionism, on the other. Toward this end, I employ a deeper conception of self-construction, examining the differences among a group of women who call themselves "lesbians," the implications of these differences for the collective construction of lesbianism, and the significance of these individual differences over time.

This book argues that the process of becoming a lesbian is not simply a matter of discovering or reclaiming that which is "inside" and seeking to break through. Nor is it solely a matter of conforming to external social roles or of enacting a performance. Women make identities—but not exactly as they please. Individuals forming their sexual identity bring a sense of self that is at least partly formed, and in constructing a lesbian identity they use the accounts, or repertoires of meaning, that are available. This is the story of how individuals banded together to challenge dominant definitions and to collectively redefine sexual identities, and how they in turn were shaped by those politicized concepts and over time modified them.

Women of the baby boom, who were adolescents and young adults during a period of radical social change, found themselves poised between two different explanations of lesbianism. The dominant account, inherited from medicine, sexology, and psychoanalysis, conceptualized lesbianism as a condition or aberration: fixed in nature, the product of birth or early childhood, and immutable. An emergent account, blending social constructionist thought and lesbian feminist ideology, emphasized the element of conscious self-reflection in choosing a lesbian identity, which was viewed as a political act.

Feminists broadened the definition of lesbianism to include many women whose sexual preferences were fluid and inchoate, who did not think of themselves as possessing strong and clearly fixed homosexual "orientations." "Any woman can be a lesbian," they proclaimed—if she was politically committed to the liberation of women. When they defined lesbianism in more expansive, universal terms, as a resistance to dominant gender and sexual norms, feminists opened up the possibility of lesbian identification to greater numbers of women than ever before. But individual differences persisted. While blurring the boundary between heterosexuality and homosexuality, lesbian feminists assumed commitment to consistent, stable sexual identities. They found themselves caught between two projects: fixing lesbians as a stable group and "liberating the lesbian in every woman." But as individuals aged and moved through the life cycle, they came to challenge these totalizing definitions of lesbianism.

This story will proceed in roughly chronological order, as we simultaneously trace the trajectory of the baby boom and the movement and culture its members helped create. We begin in chapter 1 with a look at the cultural context in which lesbians of the baby boom came of age. Drawing upon secondary sources, archival documents, and historical accounts of the lesbian/gay and feminist movements, I document how feminist activists contested medical conceptions of lesbianism, challenging the symbolic boundaries around the lesbian community and creating in their place a collective oppositional identity based on the belief that sexuality is socially constructed.

Chapter 2, which looks at individual differences among the women who formed sexual identities in the context of lesbian feminism, focuses on the coming out process as it was experienced by three women. The group of women I interviewed ranged from those who thought of themselves as deeply and irrevocably different—as "queer"—to those who experienced their sexual identities as fluid, believing their lesbianism to be a political choice. Chapter 3 examines the latter, the women who consider their lesbianism to be elective, who experienced themselves as bisexual in orientation.

Lesbian feminists created a culture that helped to reconstitute desire: by idealizing women and affirming love between women, they countered the normative ideal of heterosexual romantic love. Some individuals were able to "reinvent" themselves as lesbians; it was in this context that many first became attracted to women and consolidated lesbian identities. Through performances of identity, or "identity work," some described having successfully "become" lesbians. But differences among these women persisted.

There was a tension between two projects—a "minoritizing" project, which sought to fix lesbians as a stable minority group, and a "universalizing" project, which envisioned every woman as potentially lesbian—and chapter 4 examines how it played out in the interactions among women of this cohort. Feminism provided the ideological glue that wed these two conceptions of lesbianism, which were often at odds with one another, but it ultimately could not fuse them. Hence, the "problem of commitment" emerged as a central theme in individual and collective struggles over identity.

By the late 1970s, a combination of structural and ideological factors conspired to "decenter" the lesbian feminist project. As the baby boomers aged, they settled into families and careers of various forms.

At the same time, heightened attention to sexual, racial, and other differences helped discredit the normative assumptions of the lesbian feminist model. In chapter 5, we see how members of this generation are grappling with changes in their lives and the ideological landscape by developing a conception of identity that acknowledges both the limits of lesbian identifications and the "multiplicity" of identity. Chapter 6 explores the stories of women who came out in the 1970s and have found that a lesbian identity no longer suits their needs. Who are ex-lesbians? Why is their disaffection from the ranks so troubling to so many others? And what might they tell us about the process of constructing—and particularly reconstructing—sexual identities?

In the final chapter, I reflect upon the implications of these findings for contemporary sexual politics. The notion that one category of experience, such as sexual identity, could ever be a complete reflection of one's relationship to the world is a fiction, as recent "queer" theorizing and activism suggest. But so long as people are categorized and stigmatized according to sexuality, sexual identities are necessary fictions. The challenge is to create a politics that embodies identity and difference, that acknowledges its own categories as constructed while using those categories as a vehicle for democratic change.

Chapter One

From Old Gay to New

Symbolic Struggles and the Politics
of Lesbian Identity

Are lesbians united by a shared sexual orientation, by their same-sex desires? Do they hold in common the experience of having engaged in sexual activity or having had close, passionate relationships with members of the same sex? Or are they bound together simply by their sense of themselves as outcasts or as rebels against heterosexual society?

The boundaries separating the group called "lesbians" from the rest of women are not at all clearly or immutably marked. Historically lesbians constitute a group whose central characteristic is debatable and changing, a group upon which there is little consensus. For example, there have always been women who have had sexual/romantic relationships with other women who have not labeled themselves on that basis. There have also been women whose actual sexual fantasies or practices don't fit the common social definition of lesbianism—bisexuals, transsexuals, and others—but who nonetheless identify as lesbians. There are many possible configurations of the relationship among desire, behavior, and identity—the possibilities far exceed the capacity of social categories to describe them.

Like ethnic communities, lesbian/gay boundaries, identities, and cultures are negotiated, defined, and produced.[1] The history of lesbian social worlds is in part the story of discursive contestations for the definition of boundaries, identities, and cultures. These symbolic

struggles construct female homosexuality as a social reality; they create images, myths, and fantasies of lesbian love, desire, and fulfillment; and they shape the composition of the group of women called
lesbians.

For most of this century, medical experts have been the primary
definers of lesbian existence. Medical discourses labeled homosexual
object choice as a "condition," associated it with gender inversion,
and constructed lesbians and heterosexual women as two distinct
groups. Lesbianism, in the medical conception, is concrete and objective, a condition of being that has clear boundaries. It is something
to be "discovered," something that always exists in the individual,
albeit in a latent form before the act of identification. Subjected to
the power of institutional definitions of sexuality, individuals defined
themselves according to these understandings and organized subcultures to support homosexual desire.[2]

In the 1970s, lesbians and gay men introduced a new vocabulary
and set of concepts for understanding homosexuality. They reframed
its meaning, suggesting that the boundaries separating heterosexuality and homosexuality were in fact permeable.[3] Lesbianism was a
matter of identification, not simply desire. One could be a lesbian by
becoming "woman identified," developing "lesbian consciousness,"
making women central to one's life, and not giving oneself over
to men. Lesbians were not "failed women": they were rebels against
the oppressive sex/gender system, the vanguard of women's liberation. One could be a lesbian and a woman too. Indeed, rather than
posing a threat to one's womanhood, lesbianism strengthened and
enhanced it.

The movement from "old gay" to "new gay" worlds signifies the
transition from a world in which medicalized conceptions of homosexuality were virtually undisputed to one in which they were loudly
challenged, from a time when lesbians occupied a particular deviant
social role, focused upon homosexual desires, to a time when lesbianism became an identity, a reflexive basis for self-construction. It
marks a movement toward greater consciousness with regard to lesbianism in particular, and to sexualities in general.

Heterosexual Tensions, Homosexual Roles

The postwar period was a time of gender and sexual paradoxes. Social and economic transformations brought new possibilities for employment and education, and consumerism celebrated sexuality. Sexual exploration became central to the youth culture that emerged in the 1950s, a culture promoted by films, rock and roll, and magazines. At the same time, the Kinsey reports offered the first comprehensive examination of Americans' sexual habits, revealing a wide gap between social norms and actual sexual behavior. Through the publication of these reports, an educated public learned that many more people had engaged in homosexual activity at some point in their lives than had been previously believed.

But this growing sexualization of culture "unfolded amid prudish families and narrow, even cruel, sexual norms."[4] Heterosexual sexual tensions in the 1950s—articulated as fears of sexual chaos and translated into rigid taboos against female promiscuity—were addressed by renewing adherence to traditional gender norms and by celebrating marriage and children. Marital sex was promoted to stabilize the family; experts prescribed sex in marriage, while warning women to remain virgins. Girls were encouraged to pursue the sexual cues that confronted them but were threatened with the loss of respectability (and acceptable futures) if they did so.[5] In the face of these heterosexual tensions, female homosexuals (and prostitutes) often became the sexual deviants against which "proper" female sexuality, heterosexual and sanctified by marriage, was defined. Labeling these individuals as deviants, and creating a "homosexual role," provided a "clear-cut, publicized and recognizable threshold between permissible and impermissible behavior," ensuring that others could not easily drift into such deviant behavior.[6]

Early in the twentieth century, lesbians, "mannish women," unmarried career women, social reformers, and feminists were often lumped together. The polarization of masculine and feminine modes of behavior meant that "a complete inversion or reversal of a woman's sexual character was required for her to act as a lesbian; she had literally to become man-like in her desire."[7] Prewar New Women were castigated as gender traitors for rejecting their "proper" and "natural" social role to bear and rear children. The term "sexual inversion" was commonly used to refer to a broad range of deviant gender behavior, of which homosexual desire was only one aspect. Eventually, as women were considered able to experience and act upon sexual desire, medical concern shifted logically "from the *fact* of women's sexual activity to their *choice* of sexual and social partners."[8] The "homosexual" came to replace the "invert" as the subject of medical concern.

The image of the lesbian became particularly threatening in the 1950s; lesbians emerged as sexual demons, embodying female desire and sexual excess. Conservative Freudian analysts such as Frank Caprio, declaring that homosexuality was a medical condition, encouraged a heightened awareness of homosexuality and its supposed dangers. Caprio imagined that female promiscuity, masturbation in marriage, and "unconventional sex practices" such as cunnilingus, fellatio, and anal penetration were themselves indicative of latent homosexuality.[9] He and other psychoanalysts considered lesbians, along with male homosexuals and feminists, to be individuals perverted by childhood traumas against whom the state had to defend itself, for its own good and the good of its citizens. Hence, the U.S. government purged homosexuals, along with Communists, from its ranks.[10]

There is much debate over whether the medical experts "discovered" the lesbian or "created" her. Some historians argue that medical discourse itself constructed the lesbian as sexual subject. Before the emergence of the term *lesbian,* there may have been women who loved women, but their love was of a very different character, less central to their sense of self, and perhaps even asexual in nature. Others hold that experts simply discovered the centrality of lesbian desire prevailing in a world previously unlabeled, giving a name to that which already existed. In fact, both processes seem to have been at work. Women have for centuries loved and lusted after other women. But during the last century, medical experts publicized their existence, thereby defining the boundaries of "proper" female sexuality; as a side effect, their work gave rise to and promoted self-conscious lesbian subcultures. While the medical discourse cast lesbians as aberrations, it also allowed women who harbored homosexual desires to find some social recognition.[11]

This heightened discussion of sexual variation had an unintended result: women coming of age at this time had a degree of sexual self-awareness that was unprecedented, with a much greater chance than earlier women of being exposed to different sexual variations. Having recognized their homosexual desires, some individuals were led to medical books in the library to try and figure out "who they were." A woman I spoke with recalled her initial discovery of those books and their impact on her as a teenager in the 1950s:

> The people they talked about in those medical books were very weird. They had psychological complexes, they had unnatural desires, and they didn't look like anyone I knew. At the time I had the feeling that these were really distorted pictures, that they placed women under a microscope without taking into account their feelings at all. I didn't relate to that stuff at all. But I looked at the words—dyke, lesbian, homosexual—and I knew that they were referring to me.[12]

This discovery was a double-edged sword: on the one hand, this woman, like thousands of others who had this same experience, was shocked and ashamed that the unsightly images in the medical texts might bear some relationship to her. But on the other hand, she gained from them some social recognition, a name, and a way of thinking about herself that allowed her to find others who shared her desires.

Contrary to the histories written in the afterglow of lesbian feminism and gay liberation, lesbian life in this country did not begin in 1970. In the 1930s and 1940s, and even earlier in many places, there were lively, albeit secretive and stigmatized, lesbian subcultures in American towns and cities.[13] World War II had led to the flowering of homosexual life in the United States, mainly in port cities like San Francisco and New York, but also in many smaller cities and towns, where active communities sprang up; they were frequently working class and mixed race in character, centering mainly on bars.[14] By the postwar period, there were many subcultural niches in which women who loved other women congregated: informal networks of young lesbians of color in Harlem and other urban areas; professional networks comprising middle-class women, some of whom were involved in the first lesbian organization, the Daughters of Bilitis; homosexual resort communities; and untold other groupings.[15] Even as homosexuals were being vilified, gender roles were being shored up, and the definition of "proper femininity" was narrowing, there were unprecedented opportunities to construct a different kind of life in the relative safety of the lesbian subculture.

Outside the homosexual subculture, women who engaged in same-sex behavior learned to "manage" their stigma; being a lesbian shaped one's life choices in practically every respect—particularly with regard to one's job. Middle-class women who were upwardly mobile were forced at work to conform to feminine norms, carefully managing their identities to avoid being found out. But in the bars, women met friends and lovers, were initiated into the rules and rituals of lesbian life, escaped from the constraints of heterosexual society, and developed a sense of their common difference. Audre Lorde recalled her early gay life in New York in the 1950s: "All of us who survived those common years had to be a little strange . . . a little proud. Keeping ourselves together and on our own tracks, however wobbly, was like trying to play the Dinizulu War Chant or a Beethoven sonata on a tin dog-whistle. . . . You had to have a place. Whether or not it did justice to whatever you felt you were about, there had to be some place to refuel and check your flaps."[16] Gay subcultures allowed women, in Lorde's words, to "refuel and check their flaps." They promoted and protected the expression of same-sex desire and shielded "gender outlaws"—women who, by choice or necessity, failed to conform. What participants in these various subcultures held in common was a sense of marginality, of difference, of exclusion from gender and sexual norms and from the codes of behavior they implied. "The culture of gayness that I came out in," as one woman described the 1950s, "very much emphasized and was aware of our difference from the people who were not queer. We were constantly reminded of our difference, and built an identity that was based on it."[17]

Membership in lesbian subcultures was regulated through codes, signals, and complex in-group rules, such as those governing butch-femme roles. Joan Nestle has characterized butch-femme during this period as "a conspicuous flag of rebellion" in a highly stigmatized, secretive world, a means of survival in an age when gender rules were leaden weights. She describes butch-femme as a "style of self-presentation that made erotic competence a political statement in the 1950's."[18] Roles eroticized differences between partners. The butch, or active partner, orchestrated the sexual interaction, but her pleasure was dependent upon pleasing her partner. "We labeled ourselves," Nestle writes, "as part of our cultural ritual, and the language reflected our time in history, but the words stood for complex sexual and emotional exchanges."[19]

Butch-femme roles linked sexuality, appearance, and frequently economic position in a highly ritualized way. Dress was a reflection of sexual style, a signal to potential sexual and nonsexual partners, and a pretty good indicator of whether you were a secretary or a manual worker. The writer Ann Bannon fashioned a series of paperback novels around the character Beebo Brinker, a strapping tomboy who worked as an elevator operator so that she could wear a man's uniform.[20] The system of roles, as practiced in the 1950s, implied a great deal of permanence and consistency. Identity as butch or femme was an essential, integral part of one's being. Once a femme, always a femme—and likewise for butches. By imposing rules and placing limits on self-expression, roles eroticized difference, providing security and regularity in a tenuous, secretive world. While they were often proud statements of lesbian resistance, they were also the expression of an oppressed minority faced with a paucity of alternatives.

Butch-femme roles were not universally adopted within the subculture, however. Many women objected to roles on the grounds that they confined individuals to certain modes of conduct and limited individual self-expression. In addition, butch-femme couples may have embarrassed some because they made lesbians culturally visible, which was, Nestle writes, "a terrifying act for the 1950's."[21] Working-class butches, who wore men's suits and kept their hair short and slicked back, presented a strong visual message. Historical accounts describe in harrowing detail the brutality meted out to lesbians, particularly strongly butch women in the 1950s and 1960s.[22] Many bars monitored their clients' clothing, requiring that no more than one piece of men's apparel be worn, and frequent police raids enforced these rules. While the medical profession "policed" the boundaries that delineated the normal from the abnormal, those boundaries were quite literally policed as officers kept the subculture in line.

The effect of this is easy to imagine: those who identify as homosexual cannot escape an either/or situation. Either one is "in the closet," passing for straight and experiencing the loss of self that that entails, or one is "out" and facing the harassment, threat of violence, economic deprivation, and loss of family support that so often follow. To become a part of the lesbian world was to give up many of one's privileges. In the face of these dangers, only those who felt that they had relatively little to lose in terms of social status—or who, despite extreme social disapproval, could incorporate "deviant" sexuality into a favorable sense of themselves—came to self-identify as lesbian.[23]

It was principally sexual desire that shaped lesbian communities before the convergence of Stonewall and the second wave of feminism. As one woman who lived through this period put it, "If you weren't particularly sexually driven, if you didn't care one way or another, why put up with all the social opprobrium? If you could just as easily sleep with a man as with a woman, why go through hell to go to bed with a woman? Or if you were just as happy celibate, why not just be a spinster? The hell we went through was just not worth it unless the rewards were pretty intense."[24] One might speculate that "old gay" women, who claimed lesbian identities in the 1950s and early 1960s, were more likely to be of working-class or upper-class origin: working class, because they had little to lose; upper class, because they had access to greater resources and the freedom to maneuver outside the structures of "straight" society. These women were also less likely to have had significant sexual and emotional relationships with men, or to have developed stable identities as heterosexuals. In the 1950s and 1960s, this "core" group probably constituted the bulk of the population of lesbian-identified women.[25]

For most women, the pain and social disapproval one had to endure in order to claim a lesbian life in the 1950s were too costly. As Jill Johnston, who became a prominent lesbian feminist writer and critic, described this period:

> There was no lesbian identity. There was lesbian activity. . . . For most of us the chasm between social validation and private needs was so

wide and deep that the society overwhelmed us for any number of significant individual reasons: not running off at 20 or so with your one true love forever like the ladies of llangollen; not being able constitutionally or by naivete or distaste or poor location to be a bar dyke; not falling by chance into a fugitive salon a la paris in the 20s and colette and rene vivien and romain brooks and radclyffe hall and the like. those were three good reasons. for all three I was one of those who didn't make it.[26]

Those who did make it, who constructed a sense of community amid the violence and extreme social stigma of this period, laid the groundwork for the social movements that would emerge during the following decades.

"Smash the Categories"

What is a lesbian? A lesbian is the rage of all women condensed to the point of explosion. She is the woman who, often beginning at an extremely early age, acts in accordance with her inner compulsion to be a more complete and freer human being than her society—perhaps then, but certainly later—cares to allow her.... For she is caught somewhere between accepting society's view of her—in which case she cannot accept herself—and coming to understand what this sexist society has done to her and why it is functional and necessary for it to do so. Those of us who work that through find ourselves on the other side of a tortuous journey through a night that may have been decades long. The perspective gained from that journey, the liberation of self, the inner peace, the real love of self and of all women, is something to be shared with all women—because we are all women.

Radicalesbians, "The Woman
Identified Woman" (1970)

Now! Enter the young; the new morality; the belief that the individual has the RIGHT to be different. Basic to this attitude is the assertion that the larger society cannot legitimately dictate the life patterns or social habits of its individual members.... Fortified with this idea, increasing numbers of young homosexuals and Lesbians perceive

> *their sexuality in the same manner as other social differ-*
> *ences; placing sex practices (not just homosexuality) on the*
> *same level as variations in dress or life-style habits.*
>
>   Fen Gregory, "Before the Gap
>   Becomes a Chasm," *The Ladder,*
>   April–May 1970

Women who reached adolescence and young adulthood during the
1950s and 1960s lived their formative years in a period of relative
conservatism and conformity, only to have their assumptions about
the world radically challenged by protests against the Vietnam War
and by the civil rights movement. These movements dramatized the
glaring contradiction between American values of liberal individualism and the conventional social practices that denied rights to many.

Gay people, some suggested, should take their place alongside
other "legitimate" minority groups vying for power in American society. "The revolution must be fought for us, too, not only for blacks,
Indians, welfare mothers, [and] grape pickers," proclaimed lesbian
activist Martha Shelley in 1969.[27] That same year, a crowd of drag
queens, dykes, street people, and bar boys battled police as they attempted to shut down a bar in Greenwich Village in New York, in
what became known as the Stonewall rebellion.[28] Stonewall represented what sociologist George Herbert Mead might call a "problematic occurrence," a moment at which people become conscious of
themselves and their circumstances, of what they have previously
taken for granted, and of the need to seek alternative ways of acting.

But early gay liberationists never thought of themselves solely as
building a civil rights movement for a particular minority, in the style
of "ethnic" politics. They believed they were waging a revolutionary
struggle to free the homosexual in everyone. "New gay" activists redefined the frontiers of lesbian/gay existence.[29] They popularized a
new vocabulary, tied to a new set of concepts: "sexual identity," "gay
lifestyle," "gay pride," "coming out." They equated the adoption of a
homosexual identity with the development of "gay consciousness,"
thus making gay identity, and even desire, a much more reflexive
matter than ever before. They proclaimed that homosexuals were a
radical vanguard that posed a challenge to the dominant heterosexist
and masculinist sex/gender system.

In "Notes of an 'Old Gay,' " an important gay liberation tract, a woman who had experienced lesbian desires before Stonewall, a self-described tomboy from an early age, related her encounter with psychiatry, crediting the movement with her eventual challenge of the hegemony of medical knowledges in defining homosexuality: "I read all the usual psychiatric shit and found deviance writ large in my personal history: inadequate identification with same-sex parent; infantile narcissism; penis envy; penis-fear; body-shame; 'urethral' personality; fear of adult intimacy; degradation fantasies; equation of sex with dirt, etc. In short, I had 'introjected' our culture beautifully; now I had to be cured of it." She and others had been viewed as "not women," "the third sex," "inverts," and "dwellers in the half-world," but they had, finally, a theory that defined them as "normal women" or even an avant-garde. "I see now that I, in line with the society around me, my psychotherapist, and all my friends (gay and straight), was firmly resisting an interpretation of lesbianism that would bring into question the essential rightness of the male sexist ethic, or suggest the kind of drastic overhaul our society really needs."[30]

Gay liberationists emphasized the innate "polymorphous perversity" of individuals and the artificiality of the roles imposed upon them by society. In 1970, activist Carl Wittman suggested the radical potential of homosexuality:

> Nature leaves undefined the object of sexual desire. The gender of that object has been imposed socially. . . . As kids, we refused to capitulate to demands that we smother our feelings toward each other. Somewhere we found the strength to resist being indoctrinated, and we should count that among our assets. . . . Homosexuality is NOT . . . a makeshift in the absence of the opposite sex; it is not hatred or rejection of the opposite sex; it is not genetic; it is not the result of broken homes (except inasmuch as we could see the sham of American marriage).[31]

Wittman turned conventional explanations of homosexuality—as genetic, as the problem of a "failure" of the family—on their heads, portraying homosexuals as rebels against a failed system. But rather than substitute homosexuality for heterosexuality, he and others hoped that in a liberated society, homosexuality and heterosexuality would flourish side by side, as sexual and gender roles of all sorts became meaningless. As a popular wall poster at the time proclaimed, it was time to "smash the categories." What if every person or even a small percentage of those who had had feelings for a member of his or her own sex let that be known? If left to their own polymorphously perverse devices, individuals would reject the constraints of both homosexuality and heterosexuality and be bisexual.[32]

Sexual behavior was changing. A study by the Institute of Sex Research showed that the number of women engaging in premarital sexual intercourse had doubled in the 1960s. As Lillian Faderman observed, "heterosexuality began to look somewhat like homosexuality, as nonreproductive sex and cohabitation without marriage came to be commonplace."[33] In mixed-sex communal households, as the boundaries between friends and lovers blurred, "free love" and the practices of group sex and nonmonogamy occasionally allowed women to find one another beneath the sheets. But in a society in which men held the upper hand, could love ever really be "free"? Some women came to suggest that sexual liberation was a "male plot." "Sexual freedom has meant more opportunity for men, not a new kind of experience for women," declared one.[34] Perhaps gender was the real locus of women's oppression. And so women began to form feminist organizations and their own movement for liberation.

Lesbians were not particularly welcome in this movement. In 1970, an important anthology of writings from the women's liberation movement, Robin Morgan's *Sisterhood Is Powerful,* collected the writings of fifty-four women. Only two of the articles and one poem mentioned lesbianism. Martha Shelley, in her piece "Notes of a Radical Lesbian," provided a scathing critique of femininity in American culture:

> For women, as for other groups, there are several American norms. All of them have their rewards, and their penalties. The nice girl next door, virginal until her marriage—the Miss America type—is rewarded with community respect and respectability. She loses her individuality and her freedom, to become a toothpaste smile and a chastity belt. The career woman gains independence and a large margin of independence and a large margin of freedom—if she is willing to work twice as hard as a man for less pay. . . . The starlet, call girl, or bunny,

whose source of income is directly related to her image as a sex object, gains some financial independence and freedom from housework . . . but she pays through psychological degradation as a sex object, and through the insecurity of knowing that her career, based on her youthful good looks, is short-lived.[35]

Others within the movement had leveled similar charges: Women in American society were forced into narrow, confining roles. They were degraded and objectified for the sake of male desire, forced to work twice as hard as men for less pay, imprisoned in the house as caretakers of husbands and children. But where Shelley's critique differed from other versions of radical feminism was in posing lesbianism as the solution to women's oppression: "The Lesbian, through her ability to obtain love and sexual satisfaction from other women, is freed of dependence on men for love, sex, and money. She does not have to do menial chores for them (at least at home), nor cater to their egos, nor submit to hasty and inept sexual encounters. She is freed from fear of unwanted pregnancy and the pains of childbirth, and from the drudgery of child raising."[36] Lesbians, because they stood outside the norms of the sex/gender system, because they were financially and emotionally independent of men, childbirth, and child raising, were the only women who were truly free. The boldness of this statement was a telling indication of the growing self-consciousness of lesbians within the heterosexual-dominated women's movement. In the same year that *Sisterhood Is Powerful* was published, lesbians fled what they perceived as virulent homophobia among heterosexual feminists, forming an autonomous lesbian feminist movement.[37]

"It is the primacy of women relating to women, of women creating a new consciousness of and with each other which is at the heart of women's liberation."[38] So declared "The Woman Identified Woman," the 1970 essay that is generally considered to be the first statement of an autonomous lesbian feminist politic. This essay circulated widely among young radical feminists and achieved enormous influence. It reconceptualized the meaning of *lesbian*, equating it with female independence and suggesting that the label had been used to divide women: "When a woman hears this word tossed her way, she knows she is stepping out of line . . . for a woman to be independent means she *can't be* a woman—she must be a dyke. . . . As long as the label 'dyke' can be used to frighten women into a less militant stand, keep her separate from her sisters, keep her from giving primacy to anything other than men and family—then to that extent she is controlled by the male culture."[39] In this view, the category *lesbian* was predicated on the existence of gender inequality; the practice of labeling independent women as lesbians was intended to force their conformity to conventional gender roles.

> Lesbianism, like male homosexuality, is a category of behavior possible only in sexist society characterized by rigid sex roles and dominated by male supremacy. Those sex roles dehumanize women by defining us as a supportive/serving caste in relation to the master caste of men. . . . Lesbian is the word, the label, the condition, that holds women in line. . . . Lesbian is a label invented by the man to throw at the woman who dares to be his equal, who dares to challenge his prerogatives[,] . . . who dares to assert the primacy of her own needs[:] . . . a lesbian is not considered a "real woman." And yet, in popular thinking, there is really only one essential difference between a lesbian and other women—the essence of being a "woman" is to get fucked by men.[40]

By logical extension, in order to create a freer, more egalitarian society, these limiting categories must be destroyed.

In order to do this, however, they first must be embraced, in a "reverse affirmation" of the characteristics assigned by the dominant culture. Lesbians were not failed women, but actually rebels against gender inequality. If the "exchange of women," compulsory heterosexuality, was the bedrock of the sex/gender system, then women who made lives with other women were actually subverting the dominant order. Lesbians, Sidney Abbott and Barbara Love suggested, echoing Martha Shelley's earlier proclamation, were the only truly independent women.

> Women's Liberation and Homosexual Liberation are both struggling toward a common goal: a society free from defining and categorizing people by virtue of gender and/or sexual preference. "Lesbian" is a label used as a psychic weapon to keep women locked in their male-defined "feminine role." The essence of that role is that a woman is defined in terms of her relationship to men. A woman is called a lesbian when she functions autonomously. Women's autonomy is what Women's Liberation is all about.[41]

Once lesbians were redefined as "autonomous women," it was but a short step to argue that women's "authentic" nature, repressed by the dominant culture, was to love other women. Lesbians were born "that way," lesbian feminists asserted; indeed, *all* women were born "that way," all had the capacity to be lesbians but were hampered by the system of male domination. In this universalizing conception, lesbians were not "essentially" different from heterosexual women. They were different only in terms of their political commitment to affirm women's autonomy.

The quest for autonomy was linked to the project of rebuilding a new sense of self, of claiming an identity for women. "We must develop in ourselves everything that is strong, female, proud and build it into our *new identities*" (emphasis mine), proclaimed *The Other Woman*, Toronto's lesbian journal, in 1973.[42] As Rita Mae Brown explained, the lesbian feminist was at heart an existentialist: she makes her own world. "A woman-identified-woman defines herself in relation to other women and most importantly as a self apart and distinct from other selves, not with function as the center of self, but being. In other words, only you can identify yourself; only you can know who you are."[43] Separating from the male-dominated, heterosexual culture and affiliating with other women would make possible this self-realization, according to Brown: "[Lesbianism] is a different way of life. It is a life determined by a woman for her own benefit and the benefit of other women. It is a life that draws its strength, support, and direction from women. . . . You refuse to limit yourself by the male definitions of women. You free yourself from male concepts of 'feminine' behavior."[44]

There was little room in this politics for gay men, who, like heterosexual men, were considered to be part of the problem. Young women who "came out through feminism" believed that female homosexuality had a different source and a different meaning than male homosexuality. While gay liberationists had earlier criticized the limitations of binary identity categories, embracing the belief that everyone was naturally bisexual, feminists claimed that lesbianism was the only viable alternative to compulsory heterosexuality. Gay men, said feminists, separated sex from emotional involvement and were preoccupied with superficial issues, such as the right to have sex in public places. Lacking a radical analysis of sex and sex roles, they advocated solutions that made no basic changes in the system that oppressed lesbians as women.

In contrast, "woman identification," feminists believed, was an act of self-affirmation and love, an act of identification rather than desire. Ultimately, it was much more than simply a matter of sex, poet Judy Grahn declared: "Men who are obsessed with sex are convinced that lesbians are obsessed with sex. Actually, like other women, lesbians are obsessed with love and fidelity."[45] Reconceptualizing the nature of sexuality, some feminists perceived desire itself as a social construct; there is no essential, undifferentiated sexual impulse, sex drive or lust, that resides in the body. The part that sexual behavior played in lesbianism was only small, and not always necessary.

Adrienne Rich suggested that primary identification with women, "a range . . . of woman-identified experience," and practices designed to make women central to one's life—and accordingly to minimize the influence of men—could or should be placed along a "lesbian continuum." The operation of compulsory, or normative, heterosexuality has meant that sexual preference is never a "free choice." "For women heterosexuality may not be a 'preference' at all but something that has to be imposed, managed, organized, propagandized, and maintained by force."[46] Rich blurred the boundaries between homosexual and heterosexual women, universalizing the possibility of lesbianism. While providing a critique of the limiting definitions of lesbianism that derived from sexology, she maintained a commitment to the political utility of organizing around the category. Here we see, as Eve Sedgwick puts it, the

> re-visioning, in female terms, of same-sex desire as being at the very definitional center of each gender, rather than occupying a cross-gender or liminal position between them. Thus women who loved women were seen as *more* female . . . than those whose desire crossed boundaries of gender. The axis of sexuality, in this view, was not only highly coextensive with the axis of gender but expressive of its most heightened essence.[47]

But same-sex *desire* became secondary to same-sex *identification*. Radical feminists consciously downplayed the sexual aspects of lesbianism, at least in their public rhetoric. The process of desexualizing lesbianism may have begun when early lesbian feminists, such as the Furies, attempted to make lesbianism acceptable to heterosexual feminists who were uncomfortable with overt lesbian sexuality.[48] Lesbianism was imagined as a kind of "female bonding," a more inclusive category with which a larger number of women could identify, and for which there was a historical precedent: the "passionate friendships" of eighteenth- and nineteenth-century women.[49]

These and other social constructionist ideas had an enormous impact on the emergent lesbian feminist culture. Lesbianism was no longer assigned at birth or in early childhood. It was no longer the product of biological imprinting—the inheritance of genes or hormones—or a psychological aberration, such as a rejecting mother, unresolved oedipal crisis, or traumatic early sexual experience. Neither explanation had been very popular, because feminists were wary of both biological determinism and the psychotherapeutic system. Instead, lesbianism was a choice open to any woman.[50]

Writing in *The Ladder*, the newsletter of the Daughters of Bilitis, one woman described her transformation from "old dyke" to "new lesbian" in terms of her rejection of essentialist concepts of lesbian identity.

> I clung to the conviction that most women quite naturally were attracted to men as I was attracted to women. I found it impossible to understand, in any way meaningful to me, how a woman could love a man with the total involvement of her sexuality but nothing would shake loose my belief that somehow she did. My rationalization was that, being a lesbian, I could not expect to understand. . . . But at the same time I insisted on trying to understand them. And I experienced and observed things that did not quite fit my comfortable assumption that some women are born lesbians and most are not. I cannot pinpoint just when I took the plunge and threw out the silly assumption (as it now appears to me) that most women are naturally drawn to men, but it happened as a direct result of the women's liberation movement.[51]

That "silly assumption"—that women are naturally drawn to men—would go unchallenged no longer.

Identities in Motion

The most popular novel of the lesbian feminist period, *Rubyfruit Jungle* by Rita Mae Brown, told the story of Molly Bolt, an unapologetic, fiery young lesbian who captivated cheerleaders, heiresses, and other seemingly straight women at every turn. She briefly dates a married woman named Polina.

> The wine went directly to Polina's tongue and she told me how freaked out she was and how secretly she thought lesbianism attracted and frightened every woman, because every woman could be a lesbian, but it was all hidden and unknown. Did I get into it because of the allure of the forbidden? She then went on to say what a wonderful relationship she had with her husband. . . . and wasn't heterosexuality just grand?
> "It bores me, Polina."
> "Bores you—what do you mean?"
> "I mean men bore me. If one of them behaves like an adult it's cause for celebration, and even when they do act human, they still aren't as good in bed as women."
> "Maybe you haven't met the right man?"
> "Maybe you haven't met the right woman. And I bet I've slept with more men than you have, and they all work the same show. Some are better at it than others but it's boring once you know what women are like."[52]

Women around the nation took to heart Molly's assertion that every woman could be a lesbian, that lesbianism was the exciting, alluring alternative to garden-variety heterosexuality. A woman who had been married for twenty-two years, interviewed in the early 1970s, described the origins of her lesbian identification: "I began . . . to become involved with women's consciousness-raising groups, and I began to hear . . . of the idea of women being turned on to each other. It was the first time I heard about it in terms of people that I knew. . . . I was receptive but had no previous, immediate history. Like there was a part of me that had been thinking about it, and thinking, 'Gee, that sounds like intellectually that's a good idea.' "[53] This was a very different narrative of lesbian development than the dominant essentialist one. Fading was the image of the tomboy, the girl who had never fit into heterosexual femininity, who had been castigated by her family and shunned by schoolmates, and who became a woman forced to live her life on the margins of society.

Feminists contested popular conceptions of lesbianism, renegotiating the boundaries of permissible sexuality and creating more ways of "being" a lesbian. They constructed far more voluntaristic conceptions of desire, which many women believed could be resocialized and reshaped at will. Thus women coming of age in the early 1970s, though they had little contact with the mainly underground tradition of working-class lesbian bars, had access to a wider variety of different accounts of lesbianism than those in the 1950s, when medical discourses controlled the terms of sexual knowledge. It was more common for women, particularly middle-class women, to be faced with a *choice* about which sexual identity—heterosexual or homosexual—to adopt.

Some have suggested that for the most fervent proponents of radical feminism in the 1970s, lesbianism was often less a choice than an imperative.[54] How could one possibly support the liberation of women and sleep with the enemy? Lesbianism became the privileged option of the vanguard of the women's movement, the only viable position for those who considered themselves truly committed politically to the liberation of their sex. This does not mean that radical feminists universally developed sexual relationships with women. But many previously heterosexual women did withdraw from their relationships with men. Armed with the homosocial concepts of the "woman-identified woman" and the "lesbian continuum," which emphasized identifications over desires, many declared themselves to be lesbians.

Certainly, the new discourse of lesbian feminism enabled many women who had never considered the possibility of claiming a lesbian lifestyle to leave their husbands and boyfriends—some for political motives, others in expression of deeply rooted desires, many for both reasons. It allowed many of those living primarily closeted lives to come out and declare their lesbianism openly. Prefeminist lesbian subcultures located in the bars had been composed mainly of working-class women. Upper-class women had their own social networks and secretive institutions. By redefining lesbianism as a political challenge to male domination, feminists made lesbianism more public and opened up the possibility of homosexuality to greater numbers of middle-class women than ever before. Lesbianism became a more public, visible, and self-conscious basis for identity. As Lillian Faderman notes, "There were probably more lesbians in America during the 1970s than any other time in history, because radical feminism had helped redefine lesbianism to make it almost a categorical imperative for all women truly interested in the welfare and progress of other women."[55]

Feminist-style lesbianism resonated with many women who had long experienced their sexuality in relational rather than simply erotic terms, who had never thought of themselves as "exclusive" homosexuals, or indeed as homosexuals at all. Lesbianism had become, through the influence of feminist ideas, a highly self-conscious and reflexive identity—"on a head level and not just a 'gut' level."

> Women's liberation has made it a lot easier to be a lesbian. Feminist reasoning has given lesbians a better way of understanding, on a head level and not just a "gut" level, their rejection of males as lovers, their departure from the restrictive male-defined ideals of "femininity" and their heretofore rather mysterious admiration of their own sex. The new view of lesbianism holds that because she (the lesbian) is a woman, because she has been subjected to the humanly intolerable pressures of a sexist world, she has turned to lesbianism not only in a gesture of defiance but also as the only life-style that grants her a means of sexual and emotional expression.[56]

When lesbian feminists declared that lesbianism was a choice, an affirmative category of resistance, they succeeded in bringing into the fold many women for whom relationships with men were significant. Some were married or had positive long-term relationships with men. Nevertheless, after "discovering" women as sexual and emotional partners, they identified as lesbians. As an "old gay" woman suggested, "to read some of their accounts one almost gets the picture of a woman suddenly putting down her feminist books and lecture notes or leaping up in the middle of a consciousness raising session and in one blinding moment of satori rushing out to find a female lover."[57] And another "old gay" woman remarked, several years later:

Those of us who were active in 1971 and '72 witnessed the tremendous influx of formerly heterosexual women into the Lesbian Movement. They came by the *thousands*. Lesbians of this background now compose the very backbone of the Lesbian Movement. . . . We put the world of men on notice that we were out to give their wives and lovers a CHOICE. We got a bad reputation as "chauvinistic." Lesbian feminism was called an "expansionist philosophy"—meaning we were out to politically seduce (read—"awaken") all women. In the years that have followed, it seems ironic to this old-gay-never-married dyke, that some of the most ardent, anti-straight women . . . were 1971's HOUSEWIVES![58]

This bewildered some heterosexual feminists, who wondered, "If lesbians were sick, disturbed people from birth, how is it that my best friend, who joined the women's movement with me, is now sleeping with women? Who is she, and who then am I?" Sidney Abbott described the arrival of social constructionist ideas: "Female sexuality did not seem to be fixed but very changeable."[59]

The feminist reframing of lesbianism blurred the boundaries separating the heterosexual and homosexual worlds. The enlarged lesbian population that resulted included women whose lesbian identities were more dependent upon the social milieu than those of the "core" group, which was perhaps *less* dependent on situational factors. Some women had previously been heterosexual, and had never consciously identified lesbian attractions or engaged in lesbian behavior; they "discovered" their lesbian desires once lesbian feminists had expanded the boundaries of the category and made lesbianism more attractive.

Others who "came out through feminism" included those who had harbored lesbian desires or engaged in "intermittent" lesbianism behavior without having before self-labeled as lesbian. Some experienced themselves as bisexual, in orientation if not in practice or identity; though holding the Freudian view that all people are originally bisexual, they were convinced that bisexuality was not a viable political identity. "To fight a system," Robin Morgan declared, "one must dare to identify with the *most* vulnerable aspect of one's oppression— and women are put in prison for being Lesbians, not bisexuals or heterosexuals *per se*."[60] As Rita Mae Brown warned, "You can't have your cake and eat it too. You can't be tied to male privileges with the right hand while clutching to your sister with your left."[61]

By consorting with the enemy, bisexuals undermined the struggle against compulsory heterosexuality. Moreover, bisexuality was an inherently *sexual* category, while lesbianism, feminists suggested, transcended sexuality. Hence, many women with bisexual desires took on lesbian self-identifications. Still others came to identify as lesbians though they did not engage in sexual activity with other women; they became known as "political lesbians." They were not opposed to sex between women, yet chose to be celibate.[62]

One woman described what seemed different about many of these women who came out as lesbians through the influence of the women's movement:

> There were an awful lot of women who came out at this time, for whom lesbianism was not an intense sexual thing, and it really was about bonding with other women. It wasn't about passionate fucking. It was sometimes about a domestic relationship, making a life together where neither person is dominating the other. It is about having a more equal relationship at home where you could feel comfortable and not feel squashed by the other person.[63]

It was principally sexual desire that had shaped lesbian communities before the convergence of Stonewall and the second wave of feminism. Lesbian subcultures before feminism had formed to provide safe spaces to realize lesbian desire; these subcultures were marked by stigma and organized around sexuality. Lesbian feminism created a different breed of lesbian. She did not necessarily share "old gays' " feelings of deviance. She was less likely to be exclusively driven in a sexual sense toward women. She was more likely to be middle class and to have thought carefully about the political implications of her new identification. For middle-class women who were captivated by a political vision of women's liberation, sexuality was often secondary.

Despite the widespread suggestion that "any woman can," the image of the grown-up tomboy, the "born lesbian," continued to carry a particular cachet among "new lesbians." In "The Woman Identified Woman," the Radicalesbians had described the lesbian as a woman who "often beginning at an extremely early age, acts in accordance with her inner compulsion to be a more complete and freer human being than her society . . . cares to allow her" and had privileged the early developing lesbian as a nascent feminist. In a similar vein, the Berkeley Women's Music Collective sang:

> gay and proud
> i was born a bastard
> you know my mother she couldn't keep me
> sent me off to a foster home
> where they tried to teach me
> that girls can't go climbing trees
> or playing with certain toys
> got to stay in dresses else they're called tomboys
> well i can sing it loud now
> i can sing it loud now
> i can sing it loud now
> gay and proud
>
> we women been waiting all our lives
> for our sisters to be our lovers
> hey look around you now
> ain't you glad we finally found each other[64]

Despite the radically social constructionist rhetoric of the movement, many individuals acknowledged differences between "born lesbians"—women who "knew" from an early age that they were attracted to the same sex—and "born again" types, those who "discovered" lesbianism through the culture of lesbian feminism. The former group was drawn to lesbianism principally because of their same-sex desires; the latter searched for identity and community. Would the commonality between these two groups of women, all of whom had chosen to love women, overcome their differences?

"I came out 'in the movement' discovering my gayness through feminism, but I have become aware recently that if I were to wake up some morning with no feminist consciousness and no women's liberation movement, I would still be gay," remarked a participant in a "gay-straight dialogue" held in Los Angeles in 1972. She wondered whether there might be more to becoming a lesbian than developing "lesbian consciousness": "I prefer women and have no desire to relate to men. . . . Feminist movement, or no feminist movement, I am gay."[65]

Clearly, lesbians of the baby boom generation took many routes to identification: individuals gave markedly different accounts of the origins of their lesbianism, the meaning of lesbian activity and lesbian feelings, and their age of entry into the lesbian community. Some women possessed a greater sense of "difference" or deviance, a feeling of being "not heterosexual," than others. Much the same could be said of their "old gay" predecessors: strongly butch women in particular tended to think of themselves as being more deviant and more strongly driven to lesbianism than were their femme counterparts.[66] But feminists believed these individual differences could be subsumed in building a collective conception of lesbianism.

Aided by feminism, radical lesbians broke down not just the boundaries between the heterosexual and homosexual worlds but also the elaborate, gendered organization of secretive lesbian subcultures. They greatly expanded the pool of self-identified lesbians, particularly among middle-class women who had little, if any, prior contact with or knowledge of the strongly class-segregated and role-playing subcultures of the 1950s and early 1960s. This caused some problems. Many "old gays" came to resent "new lesbians" for disrupting the taken-for-granted rules and traditions that structured their subcultures. And even among those who had come out in the context of feminism, differences persisted. Some women felt deeply different, queer, often from a very early age. Others, who experienced their sexuality as fluid and changeable, saw their lesbianism as a choice.

In 1972, two lesbian feminist observers foretold the problems that would arise from these differences: "the political lesbian's simplicity and joy in loving women are invigorating, spontaneous, and unburdened, but her inability to identify with homosexual oppression lends an air of unreality and a feeling of emptiness to her statement."[67] Though feminists attempted to construct a universalizing, inclusive definition of lesbianism, smashing the categories was a much simpler task than remaking the self.

Chapter Two

Difference, Desire,
and the Self

Three Stories

> The individual can only be what is possible within some
> specifically constructed historical world. But individuals,
> thus constrained, construct and reconstruct such historical
> worlds by exploiting the distinctive ambiguities of interac-
> tion. They bring with them to each of their interactions a
> unique and inner self.
>
> Dennis Wrong, "The Oversocialized
> Conception of Man in Modern
> Sociology" (1961)

As we have seen, women who reached adolescence and young adulthood during the 1960s and 1970s—at a time when U.S. society was
in a period of great social ferment, when gender and sexual norms
were being publicly contested—confronted two different accounts of
lesbianism. The medical model conceptualized lesbianism in terms
of homosexual object choice or desires, which were fixed and immutable. This dominant explanation associated lesbianism with gender
nonconformity, exemplified by the mannish woman. To become a
lesbian was to reveal something that had before been hidden, to disclose something that occupied the very core of one's "being," and to
build an identity on the basis of one's stigma.

In contrast, an emergent account, influenced by social constructionist thought, considered lesbianism to be a product of multiple
influences rather than being traceable to a single cause, a lifestyle
choice that entailed conscious self-reflection and identification. In
the context of the feminist and gay liberation movements, to become
a lesbian signified coming to self-knowledge, identifying with the collectivity of other lesbians, and making political commitments.[1]

The discourse of "coming out," as it was used by my interviewees, linked these two conceptions of homosexuality. It imagined the process of homosexual identification as a coming to terms with an "authentic" self, which implied the existence of a "core" sexual orientation, an internal "truth." [2] Yet it situated the development of a lesbian identity as a voluntaristic and reflexive act that challenged the pervasiveness of "compulsory heterosexuality" and was accessible to anyone who possessed the right political convictions. The women I interviewed shared a strong belief in the idea of "coming out," which they generally understood as two linked processes: the consolidation of a personal sense of self as lesbian and the development of a social identity as lesbian, the latter entailing a certain degree of public disclosure. When I began an interview by asking someone how she would describe her sexual identity, most interviewees promptly launched into their "coming out" story.

In one instance, I sat down with a forty-three-year-old woman, a carpenter in San Francisco, and asked her to tell me about her life. No sooner had I turned on the tape recorder than she proceeded to tell me her coming out story, beginning in early childhood and moving through time to the present. It seemed to me that she had told this story many times before. In the course of my research, this scene was repeated time after time. Immediately after I asked my subjects how they would define their sexual identities, they would embark upon their stories, carefully tracing their biographies in roughly chronological order.

Coming out as a lesbian typically took several years or more.[3] Like a fictional bildungsroman, in which a character achieves self-development by making a challenging journey, the process of coming out moved the individual from one state of being to another.[4] It guided her along a path that ended with the moment of resolution: the "final" achievement of a lesbian/gay identity. The relating of her coming out story was itself an important element of this process, in part because it was an act of disclosure. Though few disclosed their lesbianism to all whom they met, and at all times, the women I spoke with were "out" in many if not most aspects of their lives.

In telling me her story, each woman constructed a personal narrative of sexual identity development that helped to organize her autobiographical experience for herself and for me, the audience. In speaking with individuals, I was often struck both by the pervasiveness of the discourse of "coming out" and by the great variety among the stories themselves.[5] Coming out was a narrative template that was expansive and adaptable enough to accommodate a diverse array of life experiences. Here are three of these stories.

Barb Herman: "Just the Way I Am"

Forty-two-year-old Barb Herman was born to a lower-middle-class Italian family in New York. Barb experienced desires for other girls early in life and acted on these desires in isolation, often thinking that she was "the only one." She thinks of herself as having been a tomboy as a child. "I never played with dolls, and hardly ever played with girls. I wore boys' clothes at age eight or nine."

Barb remembers the 1950s and early 1960s as a time when she was "young and out of control, having all these feelings, and no place to go to talk about them." At fifteen, Barb had a first sexual experience with another girl. It was 1962. At the time, she had no words to describe her feelings, though she was vaguely aware of the existence of other lesbians. It was an experience that she describes as an epiphany, or defining moment. She felt a "mixture of fear and exhilaration. This is home after all these years. I knew that this was what I wanted, but I knew that it was a really bad thing."

Lesbian pulp novels—dimestore fiction sold during the 1950s and 1960s, featuring lurid covers and titles such as *Odd Girl Out* and *Strange Sisters*—told tales of lust, intrigue, and secrecy, of being young and confused, and of being a social misfit. These books remind Barb of her own adolescence, for she "faced the very same kind of struggles" as their characters. Once she had her first homosexual experience, she said, "I felt at peace with myself emotionally. This is home." Quoting the 1952 novel by Claire Morgan (Patricia Highsmith) called *The Price of Salt*, Barb recalled the line: "Nobody had to tell her that this was the way it was supposed to be."

Barb feels that she has always been a lesbian, that it was not at all a matter of choice. To become a lesbian, she simply "discovered" what was "already there." In contrast, she described her first girlfriend, who "turned straight" after a few years: "She flipped out. She became straight after a few years, got married, had kids, and seriously repressed that stuff: her sexual experience with me, her feelings for others. Maybe she had some doubts about really being gay. I couldn't repress it. I never did. I never had any doubts."

Yet it would be several years before Barb could actually name her lesbianism to others. Through her teens and early twenties, Barb had a series of relationships with women but never claimed a lesbian identity in the sense of affiliating with the lesbian subculture. She was seeing a psychiatrist at the time, who told her that she had "trouble relating to people" and prescribed tranquilizers. Several years after having had her first homosexual experience, Barb befriended Lore, the first "flesh and blood" lesbian she had ever met—the first woman she knew who identified as a lesbian. One day, Lore looked Barb in the eye and said: "You are a lesbian." At the time, Barb said, she scoffed at the allegation, "but it planted some sort of seed." Still, claiming a lesbian identity in a social sense, as a member of a stigmatized group, was not an easy task in the absence of any public lesbian visibility.

> At the time the women's movement was just starting to struggle with lesbianism. I had no patience for it. I had no patience to struggle with them. Even if I said "I am not a lesbian," I think I always knew I was. But it's this funny thing. How you dissociate yourself from things that you're feeling, even if there is a label for what you're feeling in the English language. I always knew I was a lesbian, but I distanced myself from the word. It was too scary to consider. . . . I remember looking at the rise of feminism, and thinking it was hopeful, and that things were moving in the right direction. But I remember thinking or sensing that they're not there yet. It's not all right to be a lesbian—yet.
>
> There were all these strikes going on, and I still didn't quite get all the connections—with the war, with academic freedom, with general alternative education and feminism and black power. There were all these strikes all over campus. Kent State. Riots at Columbia. The world was going to pieces, but I was freaking out about being a lesbian. That was the most important thing to me.

But in 1970, a homophobic incident provided the catalyst for Barb's public coming out. While in college, she was living with a girlfriend and several other people in a communal house. One morning, she awoke to hear her housemates discussing whether the presence of Barb and her girlfriend was "warping the household." That was, she said, "the straw that broke the camel's back." Soon after this, Barb became involved with a radical lesbian political group that had just formed in town. She described attending a first meeting, in 1971: "It was like the messiah had come. There were all these people who were like me. They were all my age. They were lesbians. They were distributing mimeographed copies of 'The Woman Identified Woman.' I quickly realized I was a feminist as well as a lesbian."

Becoming a feminist lesbian meant that Barb could begin to think of her lesbianism in positive terms. It also meant that she could think of her femaleness and her lesbianism as compatible, rather than conflicting. She gained a sense that she could have a social as well as a personal identity as a lesbian.

> The whole period from 1971 to 1973–74 was an incredible release. It was great. Because I had gone on marches—civil rights marches and other kinds of demonstrations—before, but none of it seemed to have much to do with my life. It was a thrill to be doing it for me instead of for everybody else. Getting involved in lesbian feminism was a very personal kind of thing. Things were happening very fast; every time you turned around there was more going on, more stuff being written, more things to read and talk about. We were up half the night talking. It was like the racetrack. For a while life was really exciting.

Barb says that she would be a lesbian regardless of these historical changes, but she imagines that she would have been forced to lead a far more secretive, far more unhappy life.

Barb's narrative exhibits many elements of the "dominant" account; she sees her lesbianism as an immutable orientation, fixed at birth or in early childhood. She talked about "knowing" she was a lesbian by age eight, even before she had words to describe her feelings. Adolescent girls vary in the extent to which they know their desires. Some are not at all aware of sexual feelings, heterosexual or homosexual, while others, like Barb, are deeply conscious of them. Girls with early awareness of their sexual feelings often experience their adolescence as a period in which their embodied sexual desire is simultaneously elicited and denigrated by the dominant culture.[6] One can imagine that girls with early lesbian desires rarely, if ever, receive reinforcement either in the dominant culture or within adolescent peer groups.

Barb identified desires for girls and women at a very early age, experiencing these desires as powerful and unwavering. In the context of the early to mid-1960s, Barb saw herself as virtually alone, having no one to discuss her feelings with. She compared her experiences with those of old dykes, who had come out as lesbians before feminism. "I was sort of an old lesbian. To be an old lesbian meant you were out before feminism. I wasn't out to anyone but myself." Being a lesbian in the mid-1960s was a "long stream of unfinished business." She thinks of herself as straddling the "old gay" and "new gay" worlds because she had same-sex experiences before the late 1960s, before the lesbian/gay movements expanded the social space open to lesbians and gay men. "But I knew when I was eight years old. I probably knew much earlier."

When I asked Barb why she is a lesbian, she replied, "It's just the way I am." Indeed, she found the question itself rather curious. Barb sees her adolescent experiences of difference and her eventual homosexuality as points on a continuum. Her personal identity as lesbian was never really in question. As she grew older and began to affiliate with the lesbian community, those connections gave her a social identity as well, a sense of direction and purpose that went beyond the self, and a way to counter some of the stigma she encountered. She spoke of the important role that the lesbian community played in allowing her to normalize her sexuality.

But the fact that she experienced her lesbian desires early in life has been crucial in shaping her sense of self and the meaning her lesbianism holds for her. Indeed, her identity account resembles the "old gay" account, insofar as secrecy looms large for those who have spent their formative years "managing" their stigma, carefully determining which parts of the self they would reveal to others. She feels that she has lived much of her life in the closet.

Perhaps because of these experiences, Barb tended to accentuate the differences between herself and heterosexual women, viewing lesbians and heterosexuals as two distinct categories, much as did women of an earlier prefeminist cohort. She thinks of lesbianism largely in essentialist terms. She believes that the only "real" lesbians are "born" lesbians—women like her, who have little choice in the matter of their sexuality.

Margaret Berg:
"Coming Out through Feminism"

Margaret Berg grew up in New England; she was a red diaper baby, the daughter of Jewish leftist activists of mixed working-class and middle-class backgrounds. To be a woman in the 1950s and 1960s, she said, was to grow up with "the profound sense of oneself as a second-class citizen." Margaret spoke of her need to feign under-achievement in school in order to catch a husband. She said that she experienced her heterosexual relationships as largely unsatisfying and her sexual interest in men as often conflicted, motivated more by accommodation to male needs and social expectations than by her own desires. "I had all the feelings about men that we all had; we thought they were like zombies. I felt that I took care of all the men I was involved with. I felt like I was much stronger than they were. I felt like I gave much more than I got." She recalled, "We were grow-ing up in a world that was so invalidating of women. I straightened my hair, I was ambivalent about being smart, my physics teacher told my parents: she's doing fine for a girl."[7]

The women's movement emerged in the late 1960s to help her make sense of this alienation and situate it in the larger scheme of women's oppression. Margaret compared her exposure to femi-nism in 1969 to "coming out of a cave." Feminism, she said, was "the most exciting and validating thing that had happened in our lives." It allowed her and others to resolve the dissonance they felt between cultural codes and subjective experience. Within the context of the movement, Margaret developed an analysis and vocab-ulary for these feelings, seeing her problems in gendered terms for the first time. She began to believe that she had devalued herself as a woman and underestimated the importance of her female relationships.

Because of their growing idealization of other women—a change in attitude made possible by feminism—women like Margaret withdrew from primary relationships with men. This was less a conscious decision than the outcome of the growing separation between men's and women's social and political worlds, at least among the young, predominantly middle-class members of what became loosely called the "movement." At the time, she was romantically involved with a man, but as her women friends became more and more central, he became more peripheral. Eventually, "most of my friends were women, all of my friends were feminists, men were not part of my life. It was all very seamless." Margaret had always thought of lesbianism as something that was involuntary; it was an orientation that one either did or did not "have." But when she was in her early twenties, she became aware of the possibility of constructing her own sexuality and of electing lesbianism. As she described it, she was one of those women who "came out through feminism."

When Margaret became involved in her first lesbian relationship, she said, "the only gay women I knew (and *we* wouldn't call ourselves gay) were my friend and myself." Her friend, Jennifer, eventually moved into her apartment. The world they traveled in was that of liberated sexuality and free use of drugs, and there was "a real sense of barriers breaking." She was drawn to Jennifer as a kindred spirit, an equal. "There was a certain reflection of myself I found in her." Margaret recalled that Jennifer had "much more self-consciously identified homoerotic feelings," while hers were more about sexual experimentation and rebellion.

In an effort to make sense of her feelings, and to find support for them, she began to attend a women's consciousness-raising group devoted to discussing questions of sexuality. Practically overnight, through the influence of gay liberation and lesbian feminism, the gathering transformed itself into a coming out group. There, Margaret was socialized into the lesbian world. She began to think of herself as a lesbian and call herself one.

> There was a normative sense about discovering women and male domination and how disgusting men could be. Not to be a lesbian was

stupid, masochistic . . . something called "lesbian consciousness" developed in our heads. It's hard to reconstruct just how the process occurred. We talked about "coming out" every four or five weeks. That term started having more and more ramifications as our lives changed. Not just making love with a woman for the first time—but every new situation where you experienced and/or revealed yourself as gay.

Within the context of a coming out group, Margaret carved out a place for herself in the lesbian subculture. Earlier, "coming out" had referred almost exclusively to the process of disclosure. But now women who had never experienced themselves as deeply and irrevocably different, but who shared a sense of alienation from gender and sexual norms, could also claim lesbian identities by developing "gay consciousness." The discourse of lesbian feminism conflated feminism and lesbianism. Lesbianism was reenvisioned to signify not simply a sexual preference but a way for women to gain strength and confidence, to bond with other women.

But the political strategy of coming out to others as a means of establishing unity often had the contradictory effect of heightening differences *among* women, and the tension between identity and difference within the coming out group soon became apparent. Margaret describes the "experiential gap" separating the women in the group who were "entering a first gay relationship" and those who were "coming out of the closet":

> One woman was quite involved with a man and left almost immediately—it was never clear exactly why she had joined the group, except that she felt good about women. Another women pulled out because she felt there was a "bisexual" orientation to the group. . . . Her "coming out" was very different from the rest of ours. She wasn't entering a first gay relationship; rather, she was coming out of "the closet," entering a gay community and acquiring pride in an analysis of who she is. . . . There was a real experiential gap between her and the rest of the group. We had no understanding of the bar scene, of role-playing, of the whole range of experience of an "old gay." I'm sure a lot of this inexperience translated into moralistic arrogance—we were a good deal less than understanding when she called her lovers "girls."

In this clash of cultures we see two different visions of lesbianism: the old dyke world, which valorized gender roles, and the emergent lesbian feminist culture, which rejected gendered coupledom in favor of the communalized sensuality of the group circle dance.

> We all went to our first gay women's dance together. I was very scared by a number of older women dressed sort of mannishly. Not scared that they'd do anything to me, but wary of being identified with them. I was very relieved when a group of women . . . showed up and we all danced together in a big friendly circle. That was my first exposure to a kind of joyful sensuality that I've come to associate with women's dances. Looking around and seeing a lot of gay women enjoying themselves and each other helped me let go of a lot of my fears and validated the possibilities for growth and pleasure in the relationship with J.

The old gay world conceptualized lesbianism as desire; the new gay world reconceptualized it, more diffusely, as woman identification. Margaret saw differences in the group primarily in generational terms, evidencing the extent to which other distinctions may have been less salient at the time. For younger women, becoming a lesbian was a matter of developing lesbian consciousness, developing a personal sense of self as lesbian. For the second group, the issue was not really *being* a lesbian, a matter of personal identity, but *living* as one, developing a social identity. For Margaret, old dykes, particularly those who were very visibly butch, represented what she might become if she shunned heterosexuality. Gender inversion served as a symbolic marker of lesbianism, warning those who stepped out of their prescribed roles that the taint of lesbianism might soon follow them. But the older women also embodied a kind of protofeminism, a willingness to go against the social grain.

As she tried to figure out her place in the lesbian world, Margaret acknowledged that coming out is "an incredibly hard process." She alluded to the conflict between the dominant essentialist model and an emergent constructionist one. "Many women think there's some magic leap into gayness—that you suddenly lose all fears, doubts, heterosexual feelings. Others are afraid that they weren't 'born gay.' Come-out groups help women deal with all of those feelings. The existence of the Lesbian Mother's Group brought home to us that women are not born lesbians; that women who were both wives and mothers could decide to live with and love other women." After some initial doubts about whether or not she was "really" a lesbian, Margaret assured herself that even seemingly gender-conforming women, women who were once wives and mothers, can be lesbians. These "successful" women who had boyfriends and husbands could also become lesbians—thus, lesbians were not necessarily "failed women."

Her story suggests that some women used the discourse of "coming out" to claim authenticity and gain membership in the lesbian world. Clearly, this was a very different path to lesbianism than the one taken by women whose sense of self as lesbian was less in question, for whom coming out meant "coming out of the closet." While women such as Barb thought of their lesbianism primarily as internally driven, for Margaret and other "elective" lesbians the adoption of lesbianism as a social identity tended to precede the consolidation of lesbianism as a personal identity.

Unlike Barb, Margaret did not trace her lesbianism to early childhood experiences or have the experience of being "not heterosexual" early on—even if she expressed alienation from heterosexual gender norms. Margaret also differs from Barb in her high degree of self-reflexivity, rooted at least in part in her more middle-class background. In general she framed her lesbianism within the development of "lesbian consciousness," viewing her involvement with women rather than men as a political rather than a sexual choice.[8] Because of her history, Margaret held the belief that any woman can choose to be a lesbian. However, she recognized that there were different "types" of lesbians, who exercised greater and lesser degrees of choice over their sexuality.

Ara Jones: "It's a Changeable Thing"

Forty-year-old Ara Jones grew up in the South, the daughter of a manual laborer and a domestic worker. Ara described her life as being shaped equally by her lesbianism and her blackness. She identifies as a lesbian but has long been conscious of the fact that her own desires do not conform neatly with binary sexual categories, homosexual and heterosexual. She says she thinks of her lesbianism as "a changeable thing."

As a teenager, Ara experienced herself as fairly bisexual, though she would not have given it that name at the time. While she was sexually involved with boys, her primary commitments were with other girls.

> I was never boy crazy. I had two boyfriends. It was nice, but it was not like my relationships with girls. It was sexual more than emotional. Sexually it was fine. I think what I did a lot was . . . really separate sex and relationships—it was totally separate. Some people are very vulnerable when they're sexual; for me it was the opposite. I was less vulnerable when I was sexual with someone than when I was talking with them. I think I felt more confident about my body than with who I was.

At twenty-five she entered college and became involved with student organizations, African American and others. By this time, the period of most vocal and visible antiwar and feminist activity had already subsided, leaving behind an institutional infrastructure of lesbian/gay and feminist organizations, publications, and a more accepting climate for minorities of all sorts on her college campus.

Ara became involved with a white woman she met, who was an out lesbian. They fell "madly in love." In the context of this relationship, she began to think of herself as a lesbian. She never particularly identified with the lesbian community, however. This was in large part because it was predominantly white. "I definitely would say that I am a feminist, and a lesbian, but not a lesbian feminist necessarily. Lesbian feminism is too strict for me, and always has been. It's never felt quite right, not quite my experience, not quite comfortable." But once she and her lover broke up, a year later, Ara was forced to reassess her sexual self-definition. "I remember when she left, I felt like, okay: but what am I now? Where do I go? I felt much more connected to her than to a lesbian community. But then I didn't really feel all that connected to the black community by this time either." She continued to date men occasionally, eventually marrying a man whom she met through a friend. After two years, they decided to divorce. She described having "better" sex with men than with women. But with women, she said, she felt a "depth of emotion" that she "couldn't feel with men." She adopted a definition of lesbianism as passionate friendship: "a relationship in which two women's strongest emotions and affections are directed toward each other."[9] Becoming involved with men was "sexually possible but emotionally not." She elaborated, "Sometimes I was more aware of having sexual feelings for men than other times, but I always felt that I was a lesbian as well. In another world, it would be a lot easier. You would just go from relationship to relationship, and male and female sexuality would just sort of be . . . insignificant. But not in this world." The contradictions between these "multiple identities" may have been particularly salient for an African American woman with working-class roots, who was circulating in a largely middle-class world.

After moving to San Francisco in the early 1980s, Ara became a social worker for a county health office. She fell in love with a woman, eight years her senior, whom she met through a mutual friend. When asked whether her lesbianism is a choice, Ara replied, "Yes," adding, "but I'm not straight." Ara feels that her lesbianism is a choice insofar as she could choose to deny what she "really" felt. She could choose to be with men if she wished to fit in, but she has made a choice that fitting in is less important than being "who she is."

> Who I am is changeable. I could have lived my life as a straight person, if Sara hadn't come along. But she did, so here I am. I don't know if I'm a born lesbian, but I sure as hell know this is right for me. I love women. Maybe I'll change. Maybe I won't. So is it a choice? I don't know. Part of it is, part of it isn't.

She is not a lesbian like other women are lesbians, insofar as she was not "born" one, she says. Yet she sees herself as more sexually attracted to women than many of those who call themselves lesbians, particularly many who came out in the context of feminism. Indeed, she was involved with "one of those women" at one point and was sexually dissatisfied. For her girlfriend, she said, lesbianism was about bonding with other women. "It was about making a domestic relationship, making a life together where neither person dominated the other. It was about having a more equal relationship at home where one could be comfortable and not feel squashed by the other person." For Ara as well, lesbianism was about these things, but also about passionate sexuality and intimacy.

As we saw earlier, Barb described her personal identity as lesbian

as preceding her affiliation with lesbianism as a social category, while
Margaret said the opposite: her affiliation with the group preceded
her consolidation of a sense of "deep" identity. For Ara, separating
out the "personal" and "social" components of lesbian identification
and isolating which "came first" is impossible. She talks about her
lesbianism in terms of elements that were chosen and elements that
were not, and she remains conscious of the disjunction between "doing" and "being," between engaging in homosexual acts and claiming
a homosexual identity: "There are many women like me: women who
could've gone either way, depending upon what kind of situation they
found themselves in. I probably could've been straight and lived a
happy enough life, but women always came first—beginning with my
mama. So I became a lesbian. I thought of myself as that even though
I didn't usually use the word."

Ara's lesbianism is a choice insofar as acting upon her desires and
claiming a lesbian identity are chosen, since originally she experienced her desires as being at least partly fluid and changing. But at
the same time, she recognizes that her adoption of a social identity as
a lesbian "organized" these desires, diminishing her earlier bisexual
inclinations. While embracing a lesbian identity, Ara views it partly
as a strategic act, rather than as a direct expression of who she "really
is."

Speaking as a Lesbian

The preceding accounts are certainly not an exhaustive sample of
different ways of "being" a lesbian. Nor are they intended to be particularly representative in terms of class, age, race, or ethnicity.[10] The
stories of Barb, Margaret, and Ara suggest that individuals bring to
the process of forming sexual identity a sense of self that has already
taken on some shape, and they use the available accounts, or repertoires of meaning, to make sense of that self. These accounts are
historical constructions. As women fashion their identities, they study
those around them—selecting images to emulate or reject, fitting
themselves into the lesbian world(s). This process is historical, situational, and individual.

Coming out takes place in a particular historical context. Women

of the baby boom shared a set of broad historical and cultural experiences. The lesbian/gay and women's liberation movements figure
prominently in the three life stories, even for those who were not
actively political, providing a sense of enlarged possibilities, of expanded cultural resources.[11] Before these movements, traditional
conceptions of gender and sexuality had gone virtually unchallenged:
men and women were imagined as having separate and distinct roles;
sexology and psychoanalysis pathologized sexual "deviants" as biological or psychological aberrations. To claim a lesbian identity was to
declare oneself a deviant, an outsider, a queer.

Young women coming to adolescence and early adulthood during
the rise of feminism and gay liberation had access to an expanding
set of accounts or "scripts" for "doing" gender and sexuality. This
cultural context allowed them certain *tools*—meanings, roles, and
identities—with which to construct lesbian identities.[12] The discourse of "coming out," which suggested that becoming a lesbian was
a positive political act, was also a tool. This elastic narrative template
allowed individuals to make sense of their individual experiences and
escape the confines of normative heterosexuality and "hegemonic
femininity."[13]

Coming out is also a relational process. The family of origin is
typically the first audience for trying out one's emerging homosexual
identity. For example, some women reported that they had grown up
as "tomboys," that their families "had always known that they were
gay" and had treated them accordingly. This first testing of the waters
was typically a negative one, as their homosexual desires were invali-
dated or made invisible. It was through interaction with other self-
defined homosexual men and women later on that an identity was
rebuilt and access was gained to accounts that served to legitimate
the homosexual experience.[14] Meeting known lesbians made possible
more positive, embodied meanings of lesbianism. In the coming out
process, individuals assessed those around them, "figuring out" who
were the lesbians and whether they might "be one" as well. They
evaluated the meanings of lesbianism, questioning whether those
meanings helped them to make sense of their own subjective experiences and whether the stigma attached to such self-constructions was
manageable.

And finally, *coming out is an individual process.* Individuals negotiate the meanings, roles, and identities presented to them in different
ways. They make sexual choices amid a series of constraints, some
arising from individual psychological makeup. The experience and
organization of erotic tastes and preferences begin in childhood and
continue through puberty, partly forming the sense of self long before an individual's coming out begins. Early experiences of the body
and desire seem to play a role in adult sexual identity formation,
giving different shape to lesbian identity.[15]

For some girls this process is strongly influenced by "intrinsic"
desires and feelings, associated with "sexual orientation." Some recall
having felt an early sense of "difference," of being "not heterosexual."
Barb, who became conscious of her desires for other girls and women
when very young, described herself as having been outside of the
mainstream, not typically feminine, and not "normal." She struggled
to establish a positive sense of herself as lesbian during adolescence,
when issues of social identity besides sexuality are also being negotiated.

Those who come out later in life or who experience their sexuality
as fluid and malleable may have already dealt with these other issues
before they assume a "deviant" sexual identity. They may have established a sense of self as relatively "normal," at least in terms of their
sexuality. Margaret and to a lesser extent Ara, because they did not
think of themselves as being "not heterosexual" at an early age, felt
themselves to be somewhat less different, less deviant.[16] Taking on a
lesbian identity at a later stage means coping with somewhat different
issues. "It may involve a sense of loss in terms of acceptability and
social ease, but losing something one has had is an experience quite
different from never having had it."[17]

Experience is mediated by language, so we can never know the
"truth" of women's experiences prior to social interaction. "No inner
psychology, no desiring subject, no autonomous individual—in short,
no *a priori* entity, sexual or otherwise," Roger Lancaster asserts, "pre-
cedes social intercourse and awaits its influence." Even if it is often
felt as "inner" and "subjective," desire is not part of "nature." Nor is
it "opposed to" or "beyond" meaning. It is "a social act carried out
through social language."[18] The stories of Barb, Margaret, and Ara

suggest women can arrive at a lesbian identity in very different ways; sexual identity is formed by an interplay between factors that are internal and external, personal and cultural.

For Barb, becoming a lesbian meant that she could affiliate with the category lesbian, disclose that affiliation to others, and build a social world around the desires she had for so long kept private. Women like Barb, for whom lesbianism was a matter of deeply felt desires, made up the core group of individuals who would have lived lesbian lives, or at least harbored lesbian desires, even without the lesbian/gay and feminist movements. Their desires for girls and women, felt from an early age, were often accompanied by feelings of gender nonconformity.

Margaret and Ara, on the other hand, might be considered members of the larger grouping of women for whom lesbian identities are more highly dependent upon social context. Neither experienced exclusive homosexual desires from an early age. They did not begin the process of coming out from a position within "a closet," a subjective sense of themselves as highly deviant; their sexual drives toward women were apparently not as strong as Barb's. Margaret became aware of the possibility of defying compulsory heterosexuality when she encountered feminism and gay liberation. For her, coming out as lesbian entailed both developing a "deep" sense of self as lesbian and affiliating with lesbianism as a social category. Ara combined elements of Barb's and Margaret's stories. Like Barb, she began the process of identity formation with a sense of sexual difference, but for Ara this sense of difference was initially more inchoate and unformed. She recognized her homosexual desires relatively early, but these coexisted with heterosexual desires. Ara saw her embrace of the social category lesbian as somewhat serendipitous rather than as a firm expression of who she "is."

Despite their common use of the "coming out" template, baby boomers told a diverse array of different self stories. To some women, coming out meant "coming home," welcoming the desires they had long affirmed in secret. These individuals experienced a deep, subjective sense of being different early in life, and they saw coming out primarily as a matter of *disclosing* their lesbianism and finding a group of people who would support that disclosure. For others, however, coming out meant "discovering" their lesbianism. For these women, many of whom had "come out through feminism," identification with lesbianism as a sociosexual category often preceded a subjective sense of being different or deviant. Coming out was for them principally a quest to develop a deep sense of self, a matter of *individuating* as a lesbian. Finally, for a third group, whose personal and social sense of lesbianism appeared more fluid and inchoate, coming out entailed both individuation and disclosure in roughly equal measure.

To quote Biddy Martin, "the word *lesbian* is not an identity with predictable content[:] . . . it is position from which to speak." [19] Lesbian feminists redefined lesbianism in more expansive, universal terms, making the boundaries between straight and gay worlds less distinct and constructing an oppositional culture founded upon resistance to gender and sexual norms. Though drawing upon common cultural referents, women of the baby boom experienced the process of coming out in very different ways. One might say that they spoke different dialects of the same language of self-discovery and development, a fact that would pose thorny problems as they tried to fashion a collective identity.

Chapter Three

Becoming Lesbian

Identity Work and the
Performance of Sexuality

> Lane had always loved women, had always known that her
> life with males would be as comrades and not as lovers.
> ... There was another kind of lesbian, though, another
> lesbian history, where the woman did not know, or only
> knew somewhere in the locked attic of her own elusive
> mind, for years. This woman lived two lives in her lifetime:
> first the heterosexual, then the homosexual, the second as
> if by solemn choice and not by chance or chemistry.
>
> Sheila Ortiz Taylor, *Spring Forward,*
> *Fall Back* (1985)

When Margaret Berg first slept with a woman, her lover declared
herself to be a lesbian immediately afterward. She had what she calls
a "coming home" experience. For Margaret, however, the experience
was far less significant. "After the first time we made love, for her it
was like well, now we were lovers. And to me, it was much more:
okay, I tried this, but it was much more along the lines of sexual
experimentation. . . . Maybe I'll do it again, maybe I won't." Margaret's lover had "much more self-consciously identified homoerotic
feelings" than she did. "I hadn't thought about the whole thing very
much. It was much more consciously on her agenda," she recalled.
"She was the one to make the first moves." At times, this sense of
dissonance was echoed by others. Margaret remembered her lover
saying to her early in their relationship: "Sometimes I think I'm a
lesbian and you're not."

Laura Stone recalled her first lesbian experience as a nineteen-
year-old in 1969: "We slept together and kind of fumbled through
it." While her friend declared herself to be a lesbian immediately

after this experience, she resisted. "I knew that I didn't feel like *aha,* I was coming home. I didn't feel like: what a relief to shed this charade. I didn't feel like: where have I been all my life? But I wasn't repulsed either." After recognizing that her initial sexual response to women was muted in comparison to that of other women she knew, Laura quickly became known to others as "the straight woman who was messing around with gay women." She perceived her feelings as a source of inadequacy and therefore kept them private, confined to a sort of personal inner dialogue.

Within the culture of a social movement in which identity provided an entry into political participation and was often seen as a end in itself, some women's worst fear was that they would be unable to develop *any* identity at all. Mary Lipton recalled: "For the longest time, I was afraid that I wasn't anything. I wasn't gay or straight. That I was the only person in the entire world who wasn't anything. I was turned off to men but hadn't fallen in love with a woman. I actually slept with a woman but it was not a good experience. . . . I really wasn't sure what I was. I thought maybe I was nothing."

Unlike those who experienced themselves as more *internally* pushed toward homosexuality, some women initially experienced a lack of congruence between their "deep" sense of self (or personal identity) and the social category lesbian; they "tried on" a lesbian identity and decided it didn't quite "fit." Sometimes this incongruence appeared as a lack of emotional and physical response in initial sexual encounters; homosexual *behavior* did not itself guarantee the development of a lesbian *identity.* Sexual involvement alone was not enough to authenticate their lesbianism; it did not necessarily move them through the path of lesbian development.[1] Some left the lesbian fold, driven out by their perception that they were not "real" lesbians.

But the recognition that there were different types of lesbians, and that some women initially had an easier time claiming an identity than others, strengthened others' resolve to undertake "identity work" to claim lesbian selfhood. As Laura Stone put it,

> I knew that some part of me felt like I couldn't move further towards women, and that I was being scared off from that, being scared off from going my own route. Part of me thought that it's because it's not supposed to be. . . . So it was almost like I saw myself desensitized to

the socialization of the society, but I was straight identified. At no point in that process did I think of myself as a lesbian. But I thought I could *become* a lesbian.

Identity Work

Lesbian feminists imagined "coming out" as a journey that began with a discovery of the lesbian within one's sense of self and proceeded through time, as the individual moved from an oppressive environment to one that permitted freer and bolder self-expression.[2] Coming out signified the claiming, or reclaiming, of that which is essential, true, unchanging. But coming out is as much a practical creation of the self, a "be-coming out," as a matter of revealing or discovering one's sexuality.

"Coming out is partially a process of revealing something kept hidden, but it is also more than that," writes political philosopher Shane Phelan. "It is a process of fashioning a self—a lesbian or gay self— that did not exist before coming out began."[3] Identities do not spring forth effortlessly from individuals: individuals reflexively effect change in the meanings of particular identities. Becoming a lesbian always entails participating in particular communities and discourses, conforming to historical and localized norms for "being" a lesbian. A lesbian identity is learned and performed in many different ways. Particularly for women who "originally" experienced themselves as heterosexual or bisexual, and who became lesbians very self-consciously, through the influence of feminism, coming out as a lesbian often entailed a great deal of work.

Sociologist Barbara Ponse describes "identity work" as the "processes and procedures engaged in by groups designed to effect change in the meanings of particular identities."[4] I use the term similarly, to signify the process by which many individuals sought to make their subjective sense of self congruent with their emergent social identity as lesbian and to narrow the experiential gap separating them from other, more experienced lesbians. For women of the baby boom cohort, the identity work required to "become lesbian" took different forms, forms that often derived from feminist reinterpretations and reversals of dominant gender and sexual norms.

Erving Goffman has shown that on the surface level, individuals use gestures and symbols, "signs that convey social information," as means of self-presentation. This type of identity work signals membership in the group to others.[5] A second dimension, emotion work, concerns "deep acting," the attempt to alter one's inner thoughts so as to feel differently and also look as though one feels differently.[6] Arlie Hochschild proposes that people are more likely to seek interactional rules for both of these levels in "times of great social transition," when they often find themselves in new situations with no social rules at hand. An emergent culture would need to codify rules for management of both symbols and emotions in order to organize members' interactions successfully.[7]

Indeed, my interviewees described a period, the 1970s, when new gender norms were devised through feminist practice. Acts of identity work conveyed membership and position within the lesbian subculture to other members, while at the same time communicating information about this stigma to members of the larger society. They also effected change in personal identities, altering the ways in which individuals thought about themselves. In terms of surface identity work, individuals changed their dress and mannerisms to conform more closely to what a "real" lesbian "looked like." They also engaged in the public telling of coming out stories. But the work also went deeper, as individuals consciously altered not only such relatively superficial characteristics as symbols or gestures but also inner characteristics, such as emotions and desires. By looking at these performances, we can more fully grasp the complexity of sexual identity formation.

Telling Stories

Modern life offers individuals numerous opportunities to "confess" the "truth" of our lives. The Catholic confessional, in which individuals speak of dark secrets in order to expunge their sins, is joined by the psychoanalytic couch, where the analysand is encouraged to probe the depths of her unconscious. Among lesbians and gay men, the coming out narrative has become a kind of collective confessional that seeks both to free the individual from her or his sexual repression and, at the same time, to build a culture and community around a "reverse affirmation" of shared stigma.[8]

Many of my interviewees who came of age during the 1970s were introduced to the idea of coming out through their participation in feminist "consciousness-raising." Women talked together about their personal problems as women—their unsatisfying relationships with men, their feelings of inferiority and powerlessness. Within the context of a "consciousness-raising group," "small group," or "rap group," as they were sometimes called, many women came to recognize that the "personal is political" and began to think of themselves as members of a collectivity of women. They also came to recognize their deep feelings for other women:

> As women turned to each other for affection and support that we had previously sought in men, many sensual feelings were liberated. At meetings we gave each other hugs and backrubs; in the streets we began to walk arm in arm. We felt a new freedom to explore our feelings for each other. Some of us made love with women we loved; some of us "came out." For some women lesbianism was an extension of the desire to be completely self-sufficient. Or, many times, the women's movement provided a safe enough place to open up new sexual feelings.[9]

As gender and sexual boundaries were breaking down and the meanings of sexuality were being redefined, consciousness-raising groups often became coming out groups in which individuals were socialized into the lesbian world. In the language of the day, discovering one's lesbianism was a matter of unearthing that which was repressed and hidden, that which was negated by the compulsory heterosexuality of the dominant culture.

As Laura Stone recalled: "People didn't feel so freaked out about the idea of women loving women. It was the idea of women not loving men that was so offensive." Hence, it took a great deal of courage, and a new set of values, to go against the social grain. As a 1972 lesbian feminist tract explained, this passage entailed the fashioning of a self that, though new, was actually "truer" to the individual than had been the formerly "feigned" heterosexual self: "Readiness to become an acknowledged Lesbian seems to involve a personal and emotional restructuring of values, often with the help of friends or a consciousness-raising group. . . . The transition from a feigned heterosexual identity to a Lesbian identity may constitute a period of considerable confusion. There is a time when a Lesbian feels she is nobody, nowhere—on a bridge between an old self and a new self."[10] Coming out was conceptualized as a difficult "task" that one had to be "ready" to undertake, for which homosexual desire was not necessarily a prerequisite. The core sense of self was imagined to be malleable, a piece of clay that needed to be shaped. Coming out was a matter of "coming to consciousness" and socializing the individual into a new existence as a lesbian. Consciousness-raising was "a reconditioning experience designed to shed layer after layer of trained negative thinking and free the vital self which oppression has so effectively buried."[11]

The coming out story, the account of the passage into the lesbian/gay world, was the gay community's "development myth." It was an account of heroism in the face of tremendous odds and societal pressure: based on the ideal of being "true to oneself" and expressing one's "authentic" self, it invoked a central theme in American culture.[12] When forty-four-year-old Sarah Marcus became involved with a woman for the first time, she did not think of herself as a "lesbian." A lesbian, she thought, was a woman for whom lesbian desires had always been "primary," a woman who had never desired men. She did not fit this description. But through her involvement in feminism, Sarah joined a consciousness-raising group. There, she began to self-identify as lesbian. The coming out group helped bridge the gap between herself and more "experienced" lesbians. Sarah spoke of the great joy she took in telling her coming out story every opportunity she got. "Every time a bunch of us got together for the first time, we'd immediately launch into telling our come-out story. That's what we had in common—this feeling of having a shared secret. We'd go on and on for hours and hours." The telling of coming out stories was a public act, serving as a type of "identity announcement" that directed an individual's conduct and influenced that of others. Telling one's coming out story in effect announced one's membership in the group to others. But it also defined and sharpened the teller's interest in a situation, thus focusing attention more acutely on those situated events that are relevant to that identity.[13] In telling these stories, individuals ordered their subjective reality; isolating and recalling the defining events, contexts, or ideas gave symbolic order to their lesbian trajectory. This telling served to reinforce the teller's commitment to a lesbian identity. As Judith Butler suggests, "it is through the repeated play of this sexuality that the 'I' is insistently reconstituted as a lesbian 'I.'" In other words, the repetition of a culturally constructed characteristic produces a lesbian identity.[14]

Within the lesbian/gay community, coming out marks a change in identification, via a status passage that tends to be highly ritualized. It is a collective narrative, an "identity story," that possesses certain conventions and rules. Describing the coming out narrative as it operated among women in a Southern city in the mid-1970s, Barbara Ponse isolated five atemporal component elements that she called the "gay trajectory." First, the individual has a "subjective sense of being different" from heterosexual persons and "identifies this difference as feelings of sexual-emotional attachment to her own sex." Second, she develops an understanding of the "homosexual or lesbian significance of these feelings." Third, the individual "accepts these feelings and their implications for identity"—she comes out or accepts the identity as lesbian. Fourth, the woman "seeks a community of like persons." Fifth, the individual becomes involved in a sexual-emotional lesbian relationship. "Given one of these elements," notes Ponse, "irrespective of their order in time, it is commonly assumed in the lesbian world that the others will logically come to pass."[15]

When women told their coming out stories publicly, they tended to present a relatively homogeneous, seamless narrative. Some individuals reported the strain of rewriting their personal biographies in order to emphasize a sense of continuity and authenticity. Though they recognized that early in life they did not "feel" like lesbians, upon coming out they conceived of their new status as a personal essence, some inner quality of being, which they understood to feel "natural." As we saw, Laura Stone acknowledged that unlike the experience of many of her lesbian friends, her coming out was not a "coming home." She did not experience her lesbianism as "primary" or highly driven. Yet through the process of consciousness-raising she came to see herself as a lesbian, albeit one who was "going through a different path of coming out."

> I began to look back at my past, and think: maybe it's not such an accident that I got here. I remembered all the lesbians in my past: my guitar teacher I was in love with. I didn't know at the time she was a lesbian. . . . I ran into her at this point, at a lesbian dance, and she talked as if she had some sense then that I was going to be a lesbian. So it was this wonderful little encounter. And I remembered this other teacher, an older woman, and she stayed very vividly in my memory. . . . I remember telling my mother how much I loved her, and my mother saying to me: she's a very sad woman, that she lives with a woman. The connection was: they were very nice, but sad people.

Symbolic interactionist literature on identity construction describes how people experiencing "conversions" of identity are prone to "recasting the past" to bring it into line with the present.[16] Coming out stories, like all narratives of the self, are incomplete, selective renderings of personal history, shaped by the needs of the present as much as by the past. In interviewing people about their lives, particularly about the past, one can never know the "truth." What we know is what individuals want us to know, how they represent themselves to those around them.

Many women such as Laura or Sarah who came out "through the women's movement," who had never thought of themselves as lesbians, or even bisexuals, before their exposure to feminism, self-consciously constructed their stories to resemble those of women for whom lesbianism seemed more internally motivated. Individuals were often quite well aware of having done this. Speaking of the pressures to rewrite her coming out narrative along such lines, one woman complained: "I've gotten the feeling from fringe feminists and older lesbians that if you didn't grow up as a tomboy and fall in love with your high school classmates, you ain't no fer-real dyke. . . . When asked how I came out I have gotten into adding a fictitious struggle with lesbianism from way back in talking with some women. It helps to show your scars, even fake ones."[17]

Psychoanalytic developmental theory tends to correlate the degree of pathology in a trait with the earliness of its origins, lending credence to a pathologization of sexualities determined to have early

origins, such as homosexuality.[18] While imagining a highly constructionist conception of lesbianism that viewed sexual identities as fluid,
in practice lesbian feminists often simply reversed the standard psychoanalytic account, granting "most favored" status to those individuals who were commonly believed to be most pathological. For a
woman trying to authenticate her lesbianism to herself and to others,
early homosocial or homosexual events, relationships, and personal
feelings that may not have seemed particularly sexual or even significant at the time of their occurrence were recast to reveal a continuous lesbian history.[19] But often, despite these conscious commitments, heterosexual desires intruded. "Deeper" forms of identity
work, such as resocializing desires, were therefore in order.

Defining Desires

Lesbian feminism normalized relationships among women by depre-
cating heterosexual relationships and by generating a culture and vocabulary that valued and even *idealized* lesbianism. Feminists privileged lesbianism as the most effective challenge to compulsory
heterosexuality. They attributed a woman's heterosexual past to some
"preenlightened phase" and created a new cultural repertoire of desire, a new set of "sexual scripts" that would guide sexual desire and
behavior and provide an alternative to the dominant, heterosexual
schemas.[20]

For many women, exclusive commitment to homosexuality was
never in question. But for others, including some of those who came
out through feminism, heterosexual desires persisted beneath the
surface, despite their best efforts. Even as they identified as lesbians,
some women reported experiencing a sense of "role distance." They
felt that the term *lesbian* did not fully express "who they were."
Nearly half of the women I interviewed acknowledged various levels
of continuing heterosexual desire, even after having come out and
declared their lesbianism.

In *Lesbian Connection*, a Michigan-based national newsletter, a
pained letter writer from Madison, Wisconsin, described herself as
having been married for six years and having enjoyed "good relations
with her husband and with other men long after her marriage." But

eventually, she wrote, "It started growing in me that I was interested in women, and then I was very interested, and eventually, after my first Michigan [Women's Music] Festival, I wanted a woman so badly I cried." She described the process of identifying as a lesbian, despite the fact that she continued to enjoy sexual relations with men. "I think of myself as a lesbian who is attracted to men," she wrote,

> or a bisexual who has no desire to get involved with men but feels a sexual attraction for them. . . . I actually think there are a lot of lesbians like me but either we don't really think about the range of feelings we have, or more likely, we don't admit them for fear of not being good lesbians. . . . I will never cut men out of my life entirely but I doubt very much that if I should lose my current lover that I would ever choose to be in a primary relationship with a man.[21]

Her announcement prompted a torrent of replies, including this admission from a woman from Prescott, Arizona:

> Despite my adoration for women, I still find men (and I write this begrudgingly) cropping up in sexual fantasies and dreams (or nightmares, if you will). I have fought with myself time and time again over this and I am embarrassed to write these words on this paper. I have been unwilling to admit this to anyone but my lover, but it is a damn painful reminder of the depths of patriarchal socialization that plagues the subconscious even after it is consciously rejected. . . . I do not attribute any of my unwitting "attraction" (for lack of a better word) to men to any inherent "natural" phenomenon. It is instead remnants of the socialization I have been immersed in.[22]

Unconscious fantasies tend to pose intractable problems for "politically correct" voluntarism.[23] Among feminist lesbians, heterosexual desires were seen as evidence of "internalized oppression." Once they were recognized and brought to consciousness, the respondent from Arizona imagined that internalized heterosexuality, much like internalized homophobia, could be overcome. She made a plea for women to discover their own internalized oppression and eradicate it. Addressing the earlier writer, she observed: "Although I think I understand why men continue to invade my psyche, your letter leaves me hurting because I am reminded that all of my precious energy is not yet directed only to women. And it is scary to have to deal with my lack of control over this matter."[24]

A 1978 article on the "sexual problems of lesbians" was more for-giving, suggesting that while many lesbians continue to have fantasies about men, these desires were not fundamentally incompatible with a lesbian identity:

> Lesbians almost never talk about these experiences, many lesbians as-sume that other lesbians never have them, and literally panic when they have a sexual fantasy or dream that includes men. Many women immediately begin to question their identity: Am I really a lesbian? Does this mean that I should pick up a man and go to bed with him? . . . I bring up this taboo subject in order to reassure women that many lesbians share these feelings and experiences, and to make a plea for recognition and acceptance of all parts of ourselves. Until we recognize those parts of ourselves that are disquieting and inconsis-tent, until we respect our individual differences, the unity we built is false. More fundamentally, when we limit ourselves by imposing rigid and punitive rules for acceptable sexual feelings and behaviors, we are in fact capitulating to the same forces that we struggle against in as-serting our lesbianism.[25]

Still, having heterosexual desires was one thing, and acting on them was quite another. While conducting fieldwork in a lesbian commu-nity in the mid-1970s, Barbara Ponse found strong norms among lesbians prohibiting heterosexual contacts and mandating a high de-gree of consistency among identity, behavior, and practices. "The im-portance placed on lesbian identity," she concluded, "would tend to limit experimentation with heterosexual relationships once a woman had made the identification[:] . . . a lesbian who engages in relation-ships with men could expect censure from other lesbians."[26]

Carol Solberg, who lived in Portland, Oregon, during the mid-1970s, recalled one of the rules in her household: if a woman brought a man to stay the night, that person had to let everyone in the house know in advance. "Having men visit was okay," she explained, "but waking up in the morning to find one in the bathroom was considered heresy." Such rules, she suggested, had a "chilling effect," making men off-limits and thereby discouraging women in the household from heterosexual involvements.

In the context of a movement that was attempting to imagine an alternative sexual order, it is understandable that heterosexual involvements would be prohibited. As Margaret Berg said, "There was such a great premium placed on being a lesbian that there was no place to be if you didn't fit into the categories." When I asked her whether she would consider herself a bisexual, she recalled her formative years as a young woman coming out in the early 1970s:

> No—I felt that there was no social space for that. To say I was a bisexual was to say that I was interested in relationships with women and with men. And I didn't see myself as interested in both. Maybe there were some months where I was operationally bisexual, flirting with both men and women, but, for the most part, I was too woman identified to have a relationship with a man. Sure, there were times when I found men hot, but I couldn't have intimate relationships with them. That was too hard.

Margaret drew a strict separation between personal and social identity and, like many members of her age cohort, privileged the social over the personal. The available "social categories" were heterosexuality and homosexuality. One could think of oneself as bisexual but, said Margaret, there was no "social context" for that in her world.

The gay liberation movement had initially supported bisexuality as the ideal form of sexuality, a mode that transcended binary identity categories, questioned the homosexual/heterosexual dichotomy, and affirmed polymorphously perverse pleasures. But by the early 1970s, in many lesbian circles bisexuality was anathema: bisexuals were at best inferior lesbians and at worst collaborators with the enemy. Although lesbian feminism had attracted many women who had previously imagined themselves as heterosexual or bisexual, once they had self-identified as lesbian, they did not readily discuss persistent sexual fantasies about men. One woman told me that she had long thought of herself as being bisexual, but started calling herself a lesbian at some point because she wasn't having sex with men. "It wasn't that I wasn't still attracted to men," she said. "It was simply that they were out of the picture."

Bisexuality was not considered legitimate or authentic within the lesbian world. In the terms set forth by the "gay trajectory," women who harbored continued heterosexual desires were imagined as "having trouble dealing with their gayness."[27] Faced with these negative sanctions, some believed that even if they were originally attracted to men, and their initial lesbian experiences were not entirely positive, they could resocialize themselves to be sexually interested in women. They believed that they were originally bisexual, but had been socialized to be straight. Coming out therefore entailed identity work designed to "get in touch with one's lesbianism" and resocialize oneself to be gay.[28]

Sharon Lieberman said that after several unsuccessful relationships with men, she decided that she was not going to find a man to suit her needs, that "all men were impossible." At the time, she was working with a women's newspaper where everyone told her that she was "really" a lesbian. She recalled, "I decided to change my masturbation fantasies. I made myself. It was like an internal decision on my part: I'm not going to find the partner I want among men. So one night I was lying in bed, ready to go to sleep and I masturbated about a woman." Eventually, Sharon said, she came to have little desire for men and her sexual relationships with women became stronger and more pleasurable. Several other women told me about having consciously sought to redirect their sexual fantasies toward women. When interests and desires for men intruded, some reinterpreted them as the residues of compulsory heterosexuality and "false consciousness."

Laura Stone recalled that she "started out somewhat repulsed when I saw lesbians with each other" and through the movement became "sensitized to the possibility of sexuality being changeable. . . . It wasn't a 'wow' experience at first. But I was under the sway of the idea that it's the most natural thing in the world to do with someone you're close with. So even though the sexual experience wasn't 'wow,' I began to think about how great it was to be having sex in such a 'natural' way." Even though she "found a lot of feminists very attractive, not just physically," Laura said she was "more comfortable sexually with men." In her circle, she was known "as a straight woman who was sleeping with lesbians," or as a "political lesbian." But over time, she began to think of her heterosexuality as a product of socialization. "I was definitely one of those who always felt like I could be with men. But as I got further into my lesbianism, I thought that might be internalized homophobia, that I was carrying this thing. I began to think of my heterosexuality as a temporary aberration, a product of internalized homophobia. I didn't believe that there was some kind of primary sexual identification. I thought it was changeable." What began as "deep acting" actually resulted in a changed perception of sexuality.

"After three of four sexual experiences with women," Laura said, she "started to get turned on by it. . . . I saw myself changing. I got past all the repulsion stuff, or most of it, and had orgasms, and there were many times that it was great sexually. And I began to think back to heterosexual sex less fondly, and began to get in touch with the times when I faked orgasms, or didn't want to make love and was dry. . . . I thought I could change all the way." In retrospect, Laura thought of herself as someone, much like Margaret, for whom lesbian desires were "produced" by a sense of lesbian identity: "I would not say that my sexuality preceded my identity. My identity as a lesbian preceded my sexuality. And my sexuality was just trying to catch up. I was more mutable than other people. It seemed to me that I was a case of someone who was proof of the socialization theory."

Doing Gender

When one becomes a lesbian, gendered bodily significations of hairstyle, clothing, and even deportment are problematized. Lesbians tend to be members of, or at least travelers through, heterosexual as well as homosexual worlds. Unless they pass as men (historically the case for a very small minority of women) in order to live, work, and love, they must satisfy the requirements of both. In the straight world, they must pass as straight, or at least develop a self-presentation that marks them as female. In the lesbian world, different norms of membership apply.

Codifying and eroticizing gendered differences have long been central to lesbian subcultures. The most visible manifestation of lesbian "gender" is tied to appearance. But lesbian gender is much more than this. Joan Nestle observed the linkages among gender, self-presentation, and eroticism in the context of the working-class bar scene of the 1950s:

Lesbian life in America . . . was organized around a highly developed sense of sexual ceremony and dialogue. Indeed, because of the surrounding oppression, ritual and code were often all we had to make public erotic connections. Dress, stance, gestures, even jewelry and hairstyles had to carry the weight of sexual communications. The pinky ring flashing in the subway car, the DA haircut combed more severely in front of a mirror always made me catch my breath, symbolizing as they did a butch woman announcing her erotic competence.[29]

Members of prefeminist working-class bar subcultures eroticized gender differences. Butch-femme roles, which adapted conventional gender roles to the lesbian context, were in Nestle's words "a conspicuous flag of rebellion" in a highly stigmatized, secretive world, a means of survival in an age when gender rules bore down heavily.[30] Being a butch, or "mannish woman," was an assertion of strength against very narrow conceptions of what it meant to be a woman. To wear a leather jacket and slick back one's short hair weren't simply experiments, with style—it was an embrace of one's "true nature" in the face of the dominant culture's notions of "woman": feminine and coy.

Nearly twenty years later, in the context of the women's liberation movement, a very different politics of gender and the body emerged. Seventies feminists attempted to free women's bodies from their possession by men, which they viewed as being synonymous with their sexualization.

Women looked at their vulvas and cervix, examined their breasts and took up sports and recreational activities. . . . How we lived in our bodies, not only how we thought about our bodies, was transformed. A growing awareness of alienation from and oppression to our bodies was met not only by a new consciousness in our minds, that is, new ideology and new information, but by a new set of practices that enabled women to both learn about their bodies and live differently in them.[31]

As part of a movement devoted to empowering women by reconstituting gendered bodies, lesbian feminists attempted to erase gender differences, to recodify gender and sexuality, and to position themselves outside the dominant culture. Early lesbian feminists saw themselves as the embodiment of the androgynous ideal of a world without gender. Minimizing the differences between women and men, they embraced an antinatalist, antihousewifery politics that placed lesbians in a cross-gender position. Sidney Abbott and Barbara Love helped theorize this change:

> Lesbians have been critically examining sex roles. Instead of accepting the old explanation that was handed out to them that gay women were trying to be more male and gay men more female, they have identified cross-behavior as an important breakthrough, going beyond the confines of sex-role-categorized behavior. For the lesbian this means that she is not trying to be like a man, but that she is trying to be more of a human being.[32]

For feminists, who were committed to minimizing gender differences, the exaggerated gender roles of butch-femme were little more than a self-hating reflection of the dominant heterosexual culture. Butches, some charged, were "male-identified" in the truest sense: they looked and acted like men. Femmes were little better.

> For a variety of reasons, [butch] women prefer an appearance that is sufficiently masculine to prevent them from getting many kinds of employment and that acts to limit them to the gay subculture. . . . [They are] often of working class background, where sex roles are taught strong and early. . . . Role playing is important to the lesbian's damnation; in shouldering all the baggage of the stereotypical female image, she also subscribes to the division of gay women into two groups, male-identified women and female-identified women. She shows that she accepts the heterosexual idea that a woman who loves women is against nature.[33]

In contrast, feminists wished to free themselves from norms that associated women with their bodies and made a fetish of personal appearance. They tried to remove all traces of what R. W. Connell has called "emphasized femininity," or hegemonic rules for female gender.[34] The practice of femininity, they believed, constrained women and encouraged them to display sociability rather than technical competence, to accept marriage and caring for children rather than combat labor market discrimination against women, and to organize their lives around themes of "sexual receptivity" and "motherhood."

Jackie Henry, a therapist, remembered the scorn meted on feminine-appearing women in feminist circles in the Midwest in the early 1970s. "Where I was, you wouldn't dare wear nail polish. You really wouldn't. If you were brave enough and tough enough, you would do it anyway, and nobody would tell you you couldn't. But you would not be approved. You would certainly not build up any social relationship with that group. You would have access to that group, but you would not be welcome. The same thing with hairstyle or dress." It is not surprising that clothing, an important bodily marker of gender, would figure prominently in the effort to remake "lesbian gender." Central to all marginalized groups are struggles over identity and strategies for countering its dominant constructions; the forms of expression these groups produce reconstitute cultural codes. Like punk subcultures of the 1970s and early 1980s in Britain and the United States, lesbian subcultures construct resistance partly through style and self-presentation.[35]

Feminist lesbians wished to free themselves not only from gender roles but from high fashion altogether, which they saw as synonymous with women's oppression. Toward this end, they embraced androgynous self-presentation. They wore jeans and t-shirts, flannel shirts and work boots. They wore their hair relatively short. They forged a style that embodied ideals of authenticity and naturalness against what was seen as the artificial, feigned styles of both butch-femme and "normal femininity." Jackie Henry spoke of loose, asexual clothing as a key badge of membership in her feminist community in 1972: "I dressed in blue jeans and t-shirt or flannel shirts and desert boots—I had the outfit. I sort of dressed that way anyway. But I got more and more so as soon as I discovered this community of women in St. Louis. The radical feminist community. I discovered them right before 1972. And went out and bought a few more flannel shirts."

"We went to great pains to look as bad as we could," Jackie recalled. "That outfit—the flannel and jeans, and so on—came out of some conscious planning out of the feminist movement about restrictive clothing. There was a lot of talk about clothing as chains." Feminists burned their bras and donned flannel shirts, denim vests, and blue jeans.[36] This look, de rigueur among young lesbians and many feminists in the 1970s, attempted to replace the artifice of fashion

with a supposed naturalness, freed of gender roles and commercial-
ized pretense. It was derived, as Jackie put it, "from the wish on the
part of a bunch of upper-middle-class lesbians to identify with
working-class groups." Styled after simple, functional working-class
clothing, the lesbian look represented the wish of many middle-class
lesbians to be downwardly mobile, or at least to identify with less
fortunate members of society. One observer described San Francisco's lesbian feminist community in the early 1970s: "The women feel
that in their choice of clothing they are striking a blow against the
consumerism of a capitalist society was well as leveling class distinctions that might exist in their community. Their clothing mostly
comes from 'free boxes,' in which people discard their still usable
clothing to be recycled by anyone who wants it. Typical clothing consists of Levis or other sturdy pants, t-shirts, workshirts."[37] Clothing
was an emblem of refusal—a blow against the twin evils of capitalism
and patriarchy, against the fashion industry and the female objectification that fueled it.[38]

Several women who had thought of themselves as tomboys from
an early age spoke about the "lesbian look" in much the same terms
as they described their own coming out: as a "coming home." At age
eighteen in the mid-1970s, Carol Solberg arrived in Portland, Oregon, from New England. She spoke of the elation she felt walking
into her first lesbian cafe and finding a group of women with short-
cropped hair, dressed in jeans and men's vests: "I walked into that
room, and looked around and scanned the crowd, and saw a room
full of people who looked just like me. I had found my home in the
dykey look of the time. I had been a tomboy from an early age. That
dyke look was the way I had always dressed. Now, for the first time,
I was 'normal.' "

This sense of self-recognition was not universal, however. Though
the "dyke uniform" was intended to minimize the differences among
lesbians, disparities of style persisted and sometimes posed problems.
Thirty-four-year-old Dale Hoshiko arrived in San Francisco in the
mid-1970s from Hawaii, eager to become a part of the lesbian/gay
scene. A friend from Hawaii, a lesbian, showed her around when she
arrived, but, Dale recalled, "she didn't like hanging out with me because it pointed to the fact that we were both Asian. People would

ask if I was her sister. She liked to view herself as white." Because
Dale was Asian American, she said she was viewed as an oddity on
Castro Street, in the heart of the gay ghetto. "The men looked at me
strangely. They couldn't figure out what I was doing there. I didn't
have the lesbian look. I carried a handbag. I wasn't seen as a lesbian.
I was seen as an Asian woman." The women's community of San
Francisco, which was at that point fairly distinct from the gay male
ghetto, was much more receptive and welcoming toward Dale. But
despite the efforts of some feminists to welcome women of color into
their circles, Dale's comments suggest that dominant visual codes in
lesbian/gay communities, which determined "what a lesbian looked
like," often assumed whiteness and marked women of color as heterosexual. The identity work required of women of color was therefore doubly demanding, requiring the skillful manipulation of white-
defined visual codes.

Many women I interviewed also spoke about the persistent differences between lesbians who could pass as straight and those who
couldn't. Jackie Henry differentiated between her own experience, as
someone who appears "less threatening to the straight world," and the
harsher treatment of those who "from an early age fit the stereotype
of the butch lesbian and [are] brutally punished for it." She believed
that it was important to remove herself from the heterosexual world
and from the attentions of men, and to make herself look less feminine. But some feminine-appearing women trying to figure out how
to present their "gendered" selves found themselves in a quandary.

Sally Kirk described how, when she first came out, she "cut her
hair real short, and tried to be more butch": "When I first moved
into a household of lesbians they taught me how to dress. They
shopped in the boys' department. . . . My breasts were too large to
shop there, though. . . . They gave me butch lessons, really. It was a
whole other way of doing things." Sally, who had long hair and a
shapely figure, recalled the ways her lesbian friends helped her to
"butch it up." Jackie Henry changed her clothes to the flannel and
jeans "dyke uniform." But she experienced a disjuncture between her
public presentation and her inner sense of self. Despite her best efforts to "butch it up," her feminine hair continued to "get in the
way": "I had butt-length blond hair, which I loved and thought was

wonderful. But this is not what people did. People did not have long
blond hair and be a lesbian. Most of my friends did not know it was
bleached, but the problem was that it was long. They didn't say anything to me, except that they kept cropping their hair shorter and
shorter. And I was still trying to look like Mary Travers." Sarah Marcus said, "I tried to look more butch. I drabbed it up a bit. But I
always had a lot of trouble, and that was a source of great discomfort
to me." Women who characterized themselves as "originally" more
feminine in bearing, hairstyle, or dress sometimes felt that they had
to be "pretend butches" in order to be lesbians. And despite their
efforts to move toward androgyny, lesbian feminists were often more
sympathetic to "butchy" women. They affirmed that which the dominant culture had historically stigmatized as lesbian—the masculine
woman. But being *too* masculine was also scorned, on the grounds
that it imitated men and carried the taint of butch-femme roles.

Styles that emphasized dichotomous masculine and feminine
codes were seen as vestiges of the prefeminist days and as reflections
of an oppressive hegemonic culture. Sunny Connelly described herself as a "baby butch, through and through." During the hippie era,
there was a lot of "fluid sexuality and gender play." At that time, she
said, "it was easy to blend in the crowd. It was a time of 'anything
goes.'" In the late 1960s, she used to wear tuxedo jackets and slick
her hair back, in the "old gay" style. But with time, she said, feminists
"got on her case" for that. So she grew her hair longer and tried to
blend in. But the knotty problem of gender refused to go away.

Although they sought to neutralize gender (and race), many
women experienced a continuing disjunction between the person
they were and the person they wished to be. Some changed their
gendered self-presentation, or "surface identity," but still felt that
"deep down" they could never entirely free themselves from gender
roles. One needed to be butch to subvert femininity, but butch-
femme roles were generally anathema to baby boom women. As
Gayle Rubin has noted, "In spite of their prevalence, issues of gender
variance are strangely out of focus in lesbian thought, analysis, and
terminology. The intricacies of gender are infrequently addressed."[39]
Despite their ostensible attempts to erase gender differences, recodify gender and sexuality, and position themselves outside the domi-

nant culture, lesbian feminists were ultimately utterly dependent on the gender codes they tried to subvert.

Finding an "Other" Lover

For women of the baby boom cohort, recasting the past, resocializing one's sexual attractions, and changing one's appearance were important steps toward developing a lesbian identity. But perhaps the most important step was the establishment of a same-sex relationship, which was often virtually synonymous with involvement with an identifiable lesbian community. Many women described the erotic flavor of community interactions, the fusion of the personal and the political that made lesbianism a plausible and even exciting alternative.[40] Sharon Lieberman recalled that her sexual interest in women was inseparable from the experience of being in an all-women's community. "All our exciting activities were from being with women, and the sexual energy got turned on from doing these neat things together." It was a community that owed its solidarity partly to the fact that "it was really cut off from other stuff," from heterosexual society. The community provided an alternative sense of self and a sensibility that valued lesbianism and deprecated mainstream values.

If the community was in some sense a "significant other," which fused personal and political relationships and provided a source of potential lovers and friends, the building block of the community was the couple. For sexually inexperienced women, entry into a romantic relationship with another woman was one way of gaining membership into the lesbian subculture. Many women spoke of the importance of their first relationship, as distinct from a first sexual experience that may or may not have been considered to be significant. So Laura Stone:

> I wouldn't say that once I had good sex with women I became gay identified. I think that once I stopped being with men I became gay identified. And being in a relationship helped. But it really took my relationship with Nora for me to feel "permanently" gay. I feel like I got married to this woman. I thought I was going to be with her for the rest of my life. We had a kid together. Now, I was a lesbian, I thought. So that's when I really came out.

Women who experienced their sexuality as relatively fluid and their lesbianism as largely "elective" often formed an emotional attachment with a more experienced lesbian. The more experienced lesbian helped construct the new lesbian's coming out experience and participated in the formation of her new sexual identity. No one said that she consciously became involved with a woman for this reason alone; nonetheless, many of my interviewees were highly conscious of the role that this dynamic played in their attractions and relationships. Sally Kirk explained, "I didn't grow up being the only dyke in town. I didn't have that same sense of so many women that they were going to be the only ones, that made it seem so incredibly threatening and lonely. I remember thinking that it was a choice, but I was so mortified by that, that inside I was not a real lesbian." In 1971, soon after she declared herself a lesbian, Sally became involved with a woman who was older, who had come out before the women's movement. "I got to have the sense that I was really a lesbian because Jane was really a lesbian," she told me. It is common for an "experienced" lesbian to introduce a "novice" lesbian to a new social world and for their relationship to shape the novice's sexual identity. In this process, according to Cathy Reback and JoAnn Loulan,

> The signs and signals that form the new lesbian's identity are supplied through the cultural scripts of a woman in love: the significant lesbian is the subject, the novice the object. As the new lesbian progresses from her position as novice to that of significant lesbian, she becomes the subject, and her self-perception changes. No longer invisible without her significant lesbian, she establishes a sense of self as a romantic actor, and as a lesbian.[41]

Sally told me that in order to be attracted to women, she "always had to be attracted to people who were really different. Otherwise it was too much of the same thing." Sally was Jewish and middle class; her lovers tended to be non-Jewish and working class. "Everything was different. There was always this excitement, this dynamism." If class and ethnicity were two important ways in which her lovers differed from herself, sexual identity was an additional difference, though she did not become conscious of that dynamic until much later. Sally experienced her lesbianism as elective; her lovers all experienced their lesbianism as more primary and driven. While she was a "daughter of the movement," her lovers thought of themselves as lifelong lesbians, who would have been lesbians regardless of history, contingency, or chance.

More than half of the women who described their lesbianism as "elective" identified similar patterns in their relationships. They found themselves consistently attracted to and involved with "more experienced" lesbians. Many "new" lesbians described their involvement with "old gay" women who had then come into the women's movement. Others chose as lovers women of their own age, but "new gay" women for whom lesbianism was a "coming home" experience. Several women reported that more experienced, more internally driven lesbians courted them, attracted to what was seen as their femininity. They, in turn, were attracted to what they perceived as the more "androgynous" or masculine sense of self of lifelong lesbians.

Though few women identified with butch-femme roles per se, many spoke of eroticizing certain traits that signify gender in our culture—sexual aggressiveness, shyness, a willingness to take the initiative, and a range of others. For Toby Miller, who said she regularly became involved with "the most shut-down male-identified women," this wasn't a particularly positive dynamic. "A lot of the dynamics that were repeated in my relationships with women were sort of classic boy-girl stuff, getting involved with women who were emotionally inaccessible, and me sort of wanting more involvement. . . . I think it has to do with my brother and my childhood, and the relationships in my family. It has to do with my own stuff about what I deserve and what I don't deserve, and can and can't get." As she and others suggested, when two women come together in a lesbian relationship, they often bring to that relationship two very different conceptions of self. The eroticizing of difference flew in the face of the ideology of lesbian feminism, which imagined lesbian attachments, in contrast to those of heterosexuals or even butch-femme lesbians, as a partnering of equals, united in their similarity.

Psychologist Beverly Burch provides a psychodynamic explanation for such interactions, which she terms "unconscious bonding." The nature of the complementarity proposed in some lesbian relationships, says Burch, rests upon differences in the experiences of lesbians who have "always" and primarily been oriented toward women and those who formerly were heterosexually involved. The identity of women who begin to think of themselves as lesbian very early in life is likely to include painful feelings of being different, not in the mainstream, not typically feminine, and, often, not normal. Women who have previously identified as heterosexual or even bisexual are likely to have experienced themselves as somewhat closer to the mainstream culture. Their participation in heterosexual relationships has been authentic to a large degree, and they may more easily identify themselves as feminine. However, the sexual identity of the latter may never be as clear as that of the former; although she comes to identify herself as a lesbian, some confusion, ambivalence, or doubt may persist. At the same time, she may think of herself as more normal, as less deviant, than the primary lesbian; indeed, she may always hold out some part of her identity as nonlesbian to preserve this sense of normality. By becoming involved with a "primary" lesbian, many of my interviewees who experienced their sexuality as more malleable, found that they could consolidate their sense of sexual self.[42]

But over time, some reported that the distinctions between partners diminished. Some feminine women, for example, described becoming more like their "butchier" girlfriends. Sarah Hart identified as bisexual when she got involved with a woman whom she identified as being a lifelong lesbian. "When Sue and I first got together, if anyone had looked at us, you would know that she was butch and I was femme." But over time, Sarah said, "I butched it up a bit, toned down my femininity. Sue, my lover, did the opposite: she became a bit softer." This might be taken as illustrating the tendency, described in psychoanalytic literature on lesbian relationships, for women lovers to "merge." Such relationships are more likely to produce fusion, or loss of self, it is suggested, because the pairing of two women offers a greater possibility of bodily and psychic oneness. Lesbians in relationship enjoy an "intimacy of familiarity, comfort, and reciprocity," writes Joyce Lindenbaum. "There is a sense of shared identification, of knowing what the other feels." But as merging progresses, any differences between partners come to be experienced as a threat and are thus suppressed.[43] In terms of gender roles, masculine women may become "femmier," and feminine women "butchier." The qualities that once attracted two individuals to each other—their differences—diminish.

The Actors behind the Acts

The dominant sociopsychological conception of lesbian development, reflected in stage models of sexual identity formation, claims that lesbian identity forms in an objective, unilinear process that ends at the moment at which one "comes out," or consciously identifies as lesbian. As the preceding suggests, such models offer little insight into the production of gendered and sexed subjectivity, with all of its inconsistencies. Identity is not a "truth" that is discovered: it is a performance enacted. Identities often do not spring forth effortlessly from individuals: rather, individuals effect change in the meanings of particular identities. One is not born a lesbian; one becomes a lesbian through acts of reflexive self-fashioning. The formation of a lesbian identity is at least partly a matter of developing proficiency in manipulating codes and symbols. It involves conforming to historically specific and localized norms of identity and culture.

Women of the baby boom performed their lesbianism by rewriting their autobiographies, or by consciously trying to resocialize themselves to be sexually attracted to women and to repress their feelings for men. Sometimes they changed their self-presentation to bring it more into line with what they considered to be "authentically" lesbian. At other times they pursued relationships with women whom they identified as "real" lesbians. In the 1970s, when feminism and gay liberation were very influential, such performances took place within a system that highly valued authenticity—the idea of being "true to oneself." Lesbian feminism was founded on the belief that women could retrieve a self that had been denied to them by the dominant culture. Authenticity was an important criterion for building trust among individuals within lesbian communities, particularly as the stigma of lesbianism persisted. By the standards of the dominant culture, lesbians often felt like inauthentic, deviant, "failed" women, but within the lesbian subculture, they imagined that it was possible to "be themselves." The effect of this identity work was often, paradoxically, to impose a rather rigid normative conception of what it means to be a "lesbian." To become a lesbian in the context of the gender/sexual politics of the 1970s was to be implicated in that which one opposed: binary sexual and gender categories.[44]

While identity may consist of a string of performances made coherent only through their repetition, individuals, I have suggested, varied in terms of their "skills" as performers and the success of their performances. For many women, performing lesbianism came relatively easily and effortlessly; becoming a lesbian meant reengaging with what they already believed to be their authentic self and claiming their long-standing, if secret, desires. It permitted them to adopt a *surface* identity as a lesbian that matched the *deep* sense of difference they already possessed.

To others, who had experienced themselves as originally heterosexual or bisexual, coming out meant "discovering" their lesbianism. For these women, desire was often not the primary determinant of a deep identification as lesbian; first, they identified with lesbianism as a sociosexual category. Even after having come out, some in this group felt that their sense of lesbian self was inauthentic; it seemed that they were just "going through the motions." They felt compelled to undertake much more rigorous "identity work."

By engaging in such identity work, some individuals in this latter group were able to narrow the experiential gap separating them from other, more experienced lesbians. They "became lesbians." But others continued to suffer a dissonance between who they felt that they "were" and who they wished to "become." Identity work did not make their subjective sense of self match the sociosexual typology "lesbian." For some of these women, lesbian identity often felt "put on" or "not part of them."[45] They changed their self-presentation, which operated as a surface identity, but still felt that "deep down" they could never entirely free themselves from their essential selves. For them, gender and sexuality inhered in traits "possessed" rather than in presentations enacted.[46]

Chapter Four

Is She or Isn't She?

Constructionism and the Problem
of Commitment

There appears to be a tendency for people to like the
groups with which they identify themselves most deeply to
be so enduring as to be eternal; that is, timeless.

Everett Hughes,
The Sociological Eye (1971)

Becoming a lesbian implies a sense of permanence: having
a gay present and also looking forward to a gay future.

Laura Stone, interviewee

Like virtually all marginal groups, we cling to a center—a
fixed point that guarantees our identity and our place
within a recognizable and definable community.

Bonnie Zimmerman,
The Safe Sea of Women (1990)

After the initial euphoria of "coming out" faded, then difficult, vexing
questions emerged: who is a lesbian, and what do members of
the group called "lesbians" have in common? If individuals have an
open-ended ability to *construct* themselves, did that imply that they
also had an open-ended ability to *reconstruct* themselves? Would
women who became lesbians in the heady days of feminism be committed to remaining lesbian, or if given the opportunity would they
turn their backs on their deviant sisters and reclaim "heterosexual
privilege"?

Feminists redefined lesbianism in expansive, universalistic terms,
emphasizing the possibility for individuals to self-consciously create
and recreate their sexual identities. But the political strategy of coming out to others as a means of establishing unity often had the contradictory effect of making differences among women very visible.

Though the rhetoric of the movement claimed that lesbianism was a choice, and that any woman could resocialize herself to love women instead of men, many women secretly and not-so-secretly wondered whether in fact some lesbians were more "real" than others. Those who were strongly committed to social constructionism in theory often privately differentiated between "real lesbians"—women who were strongly driven to lesbianism and therefore committed to it—and those who were not.

Women of the baby boom placed a very high value on commitment to lesbian identity. They believed that someone who can achieve a stable sense of identity can maintain a sense of coherence even amid flux, instability, and change, holding on to that identity as she passes through different periods of life. They seemed to echo Erik Erikson's suggestion that in achieving an ego identity, one achieves an "accrued confidence that one's own ability to maintain inner sameness and continuity . . . is matched by the sameness and continuity of one's meaning for others."[1]

Most individuals I spoke with assumed that once a woman had come out as lesbian she had made a permanent decision. They suggested that when a person stabilizes her lesbian identity, she is making a long-term commitment to the well-being of other lesbians. Wavering in that commitment was evidence of disloyalty both to friends and to the larger lesbian community. Indeed, in the narrative of coming out, which marks the entry of the individual into the gay world, the final achievement of identity is typically marked by the moment of identity "stabilization" in which an individual makes a permanent decision about her or his homosexuality and forecloses the possibility of bisexual or heterosexual identity.[2]

In this chapter, I examine the conflicts that arose around the problem of commitment, as they were described by my interviewees and by lesbian feminist periodicals in the early 1970s. Sometimes conflicts over differential commitment to lesbianism emerged along generational lines as in the "old gay–new gay split"; sometimes they followed class divisions, as in the clashes between feminists and "bar dykes." It seemed that lesbian feminists' social constructionism had difficulty explaining the persistence of individual differences and dealing with the conflicts to which they gave rise. Though problematizing and denaturalizing heterosexuality, women of the baby boom failed to acknowledge the constructed, and fragile, nature of their own collective self-concepts. This led to group efforts to politicize commitment, which reached their logical extreme in efforts to fix the boundaries of a recognizable, definable community.

Difference and Commitment

Commitment, says Rosabeth Moss Kanter, refers to "the willingness of people to do what will help maintain the group because it provides what they need." It arises "as a consideration at the intersection between the organizational requisites of groups and the personal orientations and preferences of their members."[3] Many communities in modern society face the problem of attracting and retaining members. For example, trends toward intermarriage, tendencies toward secularization, and declining fertility rates have led Jewish community leaders in the United States and abroad to try to promote a greater sense of commitment among younger adherents. Fears of community decline have also given rise to educational efforts focused upon Jewish community preservation.[4]

Typically, lesbian identifications, unlike Jewish and other ethnic identifications, are not structurally reproduced via processes of "primary"—that is, family—socialization. Cultural continuity, if it exists, is maintained largely through individual actions. Yet just as lesbians are divided by age, race, class, sexuality, gender identity, and any number of other splits, so too are they divided in their levels of commitment to a lesbian identity. Observers have long been highly cognizant of differences among individuals that might lead to differential commitments to lesbian identity.

Historically, Vera Whisman suggests, the lesbian world has often been conceived in terms of a set of binary pairs: masculine versus feminine gender identity, determined versus elective sexuality, "real" versus "false" lesbianism. Sexologist Havelock Ellis, writing in the early years of this century, distinguished the "true invert" from her partner. The "actively inverted woman," whose "essential character" is marked by "a more or less distinct trace of masculinity," Ellis suggested, tended to be attracted to women whose homosexuality was less marked. These "unmarked" lesbians were characterized as being more feminine, and as having "chosen" to be lesbians, if only because they were "not repelled or disgusted by the lover-like advances from persons of their own sex."[5]

Evidence of schoolgirl crushes and adolescent sexual experiences, of passionate friendships between married women, and affairs of the heart (and body) among women in the military all point to lesbian activity being much more widespread than lesbian identity and to the vast differences of experience that divide even lesbian-identified women. There have long been "intermittent lesbians," women who have had romantic and often sexual relationships with other women at some point in their lives without forming a lesbian identity. Sometimes this activity is purely situational; often it is more than that, though it is frequently repressed and forgotten.[6]

Subcultures emerge, at least in part, in order to stabilize and regularize lesbian contacts, providing some assurance to those who congregate within their boundaries that members have made some commitment to a lesbian identity, as opposed merely to lesbian activity. In the butch-femme lesbian communities of the mid-twentieth century, femmes were sometimes characterized as women who could—and so therefore might—return to a heterosexual life.[7] Butch women, some suggested, had a tendency to become involved with femme lovers who seemed less committed to living an exclusively lesbian life. The implication here is that "real" lesbians are masculine in appearance and have a fixed, unwavering homosexual orientation; women whose gendered appearance is feminine, and who experience their sexuality as fluid and elective, though they are not "really" lesbians may at times place themselves in the lesbian category.

It would be erroneous to suggest that some women are more "authentic" lesbians than others. Indeed, social constructionist theory rightly calls such essentialist assumptions into question. Yet, at the same time, differences within the lesbian world do exist: they are "real." Some women experience their same-sex desires as deep, enduring, and unchanging. For others, these desires may be fleeting or may emerge later in life.[8] In chapter 1, I set the image of the tomboy, the lifelong lesbian, against that of the housewife-turned-lesbian feminist who came out "through the movement," never having experienced lesbian desires before. Certainly there were many individuals whose experiences lay somewhere between these two poles. Nonetheless, this juxtaposition is useful for understanding the internal complexity of the group of women who came to call themselves "lesbians" in the wake of the feminist movement.

In a culture in which lesbianism is deeply stigmatized, lifelong lesbians, particularly those who present a more masculinized gender identity, could expect to experience a greater degree of marginality and oppression than those whose same-sex desires or gender nonconformity is less marked. This sense of marginality has implications for how individuals see themselves, and for how lesbians view one another. On the one hand, "primary" or lifelong lesbians may be more likely to think of themselves as deviant even after they come to think of homosexuality as positive. They may continue to feel different, not normal. Women who have previously identified as bisexual or heterosexual, and who see their lesbianism as a choice, on the other hand, are likely to have experienced themselves as somewhat closer to the mainstream, less deviant.[9] At the same time, some confusion, ambivalence, or doubt about their lesbianism may persist.

One can imagine that these differences would make it difficult to construct a collective sense of lesbian identity. Lesbianism, particularly after the 1960s (when a lesbian social identity was firmly established in a public sense), is more than simply a sexual preference. It is a *social* identity, an objectification of self in relation to culture and community—a community that perceives the self over a longer period of time, with purposes that exceed the immediate situation, in relation to others who are not immediately present.[10] Perhaps it is not surprising, then, that following self-identification, individuals often experienced acute pressures to remain committed to their lesbianism.

"It Takes One to Know One"

In the early 1970s, young radical lesbians were extremely active. In Chicago, as in other cities through the country, they established a theater group, a car repair group, a speakers' bureau, a Sunday afternoon open softball game, a gay counseling group, a nurses' group, a social workers' organization, study groups, and concerts and lectures. The newspaper *Lavender Woman* was a product of this period of energetic institution building. The first issue, published in 1971, included a statement of purpose:

> This newspaper, written by and for Lesbians, is a powerful weapon against the society that tries, in vain, to keep us closeted and out of sight. More important, the paper will be a tool for growth. Through it, we can create a positive, viable Lesbian community; increase our political consciousness; communicate our feelings to one another; share with each other our knowledge and gifts and, above all, thank ourselves again and again for each other. We are not Lesbians in spite of ourselves, but because of ourselves. The paper will affirm that.
>
> We welcome comments and suggestions. We urge all Lesbians to contribute a bit of themselves; letters, articles, poetry, photos, drawings, etc. It is our intention to print as many of the letters and articles as space allows. All letters written to us will be answered, if not in the paper, by personal correspondence. The Lavender Monthly will be published monthly, providing our financial situation allows for it, and above all, depending upon the feedback we get from our Gay sisters.[11]

Cindy Ross, who moved to Chicago from New York and had gotten involved in radical lesbian activities, was part of the founding collective of the newspaper. She recalled that she would

> go out on the street with a bunch of issues and ask: would you like to buy a copy of Chicago's first lesbian newspaper? And people would look at me like I'd just come up from the sewers.... I remember putting myself into a lot of people's faces. But I remember selling it and feeling really good about it. When you're a Jewish girl from an atheistic household in New York you don't get to evangelize about much. And this was my chance and I loved it. I really believed that every woman was born a lesbian if she only knew it.[12]

Not everyone shared Cindy's youthful enthusiasm and expansive definition of lesbianism, however. A reader complained,

> It upsets me a lot to hear in your collective statement that you think of yourselves as lesbian/feminists rather than as lesbians. . . . Lesbian/feminists, to my way of thinking, are women who have become lesbians as the ultimate (political) act of rage against men. They have never known the same kind of oppression we, as lesbians, have had to en-

dure. They hold hands in public and don't care what people think. They don't have to, because they are still young. They never had to fight to be what they are. They use the word feminist to dilute the word: Lesbian. . . . I think that the straights have taken over our sexual habits as well as our newspaper under the sheep's clothing of feminism.

While some women who were gay before the women's movement came to extend their definition of lesbianism to include many women who came out "through feminism," others, like this letter writer, who had consolidated a sense of self in the old secretive subcultures and who rarely if at all came out publicly outside that world, did not. They resented the young Turks, whom they saw as threatening the stability of the old gay world, creating a new culture of lesbianism that they found largely incomprehensible. The older lesbian continued:

You should think about your sisters who never went to college, who are looking to you, not to have their conscience [sic] raised, but to be in touch with other lesbians. It is not an army we are in, but a way of life that revolves around loving women, a fact that you seem to have forgotten. . . . We aren't a club that you join. We are women, living and loving with other women. I think your newspaper could be better if you paid more attention to ordinary lesbians instead of the crazy people in California. . . . A long time ago you wrote about the problems lesbians have and how they solve them. I miss that in your paper. I used to feel that it was my paper too, but not so much anymore. Are you still lesbians? [13]

"Old gay" women, who had come out before the arrival of feminism, imagined that the products of the lesbian and feminist movements weren't really gay at all—at least in terms of membership in a tightly bounded gay subculture organized around homosexual desire. The "true" lesbian experienced strongly felt homosexual *desires* and a strong sense of being different, deviant. Younger women, some claimed, had more interest in the *politics* of lesbianism than in actual sexual activity with other women. Women who came out "through feminism," they suggested, were all "political lesbians"—straight women who had become lesbians when the movement made lesbianism sexy. They could not possibly be "real" lesbians, because real lesbians had little choice in the matter of their sexuality. Why would anyone *choose* to become a social pariah? In this view, the degree of reflexivity involved was inversely related to the authenticity of one's lesbianism. The more "thinking" one needed to do to become a lesbian, the less "real" one was. In other words, a real lesbian didn't have to *work* at being one.

Karen Savo recalled how older lesbians in Los Angeles in the early 1970s reacted to her and other young feminists:

> They were resentful. Oh, these chicks, they think they're so hot, they said. They were really hostile to feminism, they thought it was a bunch of bullshit. I don't think they knew why. They thought it was some new modern trend, and they were not getting on any boats. They were going to be who they were, and they were always going to be who they were. . . . They didn't have a real big analysis . . . they were probably excited that there were a lot of women around, more potential girlfriends, a lively scene. But it made them think about too many things that bothered them. When they started thinking about their own plight, their own pain, it was just too heavy.

In order to build a collective identity, lesbian feminists had suppressed the differences between those who described their sexuality as fixed and those who saw lesbianism as a choice. These differences finally emerged under the guise of generational rifts, which came to be known as the "old gay–new gay split." As Karen's description suggests, many of the older lesbians thought of themselves as deeply deviant, queer. They experienced their sexuality as fixed, and often they embraced the "butch" role. For them, lesbianism was synonymous with oppression and marginalization in the dominant culture. The secretive world of the lesbian bar was the only place they truly felt safe. "New" lesbians seemed to challenge the very basis of their sense of self and community.

In many cities, young feminists entered the bars and deliberately broke the rules of the old gay world. In San Francisco in the early 1970s, they would often pack the bars and engage in circle dances; these large, communal group dances were designed in part to discourage old gay women from dancing in butch-femme couples. Carrie Brown, who came out as a lesbian in the late 1960s, described her ambivalence toward "old dykes": "Inside myself, there was this feeling: I don't want to be like them. I wouldn't feel comfortable. But I know that there were lots of times when you'd be sitting with some-one who'd be considered old gay, and you wouldn't feel a difference. You'd be talking about something, and you'd be queers." Sometimes, she said, she went to the bars and was "awed by the old dykes. But they were mystified by us."

The rhetoric of the movement claimed that any woman could choose to be a lesbian. But for the older generation, who lived with a sense of marginality, being a lesbian meant "toughing it out" and also being accepted as part of the lesbian community. It meant con-forming to community norms and defining oneself as outside of het-erosexual culture. To die-hard dykes, many young feminist lesbians were not meeting formal criteria of membership. In the February 1973 issue of Los Angeles's *Lesbian Tide,* one self-identified "old dyke" observed:

> Having seen and heard of the "sisterhood" among straight women and lesbian feminists from a heterosexual or "feminine" identified back-ground, I am aware that: (1) it is beautiful and strong (when it is real) and, (2) I can say all the same things (i.e. "men are fucked") and do all the same things (i.e. go to abortion hearings) but at the most funda-mental level I am not them. I never related to men in that most per-sonal way, I've never lived with my oppressor, and I never remotely expect to.[14]

For many old dykes, being a lesbian was synonymous with having endured hardship and social disapproval—"hard knocks." The sense of deviance or difference on the part of lifelong lesbians made them "queer" and also special.[15] It created a deeper, stronger sense of iden-tity. As an "old gay" lesbian wrote in April 1974, "I am tired of telling my straight lesbian feminist sisters, I'm angry and gay. Sometimes I think my sisters who have found loving another woman through the rosy glow of a women identified supportive community forgot—or never learned—loving another woman is *also* being queer."[16] Be-cause younger lesbians, on the whole, had an easier time of their sexuality, she and others felt that they were less committed to it.

But some lesbians of the baby boom had much in common with the queer identity of these old dykes. In the late 1960s, when she was a teenager, Sunny Connelly moved away from her working-class Midwestern community to escape the "suffocating pressures" she experienced there. She befriended a woman with whom she worked, someone who was ten years older, whom she felt to be a kindred spirit. They drove cross-country to California and became lovers on the way. The older woman "brought her out," both sexually and culturally, introducing her to the old gay world and its rituals. She became a part of the lesbian bar scene in San Francisco and began to identify as a butch, a "queer," and a bohemian.

Though Sunny was a member of the same age cohort as those who had come out through feminism, her sensibilities lay with older lesbians. For her, being a lesbian meant "toughing it out." It meant the experience of being marginal, of being outside of heterosexual culture. To her it seemed that many feminists identified as lesbian without having felt the childhood terror of being "queer" in a heterosexual universe. For them, loving women was an adventure, not something hidden and shameful. They did not get hassled on the street for being a lesbian—they could pass.

During much of that period, Sunny hung out in bars, shying away from political activities. In 1970, she was in a consciousness-raising group with a group of women who tried to assure her that "there was no difference between [them] and [her]." But whenever she mentioned her sexuality, she said, they would get angry and say "we're not queer, but we're mad at the same things you are." In feminist consciousness-raising groups, even ones with lesbians in them, she felt that she couldn't talk about sex at all, and certainly not about the positive aspects of male sexuality. "You could only talk around the subject of sex, in terms of 'cultural roles,' " she said.

Though Sunny was excited by the arrival of the movement, she often had trouble understanding it. Feminist lesbians were very expressive about their feelings, and they talked endlessly about themselves. She was accustomed to a different behavioral code: "In the bars you didn't give a lot of personal information. You didn't sit around and have heart-to-heart chats about your family, what happened to you, what you saw. You just didn't do that. So I couldn't quite follow why those things were important. I felt like I didn't understand why they were talking about this stuff exactly in this way."

Feminists emphasized self-revelation, consciousness-raising, and the politicizing of personal life. They spoke in a style that was unfamiliar to the working-class world that Sunny knew, and they had a different set of values. In the bars, sexual competence was a "skill" that was highly valued, and reputations were sometimes made and unmade on that basis. But once the movement broadened the base of lesbianism and subsumed sexuality under larger political goals, Sunny felt that showing others her "sexual confidence" was akin to "eating raw steak in front of people." It made her feel crude. She felt sexually unappreciated in the new gay world, which tended to shun public discussions of sex and to place sexuality in the service of feminist political goals.

These feelings of disenfranchisement were often mixed with concerns about whether other women were similarly committed to "being" lesbians. In the previous chapter, we saw how some women who "came out through feminism" learned to "become" lesbians in part through their contact with more experienced lesbians. Relationships often brought together women from different "areas of conversation," who lacked a shared past.[17] These differences were a source of attraction, but they also carried the seeds of conflict, testing lesbian commitments. As Sunny explained, "There is a sort of attraction that happens through repulsion . . . it is an electricity thing that keeps you bonded. These attractions and repulsions keep everything moving. . . . But ultimately, my femme lovers weren't as committed to queerness as I was. They weren't willing, or weren't forced to pay the price." Differences were a source of attraction but they also contributed to the instability of many relationships. Intimate relationships in modern life presuppose a conscious commitment that replaces the external anchor more common in premodern life.[18] Because they are more easily established, they are also more easily dissolved. Homosexual relationships, which exist outside of traditional family and kin networks, and which exist only as long as both partners wish them to, may be particularly susceptible to instability. Within the context of a lesbian relationship, the problem of commitment often transcends the particularity of the relationship; it often encompasses commitment to lesbian identity itself.

In the days before feminism, when butch-femme roles eroticized

and structured sexual interactions around the principle of gender difference, things seemed clearer. In order to gain membership in the
lesbian world, one simply had to know one's place. As feminists replaced butch-femme with a lesbian world that emphasized sameness
rather than difference between partners, the lines separating love
and sex became exceedingly blurry. Indeed, "old gay" women were
not the only ones confused by the fluidity of sexual boundaries.

In 1971, soon after she came out and openly declared her lesbianism, Barb Herman participated in a demonstration to force her
university to establish a women's center. She recalls thinking to herself that she didn't trust a particular woman at the demonstration
because "she might be with a man next month." When asked how she
could tell how a particular woman was a "real" lesbian, she replied, "I
don't know. I just felt that she felt comfortable with it. And when she
would talk about it, it didn't sound stilted, or overly rhetorical. It was
real language. . . . Some of the language that other women used
didn't seem right to me. They would talk in ways that I agreed with,
but they didn't really feel the words they were saying. Being a lesbian
for them was too much of an intellectual decision." Barb said she had
an intuitive sense about certain women, a sense of who was a "real"
lesbian and who was not. She and others described this as "lesbian
radar," or the belief that "it takes one to know one." Some wondered:
If lesbianism is truly a choice, why doesn't it feel that way to *me*?
Because she had had same-sex experiences before the late 1960s,
before the lesbian/gay movement expanded the social space open to
lesbians, in many respects she saw herself as straddling the "old gay"
and "new gay" worlds. Like old gay women, she defined her lesbianism primarily in terms of desire and marginality. She considered
her orientation a basic, irrevocable part of who she was.

Some shared many older women's skepticism toward lesbians who
had come out "through feminism," wondering whether the definition
of lesbianism had become so broad as to be meaningless. A contributor to *Lesbian Voices,* a newsletter in San Jose, California, searched
for a way to describe lesbianism in more precise terms.

> Jill Johnston said "all women are lesbians"—after all, we love our-
> selves, don't we? And women who masturbate have come to regard

that as a lesbian experience, so I'm told. And much of the warmth and sisterly affection in the feminist movement has come to be described as "lesbian," even when the only touching is on the spiritual level (and not the mental, emotional and sexual levels). It seems to me that the word "lesbian" is in danger of losing all meaning.[19]

She and other "new gay" women began to reject the popular feminist notion that sexuality was freely malleable. "Is a Lesbian Born or Made?" asked a contributor to *Leaping Lesbian* (Ann Arbor, Michigan). It was a little of both, she explained. Being a lesbian was a little like being "left handed, or being musically talented": "I'm not saying that we should assume the posture of 'I can't help it, I was born that way.' That's a ridiculous apology that assumes different is bad. . . . Look, I'm big on choices—and I'm happy—so if I could, I'd choose exactly the life I'm leading. But as far as I can see, the only real choice we have is whether or not to be true to ourselves."[20] Suggesting that being a lesbian was first and foremost about homosexual desire, some insisted that they would have become lesbians even if the movement had never come along.

Sue Hammond, who identified as a "bar dyke" in the 1970s, talked about how she became involved in two different relationships with women she called "pretend dykes," "politico types" whom she had met through a community organization. She and others conflated the terms "pretend dykes," "political lesbians," "lesbian feminists," and "femme" women, often using them as a coded way to speak about class privilege. Women who could choose their lesbianism, said Sue, had the economic resources to do so. "I was working in an office, and I constantly had to look over my shoulder all the time, to make sure I was passing right, putting on a good act. I had to hide well. A lot of those other women didn't have to work, or maybe they were in school, or something. They had a lot more freedom. They could do what they wanted." Similarly, Shirley Alvarez, who came out in San Francisco in the 1970s, having grown up in a working-class Mexican American family, stressed the economics of lesbian desire:

It's an economic thing. Whereas a lot of white middle-class women have a lot more choices. They can stay married, fuck women, whatever. They don't have the same kind of constraints. If you're a brown person, and you're going out on a limb, out of your little culture thing, to be with someone of your same sex, it's not just a play thing. It's more of a heart thing. You're not thinking: I'm not in touch with my feminism. You're thinking: I really want to be with some women. It's not that kind of choice. Why put up with all that shit that you get just for fun, for experimenting? For me, it would be like no way. It's gotta be the real thing. Whereas, I feel that a lot of people like to experiment, explore different parts of themselves.

Access to economic resources undoubtedly made the choice of an unconventional lifestyle more possible, but sexuality was clearly not reducible to such economic considerations. For one thing, many middle-class women reported that they lost access to family resources after they came out. And some working-class women who came out as lesbians reported that they had more freedom to do so because they had "less to lose." Moreover, class boundaries were often indistinct. Middle-class women were more apt to talk about their sexuality in terms that emphasized reflexivity, self-identity, ideology, and changed consciousness, emphasizing the belief that lesbianism was a political choice. They employed language that was unfamiliar to many working-class women. But many women from working-class backgrounds, particularly those who attended college, learned to "talk the talk."

Sue Hammond, who has spent most of her life working in odd jobs, distinguished between women who claimed to be lesbians but were "really straight" and straight women who occasionally socialized in the lesbian community, but who never self-identified as lesbians. The latter group was okay, she said, because "the vibe wasn't there, the subliminal messages weren't there. They were clear about their orientation." Straight women who "masqueraded" as lesbians were another story entirely. Sue came to question the authenticity of some "new lesbians"—particularly the ones that "tried to butch it up." "Deep down," she said, she felt that women who elected lesbianism because they were feminists were mostly "femmes": "I thought: maybe you're not wearing lipstick, but you kind of act to me like a feminine woman—flirtatious, jewelry, shawls, or ponchos. The butches would be in the peacoats or the green army jackets. There were women who came out of the feminist movement who wore butch clothes, but to me it seemed like most of them were femme. That's the hit I got." For self-identified butches like Sue, commitment meant very different things depending upon whether one identified and was seen by others as "butch" or as "femme."

When she and others referred to "butch" and "femme," they meant ways of coding identities and behaviors that are both connected to and distinct from standard societal roles for men and women. Among lesbian and bisexual women, as well as in the general population, "there are individuals," Gayle Rubin points out, "who strongly identify as masculine or feminine as well as individuals whose gender preferences are more flexible or fluid."[21] While the rhetoric of the lesbian feminist movement claimed that butch-femme roles had been erased, for many women I spoke with they persisted through the 1970s.

However, for my baby boom interviewees there was little agreement on exactly what "roles" meant. Some women used the term *butch* to refer to those women, not at all interested in male gender identities, who use traits associated with masculinity to signal their lesbianism or to communicate their desire to engage in the kinds of active or initiatory sexual behaviors that in this society are allowed or expected from men. Others used the term to describe women who adopted "male" fashions and mannerisms as a way to claim privileges or deference usually reserved for men. In other words, butch-femme roles had both public (visual) and private (sexual) aspects. Many spoke about the power differences embedded in butch-femme and about the attraction of opposites.

In bed, power differences between butches and femmes were often consensual.[22] But in public, in the context of the heterosexual world, femmes had the upper hand. Identifiably butch women drew fire from people on the street or at work and were often subjected to verbal and physical abuse. But for femmes, the opposite was true, according to Sunny Connelly: "they had to keep telling people that they were queer." If you "look like everybody else, and you want them to know, then you have to make a special point. And that's a different way of being recognized. A different kind of struggle." Femmes could hide their lesbianism and had more social power, or heterosexual privilege, in the dominant culture. But in the realm of the subculture, it was the recognizable lesbian, typically the butch, who had more status, because she was seen as more "authentically" lesbian.

The problem of differential commitment to lesbian identity, as it was experienced within relationships with marked butch-femme differences, prompted many lesbians of the baby boom eventually to reject lesbian feminist sexual constructionism in favor of a more essentialist conception that differentiated between "true" and "false" lesbians. Sue Hammond told me that her relationships with two different feminist lesbians ended bitterly—both left her for men. This was much more difficult than being left for another woman, she said, because "not only are you being rejected, but your whole life is being rejected." Many women had similar experiences of being left for a man, sometimes more than once. They often shared Sue's sense of bitterness about it.

Faced with this uncertainty, Sue resolved to become involved only with women whom she determined to be similarly committed to lesbianism—with "real" lesbians. "It didn't happen again after the second time. After that I only hung out at the bars, and I only got involved with bar dykes, because bar dykes are real dykes. You can trust them to maintain their sexual orientation and not go flitting off to something else. I hung out with dykes who had a dyke history and who stayed dykes." As their old gay sisters did before them, many "new gay" women began to wonder whether, with the onset of feminism, it had gotten "too easy" to become a lesbian. They came to associate lesbianism with having endured hardship and social disapproval, with feeling different, deviant; they believed that the secretive nature of these desires made them even more central to the self.[23] Women who felt that their lesbianism was highly driven believed that many who elected lesbianism were not "authentic" lesbians: they did not share those feelings of difference and the shame of being "not heterosexual. "They wanted to have their cake and eat it too," said Sue. Distinguishing between those who were committed to lesbianism and those who were less committed was far from simple, however. What did it mean to be a lesbian, anyway? Was it defined by desires and fantasies, by sexual practices, or simply by a feeling one had?

Politicizing Commitment

Twelve hundred women attended the first West Coast Lesbian Feminist Conference, held in Los Angeles in June 1973. The goal of the conference was to unify lesbian feminists under a common program. "If there [is] any point of unity it [is] that almost all lesbians are conscious of and hopeful for the development and existence of a lesbian-feminist culture/movement," reported *Lesbian Tide*.[24] But almost immediately, the gathering was wracked by internal disputes over the definition of lesbianism and over who would be permitted to attend. A male-to-female transsexual guitarist was shouted down by the crowd and prevented from performing; Robin Morgan, a prominent feminist writer and theorist, was roundly chastised for living with a man. Heated debates about class broke out.

In surveying lesbian feminist periodicals of the early 1970s, I was struck by the extensive play the gathering had received, particularly on the West Coast. In the course of my interviews with baby boomers who were living in Los Angeles or the San Francisco Bay Area at the time, I heard frequent references to the conference, over fifteen years after the fact. Though designed to unite women, the Los Angeles conference came to symbolize the difficulties of devising a collective conception of lesbian selfhood. Similar clashes took place in other parts of the country. The universalizing lesbian feminist project, which sought to open the lesbian category to all those who wished to claim it, had been challenged by the "problem of commitment." How could lesbian feminists respond to this?

Two collective solutions emerged to politicize the problem of commitment and transform it from a personal to a collective issue: the first was cultural feminism; the second was lesbian separatism. These two movements, which emerged distinctly, were animated by very different understandings of lesbian identity and the political uses of identities. But in practice they often overlapped and had similar effects: they policed the boundaries of lesbian feminism and discouraged disaffection within the ranks.

Cultural Feminism

In the face of the divisions at the Los Angeles conference in 1973, writer and critic Robin Morgan, who was a keynote speaker, made a plea for feminist unity. What is needed, she suggested, is "a real feminist revolution . . . not a Lesbian nation, not an Amazon nation, but a feminist revolution, a gynocratic world run by woman's power." In Morgan's view, a feminist revolution would be facilitated by a new definition and use of the word "Lesbian." As the periodical *Lesbian Tide* described her speech, Morgan urged lesbians to bridge the "male-created dichotomy of sexuality—lesbian vs. heterosexual. . . . We are Lesbians who love our mothers and our daughters, who love each other, who face the male world and fight it with the support of our world—a world of care and tender unity." [25] Morgan's "solution" to the collapse of lesbian feminist unity and the explosion of difference that ensued was to encourage women to unite under the flag of feminism, a position that would come to be known as "cultural feminism."

Cultural feminists favored a universalizing definition of lesbianism, one that emphasized the commonalities among all women and the importance of female values. They sought to "reverse the cultural validation of the male and the devaluation of the female." [26] They suggested that female relationality, mothering capacities, and "ethic of care" were elements of women's distinctive culture. Cultural feminists defined connection as the core of female selfhood, emphasizing identification between women rather than their desire for one another. [27] This radically universalizing strategy suggested that the label *lesbian,* which was never more than a tool of the patriarchy anyway, should be abandoned in favor of a "women's culture" that submerged discussion of sexuality.

As Adrienne Rich suggested, a "lesbian continuum" connected all women; lesbians and heterosexual women were basically the same, not fundamentally distinct types of beings. The experience of infancy creates different psychic structures in men and women, and as a result most women experience relationships as central to their identities; it is out of the intimacy of a relationship that the ability to experience sexual desire and pleasure emerge. Gender, she and others suggested, was a much more significant division than sexuality. Hence, cultural feminists tried to create a women's culture that embodied these ideas of intimacy, reciprocity, and relationality.[28] In many parts of the country, the movement was splintering over class and race issues, in addition to those of sexuality. Out of these political struggles, cultural feminism had emerged, claiming that one did not have to be a member of a formal organization, or even sleep with women, to be a lesbian/feminist. Listening to women's music, reading lesbian fiction, and thinking "like" a lesbian feminist was often enough—for any biological woman, that is.

Thirty-seven-year-old Meg Dunn recalled that when she moved to Boston in 1976 and went to look at roommate listings in the local women's center, she quickly learned to associate the term "lesbian" with "vegetarianism, collectivism, cats, herbal teas, and smoke-free and drug-free environments." Meg, who grew up in a white working-class family in south Florida, was struck by how different this lesbian world was from the one she knew in Florida, where "it was a total sexual thing which had no political connotation at all." Suddenly, Meg recalled, "I was in this world where lesbianism meant a lot more than sex. It was a whole way of life. It was a lifestyle, a set of values, a politics. It was a whole different way of doing things."

Armed with the belief that women embody particular relational and political capacities, lesbians in cities and towns throughout the nation formed communal households; women's bookstores, bars, and coffeehouses; and myriad nonprofit community organizations—battered women's shelters, printing collectives, artists' cooperatives, and so forth.[29] They built an alternative culture, establishing institutions that embodied female values. Carol Solberg, who was living in Portland, Oregon, at the time in a lesbian feminist household that shared resources, recalled that "every lesbian event was sliding scale. No other community was doing that at the time. . . . We believed that we were creating a whole new world, a world that lived by different values. We didn't buy into capitalist ideology. We treated each other the way we wanted others to treat us. It was incredibly heady, empowering." Such reciprocity, practiced on a daily basis by collective households, food cooperatives, and other small-scale organizations—in what might be called a "prefigurative politics"—allowed individuals to step outside of bourgeois individualist values and live by an alternative set of ideals.[30] There was much that was positive in the struggle to change culture and consciousness, live one's politics, and build "women's community." It gave many women the strength and support to claim their desires for one another, and it allowed many to withdraw from difficult and often abusive situations, opening up social space never before available in this country.

"Women's music" was an important product of this period of cultural innovation. Though rarely explicitly lesbian, particularly after the early 1970s, women's music was created and performed primarily by lesbian feminists. In addition to encouraging innovation in terms of musical content, it politicized the *process* of musical production. As singer-songwriter Holly Near explained, women's music sought to create new institutional forms.

> Women's music was not just music being done by women. It was music that was challenging the whole system, a little different from disco, a little different from David Bowie playing with androgyny. . . . We were dealing with a lot of issues David Bowie wasn't dealing with, questions his management wasn't asking. So it was not just the music. It was like taking a whole new look at systems and societies and letting a music rise out of those systems.[31]

Like other forms of women's culture, women's music was imbued with a belief in a universal female sensibility, expressed in the idea of "woman identification." Its identity was defined in large part by its opposition to masculinist forms of culture, such as mainstream rock and roll—"cock rock." In 1974, *Ms.* magazine asked, "Can a Feminist Love the World's Greatest Rock and Roll Band?" and critic Robin Morgan replied with a resolute "No!" She warned that feminists who listened to the Rolling Stones were no better than those who advocated nonmonogamy or those who accepted transsexuals as allies: they had all adopted a "male style," which would destroy the movement.[32] An understanding of feminism as a social identity came from an articulation of what it was not: it was not, first and foremost, about maleness and masculinity.

Like the cultural feminist impulse from which it was born, the vision of women's music—positively valuing women's (and lesbian) lives and accomplishments, and serving as an organizing tool—was ambitious. But the narrow way in which women's music was defined—as music produced by, of, and for feminists—may have inadvertently limited its appeal. By the late 1970s, women of color charged that women's music had become firmly entrenched in what was, for the most part, a European tradition. Confirming their suspicions was the failure of albums and tours by Black artists on women's music labels such as Olivia to attract much-needed sales and audiences.[33]

Similarly, white women such as Meg understood the limitations of women's music to be rooted in the ghettoization of the "women's community."

> The lesbian community to me is all those women who go to Holly Near concerts or something, and I just don't identify with that at all. I never did. The first Holly Near concert I went to . . . I liked Holly, but I prefer rock and roll, and I find women's music boring. I couldn't never bring myself to use the spelling "wimmin." No way. I always think of those people when I think of lesbian or "women's" community. And I've never really identified with that.

She and others questioned the belief that women's culture could truly reflect an essential "femaleness."

When members of the baby boom referred to the "women's community," they typically meant a very specific type of lesbian community—the politicized group of lesbian feminist women. While publicly promoting inclusivity and universality, the lesbian communities that took shape in many cities and towns throughout the nation, particularly during the late half of the 1970s, were in effect rather exclusive. This "community" is different from both the lesbian population and the lesbian subculture. The *lesbian population* might be said to consist of all women who, at any one time, identify as lesbians. The *lesbian subculture* is a more specialized term, encompassing social networks and group identity. The features of *lesbian/women's community* are even more specialized, comprising social networks, group identity, shared subcultural values, and an institutional base.[34] While attempting to universalize lesbian experience, cultural feminists often created stringent normative prescriptions about who belonged in the "women's community" and what women's culture should look and sound like—excluding women who possessed the "right" desires, but the "wrong" ideologies, dress styles, or personal habits. As Mo, a character in Alison Bechdel's popular comic strip "Dykes to Watch Out For," queried: "Are you a dyke if you call yourself a dyke? Does eating tofu and not shaving your armpits automatically make you a dyke?"[35] What if one disliked tofu, and was not enamored of body hair?

But by the mid- to late 1970s, the loudest critics of cultural feminism were motivated by a quite different impulse. Cultural feminism, one woman suggested in the pages of Ann Arbor, Michigan's *Leaping Lesbian,* was diluting lesbian power:

> The Michigan Women's Music Festival is obviously a lesbian music festival—to call it a women's music festival is a failure of nerve. Many events that are overwhelmingly lesbian we don't dare label as such, for fear of alienating women. We are so afraid of being deserted by straight women that we will shut up in order not to alienate them. . . . I am definitely not against women's events—they have a vital part to play—but that's all there is, and I don't think it's enough. As lesbians we have no legitimacy in the eyes of society, and rather than strike out on our own and find it for ourselves, we continue to cling to the past.[36]

In response to the failure of cultural feminism to articulate lesbian specificity and ensure commitment, a small but significant minority of lesbians came to embrace the minoritizing strategy of lesbian separatism.

Lesbian Separatism/Nationalism

Separatists asserted that "lesbian continuum" and "women's community" were euphemisms that actually did lesbians more harm than good, and that cultural feminism fed lesbian invisibility. The cultural feminist impulse, as exemplified by Adrienne Rich's "lesbian continuum," was to blur the boundaries between lesbians and heterosexual feminists. In response, lesbian separatists attempted to separate lesbians from straight women, as well as the lesbian community from the heterosexual world. They became dedicated to rooting out male influence in all its forms. Males, separatists believed, could never be allies and could never be reformed—not even male children; lesbians, they believed, must also assert their independence from heterosexual women, who were in effect collaborating with the enemy.

The beginning of lesbian separatism is often traced to the 1971 founding of the Furies, a group in Washington, D.C. Responding to the purge of lesbians from feminist organizations such as the National Organization for Women, the Furies recast lesbianism as a political strategy that was the outcome of feminism. Drawing upon nationalist rhetoric borrowed from the Black civil rights movement and the liberation struggles of third world countries, writers such as Jill Johnston, who popularized the term "Lesbian Nation," saw separatism as a strategy for self-determination, a means for lesbians to come together to create an affirmative sense of selfhood and to build their own cultural and political institutions, apart from heterosexual feminists and gay men.[37] It was a rejection of the early universalizing impulse of lesbian feminism in favor of a conception of lesbian difference: "Like every other minority group we need a place to assert and explore our identity in the face of a hostile culture. If anything, we need this more than other minorities for lesbians have been so scattered, hidden and isolated, and none of us have grown up within a lesbian community; rather, we have to search out other lesbians as adults. A basic issue is how to assert and explore our identity as lesbians."[38] Charlotte Bunch, a theorist and one of the original founders of the Furies, drew a parallel between lesbian separatism and the plight of "old dykes." "The lesbians who had been gay prior to the existence of the feminist movement," she explained, "were less surprised by our rejection [of straight feminists] than those of us newly gay and full of enthusiasm for our recent discoveries. The older lesbians knew something that we had just begun to learn: lesbianism is not only a threat to men, but also to many heterosexual women."[39]

This early variant of separatism embodied what some have called "strategic" essentialism. Early separatists embraced the idea of a Lesbian Nation, and the essential oneness of all lesbians that it implied, less as a programmatic design for a lesbian-only world than as a metaphor for political solidarity—an intermediate strategy, not a solution. Bunch defined separatism as a "dynamic strategy to be moved in and

out of whenever a minority feels that its interests are being overlooked by the majority or that its insights need more space to be
developed." She stressed, at times, the importance of "working with
straight feminists" and becoming involved "with other feminist projects and analytical developments"—"since the core of a lesbian-
feminist politics and community had been developed."[40] As a strategy of self-identification, women of the baby boom differentiated between two forms, or moments, of separatism. Many described separatism as a stage they passed through in their coming out process,
as they separated themselves from heterosexual society in order to
consolidate a sense of lesbian identity. They spoke of separatism as
process and *strategy* rather than as a "permanent" identity.[41] At times
during the 1970s, they lived in a largely lesbian world, attended lesbian events, and tried to minimize their contact with nonlesbians.

In the early 1970s, through the influence of the women's movement, Sally Kirk "discovered" her lesbianism, after having been involved with men. Indeed, as we saw in chapter 3, Sally tried very
consciously to solidify that fragile sense of identity. By the mid-1970s
her life was spent, for all intents and purposes, entirely among
women, which she describes as her "separatist phase." For almost ten
years, Sally lived and worked almost exclusively within the lesbian
subculture. For a few of those years, she consciously refused contact
with men: her friendship circles were composed entirely of lesbians;
her organizational commitments were entirely lesbian. She removed
herself from her family of origin, who were unsupportive of her lesbianism.

Perhaps half of the women I spoke with would characterize themselves as having once been a separatist in this sense, during the hey-
day of lesbian feminism. For women of the baby boom cohort, this
"separatist phase" typically lasted a few years. Rarely was it seen as
an end in itself. As Sally suggested, "because I had taken on this
identity, in order to have it, there had to be a certain ironcladness
about it. And in order to have that ironcladness, we had to exclude
men." Mary Lipton similarly described her separatist phase as an
important step in developing a lesbian identity, part of a search for
community. "I'm not somebody who has close family ties," she explained. Having grown up in the suburb of a northeastern city, in

a family from which she was estranged, Mary found in the lesbian community her substitute family: "I really was alienated from my family from a very early age, and didn't have that support. And really needed to make distance from them. And I come from a really WASPy background where I didn't have any cultural identity which was really important to me. I had nothing to hold onto. I think that lesbian identity gave me something, some kind of community I've never had." For Mary, becoming a part of the lesbian community entailed struggling to construct a more positive sense of personal and collective self and forming a shared conception of identity with some positive characteristics. The quest for a community of like-minded persons was an integral part of the search for identity. Identification typically involved disidentification—separating from one's family, as well as from those considered to be less committed to feminism. Mary talked about how when she came out, she felt that she "had crossed this line": "I had a real need to separate myself from women who weren't so different from me. Certainly they were not so different than I had been just a few years before, when I had a boyfriend. I really had to make distance." When I asked her who was included in her community, Mary listed friends, women she saw at demonstrations, and "overlapping friendship networks."

The question of who were the most fervent proponents of separatist ideology aroused some controversy among my interviewees. One might imagine that lifelong, "primary" lesbians would be the strongest proponents of separatist ideology, utilizing it as a mechanism to control entry and exit from lesbian communities and thus encourage commitment. Separatism would give the lifelong lesbian some insurance that women she became involved with would not leave her for men. It would allow her to be certain (up to a point) that women with whom she became involved did not consider lesbianism as merely a passing fancy. It might provide a sense of permanence and security and allow her to surround herself with other women who made "exclusivist" commitments to the lesbian community. This type of identification would seem to be very appealing to someone seeking certainty and consistency.

But I have found quite the opposite: it appears that the strongest proponents of separatist ideology were formerly heterosexual women who had elected to become lesbians. Many women I interviewed felt that there was a connection between separatist politics and lack of "real" desire for women. They said the most doctrinaire separatists were those who were least attracted to women, who were least "in it for the sex." Joan Salton told me,

> Quite a number of women who became separatists were women who had just recently become lesbians, and they became lesbians out of bad relationships with men. At least a number of women I met, and also heard about. They were not old dykes who thought their way through and decided to become lesbian separatists. They were women who were bouncing off of painful relationships with men and grabbing onto an ideology which would give them that kind of space.

Sarah Marcus, who had come out as a lesbian in the San Francisco Bay Area in the context of radical feminism, agreed that separatism was a "phase" that many women went through in order to consolidate a lesbian identity. She suggested that separatists were more likely to be women who had been in abusive relationships with men. "They were man-haters, you know, women who could not stand to be in the same room as a man because they had been abused by their fathers, or brothers, or husbands." Shirley Alvarez, who lived on a separatist commune of women's land in Oregon, differentiated between "women who just wanted peace" and ideological separatists, or man-haters.

> I was one who just wanted peace. But I used to fight with the most incredible separatists, the man-haters. They're all straight now. They went to such extremes. . . . Those people are now married with children, gone back to Jesus. I think when you get too out there. . . . This one woman, she talked a blue streak about how she hated men. Now she's Miss Bible Thumper, married. She went from being a shaved head, pierced nose separatist. . . . She's not the only one.

For many, separatism operated as a form of identity work, a way to reshape the self and consolidate a lesbian identity.[42]

Perhaps separatism was initially seen as a strategy for lesbian empowerment and as a way of building identity and community; but by the mid- to late 1970s, in many towns and cities, lesbian separatism became an end in itself, a collective *identity* as much as a strategy.

Separatists tried to fix boundaries, make membership more exclusive, and harden the notion of an essential lesbian difference.[43] They took the idea of a Lesbian Nation, which had before been used metaphorically in lesbian feminist circles, quite literally, imputing to lesbians an essential core character; they asserted the superiority of lesbian culture and called for the separation of lesbian communities from the dominant culture and from those deemed less committed to lesbianism.

Separatists valorized stability, commitment, and solidarity. They conceived of the universe of women as consisting of two groups, straight and gay; suggested that lesbians held in a common a "core" attribute that made them distinctive and different; and encouraged searches for *authenticity,* for the "real" or "true" lesbian, differentiating between women who were committed to becoming and remaining lesbians and those who were less committed. As separatists constructed group boundaries, they made use of highly essentialist definitions of lesbianism, excluding all but the most dedicated and mandating individual commitment to the good of the larger group. Gone was the understanding of separatism as strategy; it was now an end in itself.

By the time of my interviews, only two of the women from my baby boom sample continued to identify themselves as separatists. Longtime activist and writer Andrea Brum was one of them, a self-described separatist who railed against those who "dabbled." "Lesbian identity," she stated, "isn't just a casual commitment, one among a smorgasbord of possibilities. It's a way of life." A firm believer in making membership requirements as stringent as possible, Andrea related her impressions of her visit to Spain while Franco was in power. Under fascism, she said, "only lesbians were lesbians. You were a lesbian with a knowledge that you risked your life." Andrea lamented that the end of fascism, and the revival of the left and feminism, has meant that "more and more women are dabbling."

She and others came to believe, against the claims of many feminists, that lesbians were in fact a clearly bounded minority group that stood outside of heterosexuality—or that ideally *should.* They questioned whether social constructionism, and the lesbian feminist ideology it spawned, could accurately understand lesbian experience and guide lesbian political activity. Equating political lesbians with consumerism's throwaway ethos, Julia Penelope, a separatist theorist, proclaimed: "My lesbianism was never a choice in the way that many speak of it now. My Lesbian identity has never really been a 'preference' for me; it's not an identity I casually selected from a Baskin-Robbins sexuality counter."[44] Like old dykes, many separatists saw individuals who experienced their lesbianism as a relatively fixed "orientation" as the only "authentic" lesbians. Fading were the dreams of liberating society by releasing "the lesbian in every woman."

Elaborate classification systems were sometimes created to separate the wheat from the chaff. Cindy Ross recalled being a member of a separatist group in the late 1970s that had a formal hierarchy in which " 'butch' lesbians who had never slept with a man occupied most favored position; women who had been lesbians before the women's movement were in the second most favored position; 'femmes' who had prior heterosexual experience, and who came out during the women's movement, were in the third position; bisexuals were at the bottom." This blend of gender and sexual essentialism created a formal hierarchy of lesbian "realness." Here we see the emergence of a highly essentialist conception, a "reverse affirmation" of the medicalized account of lesbianism that attributes "most favored" status to those individuals who are considered in the dominant culture to be most pathological. However, for ideological separatists it was not enough to "be" an authentic lesbian; one also had to develop a political stance that separated one from the dominant culture.

As these comments suggest, separatism was in essence a defensive posture, whose meaning developed primarily in opposition to an "other" comprising men, straight feminists, and less committed lesbians. Its goal was to narrow the boundaries around the lesbian group and toughen membership standards. While cultural feminists blurred the boundaries between lesbians and straight women as they emphasized the fluidity of identity, separatists suggested that only biological women who do not sleep with men could claim the lesbian label. One woman suggested the following definition of lesbianism: "A lesbian is a woman whose value system is such that she can be fulfilled spiritually, mentally, emotionally, and sexually only in a romantic relationship with another woman."[45] This definition excluded transsexuals, nonfeminist lesbians, practicing bisexuals, political lesbians, and even many "elective" lesbians.

Though directing their ire against patriarchal culture and male sexuality, separatists were as much concerned with regulating female sexuality as with shunning male sexuality. Indeed, one observer noted that separatism was, in effect, "a vehicle to establish the proper parameters of lesbian sexuality so as to diminish the possibility that lesbians will defect to 'male-identified' sexual expressions, whether these be s/m, roles, or heterosexuality."[46] Like ethnic separatists and fundamentalists of various sorts, lesbian separatists sought to construct an organic community within modern society, with boundaries that marked their community as separate from the dominant culture. They embodied the most radical version of a politics of identity, asserting a notion of group difference as real and not arbitrary and downplaying the differences within the group. The formation of a collective identity through such in-group/out-group differentiation assumes that the in-group possesses the truth, in contrast to the outsiders who suffer from error or display indifference.[47]

Despite their relatively small numbers, ideological separatists were able to exert an enormous impact on lesbian political culture, particularly after the mid-1970s, because they were well organized and very vocal. They were responsible for border skirmishes around transsexualism, boy children, bisexuality, and other issues that divided many lesbian conferences, women's music festivals, and local communities in the 1970s through the 1980s. In the pages of *Lesbian Connection*, separatists railed against those who brought children to women's music festivals, who admitted to lingering bisexual urges, and who suggested that men be allowed into women-only events; all were roundly chastised in the name of lesbian solidarity.[48]

"Women who couldn't bear to be around men took it to absurd extremes," commented Joan Salton, as she told me a story about a woman who was invited to a feminist writer's conference in Chicago in the late 1970s and who wouldn't stay in a house because there was a male dog on the premises. "Bizarre theories came up, to the effect, not only were women the superior sex, but men are mutants. Men are a different species." Shirley Alvarez recalled that on her communal farm, some women "didn't want to deal with machinery because it was man-made."

Separatists exemplified what Albert Melucci calls "integralism," the yearning for a totalizing identity, for a "master key which unlocks every door of reality." They rejected a pluralist attitude to life, encouraging people to "turn their backs on complexity" and become incapable of accepting difference.[49] By the mid- to late 1970s, the very qualities that were once seen as the special contribution of the lesbian feminist movement were undermining its existence. Communities of intimacy, it turned out, were also communities of exclusion.

Constructionism, Commitment, Solidarity

As we have seen, during the early days of the movement, the early 1970s, lesbian feminists rejected medicalized essentialist definitions of lesbianism in favor of a universalizing conception. They declared that every woman was a potential lesbian and sought to "liberate" the lesbian in every woman. Denying a clear division between the heterosexual and homosexual worlds, they suggested that lesbianism was open to anyone with the right political convictions. As Kate Millett declared, women's liberation and homosexual liberation were "both struggling together toward a common goal: a society free from defining and categorizing people by virtue of gender and/or sexual preference."[50]

But this universalizing strategy was soon called into question. Despite their efforts to consolidate and stabilize their lesbian identities, many women continued to experience a strain between their personal and social identities as lesbians. Publicly, they identified as lesbians, but "deep down" many wondered if they were "real" lesbians. Old dykes, as well as some "new lesbians" who had subscribed to social constructionist accounts of identity, began to question the liberal way in which the boundaries around the lesbian community had been drawn.

Two approaches emerged to politicize the issue of commitment: the first was an even more radical *universalizing* strategy, cultural feminism, which sought to further erase the boundaries separating lesbians and straight women. The second was a *minoritizing* strategy, lesbian separatism, which embraced an ethnic model of lesbian identity that tried to inscribe fixed boundaries around the lesbian world. Cultural feminists collapsed sexuality into gender, suggesting that feminists should overlook their sexual differences in the interest of solidarity. In contrast, separatists conceptualized lesbians as wholly distinct from heterosexual and bisexual women (and homosexual men). For some individuals, these strategies temporarily resolved the dissonance between their personal identity (as heterosexual or bisexual) and social identity (as lesbian).

Despite their ideological differences, cultural feminism and separatism often overlapped. Members of both groups collapsed sexuality, politics, and identity, relegating desire to a secondary position.[51] And in the end the effect of these strategies was much the same: they transformed lesbianism into a totalizing identity that required exclusive commitments and they carefully controlled entry into and exit from the lesbian world. Collectively, they embodied an "ethnic" model of sexuality that made the boundaries between the homosexual and heterosexual worlds more rigid.[52] One might say that separatism did so intentionally and cultural feminism, unintentionally.

Why, we must ask, did many lesbian feminists abandon their early constructionist convictions? In part, the answer lies in the nature of identity-based politics. It is the dominant group that tends to create boundaries to accentuate the differences between itself and minority populations; indeed, for lesbians, the medical profession was long a primary generator of these distinctions. But for groups organizing to pursue collective ends, such as destigmatizing homosexuality, the process of asserting "who we are" often involves a kind of reverse affirmation of the characteristics attributed to it by the dominant society. As Steven Epstein asks: "How do you protest a socially imposed categorization, except by organizing around this category? Just as blacks cannot fight the arbitrariness of racial classification without organizing as blacks, so gays could not advocate the overthrow of the sexual order without making gayness the very basis of their claims."[53]

In addition, life cycle changes certainly played an important role. That the hardening of group boundaries I have described occurred in the mid-1970s was no accident. By this time, many of the women who came out "through feminism" were approaching their thirties and were beginning to lose their youthful enthusiasm for a movement in which all things no longer seemed possible. In that group, many women were in the process of stabilizing their identities, making a permanent decision and commitment to lesbianism, and foreclosing the possibility of bisexuality or heterosexuality. Others were beginning to question their lesbianism, finding that it did not in fact suit their sense of self. The development of a collective conception of what it meant to be a lesbian—paradoxically, one that resembled the "dominant" essentialist account—provided a solution to this problem, albeit a partial and temporary one.

Chapter Five

Sex, Kids, and Therapy

The Decentering of Lesbian Feminism

"A commitment to the liberation of gay women means a re-arrangement of priorities. Gradually a new hierarchy develops. What seemed important before—job, family, career, home—cannot compete with the compelling vision of liberation." So wrote Sidney Abbott and Barbara Love in 1972.[1] But fifteen years later, as life cycle changes drew many lesbians into motherhood, families, and the labor force, two of the largest and most active lesbian organizations in San Francisco were a professional grouping of "career women," devoted to business and professional networking, and a support group for lesbians "choosing children." Similarly, in Boston during this period, "it seemed as if virtually every lesbian in her thirties was either having a baby or thinking about it."[2] Individuals came to view their lesbian identification as one among many identities, or roles, they possessed.

It was easiest to fulfill commitments to a demanding community when one had few, if any, other obligations. Indeed, the most visible sectors of lesbian communities have long been composed of women in their early twenties, in large part because when one first comes out, takes on a personal identity as lesbian, and seeks out other lesbians, issues of sexual identity are often most salient.[3] But as they entered their thirties and forties, individuals found themselves attending PTA meetings, immersing themselves in work cultures, and renewing links to their biological families of origin.

At the same time, the public face of lesbian feminism was changing.

In 1978, a San Francisco conference organized by a group called Women Against Violence in Pornography attracted women from over thirty states. The same year, lesbian sadomasochism made its public debut, as a contingent from the lesbian s/m group Samois marched in the city's annual lesbian and gay pride parade. Within a few years, issues of pornography and sadomasochism were propelled to center stage throughout the country. Polarized battles raged in the pages of feminist publications, as "sex radicals" and antiporn activists traded barbs; they came to a head in the unlikely setting of an academic conference in New York in 1982, when anti-s/m activists picketed a speak-out on "politically incorrect sex."[4]

Though the "sex debates" or "porn wars" that ensued rarely addressed the subject of lesbianism explicitly, lesbianism was a significant subtext. "The traditional notion of femininity as gentle and nurturing creates the stereotype that lesbianism is just a hand-holding society," said Susie Bright, the self-described San Francisco "sexpert" and pro-sex activist. "Lesbians don't have sex, the story goes. Or if they do, it is this really tiresome affair—five minutes of cunnilingus on each side, with a little timer nearby, and lots of talking about your feelings and career."[5] Somewhere in the midst of defining sexuality as male, and lesbianism as a blow against patriarchy, the specificity of lesbian existence as a *sexual* identity seemed to get lost.

In their search for a different, more sexualized, model of lesbian identity, Bright and others invoked the tradition of pre-Stonewall lesbianism, which they saw as rooted in working-class bar culture and butch-femme roles, unencumbered by feminist prescriptions.[6] In centering post-Stonewall lesbian identity on a rejection of men and patriarchal culture, lesbians had earlier disengaged from a gay liberation movement that was largely blind to their needs. Some now came to praise the sexual license of gay men, who had created subcultures that actively promoted the search for pleasure. In addition, the onset of the AIDS crisis in the early 1980s drew many into working alongside gay men.

A less noisy but perhaps even more significant challenge to lesbian feminist ideology came from women of color. As early as 1974, the Combahee River Collective, a group of black feminists that included lesbians, pointed out that feminism, particularly in its separatist tendencies, "leaves out far too much and far too many people, particularly Black men, women and children . . . [and] so completely denies any but the sexual sources of women's oppression, negating the facts of class and race."[7] Several years later, in a similar vein, Chicana writer Cherríe Moraga wrote urgently, "Lesbianism is supposed to be about connection. What drew me to politics was my love of women, the agony I felt in observing the straight-jackets of poverty and repression I saw people in my own family in. But the deepest political tragedy I have experienced is how with such grace, such blind faith, this commitment to women in the feminist movement grew to be exclusive and reactionary. *I call my white sisters on this.*"[8] At conferences and other gatherings, African American, Latina, and Asian women brought to the fore the divisions of race and class that had been submerged in the interest of building a unified culture and movement. In cities throughout the nation, women of color began to organize autonomously, on the basis of their own oppression.[9]

These challenges pointed toward an understanding of lesbianism as situated in a web of multiple oppressions and identities. Problematizing the once-uncontested relationship between lesbianism and feminism, these critics questioned the belief that lesbian life could ever completely divorce itself from the structures of the dominant culture. And they shifted lesbian politics away from its focus upon the "male threat" and toward a more diffuse notion of power and resistance, acknowledging that lesbians necessarily operate in a society marked by inequalities of class and race as well as those of gender and sexuality.

This chapter examines how the baby boom cohort contributed to and was influenced by these cultural and political shifts. The women who came of age during the 1960s and 1970s, the products of the postwar baby boom, were a "decisive generation" who remade lesbian life in the United States. In adulthood, they continued to play a pivotal role in shaping the public face of lesbianism. By the early 1980s, many of these women had been out as lesbians for ten years, and they felt that their sexual identities were firmly established. As they aged and settled into their careers, long-term relationships, and alternative families, they became less interested in making new connections. Many were less driven by sexual desires.

While some of them came to reassess their former convictions, most looked ahead rather than back: as the substance of their lives shifted, so did their identities. They found themselves again grappling with many questions: What does it mean to be a lesbian? How central is that identity to my sense of self? Exclusivist conceptions of lesbianism had always been suspect among lesbians of color, but by the late 1970s and early 1980s, many white middle-class lesbians who found themselves drawn into increasing contact with the heterosexual world by choice or necessity were also forced to balance their loyalties to the "lesbian community" and their obligations outside it. Resisting the encroachments of the community upon their lives, many began to resist totalizing strategies of identity.

Two themes emerged in my discussions with baby boomers as they moved into their thirties and forties. First, work and family commitments figured more prominently in their lives now than in the past. Second, lesbian self-concepts changed, reflecting these changes in their lives and in lesbian culture. Together, these and other developments signaled that the locus of lesbian life was shifting away from communal attachments; lesbian identity and community were being reconstituted in new, "decentered" ways.

Getting Saved from the Seventies

Feminists had constructed a set of positive images of the potentially transformative possibilities of lesbian relationships. Often they "aristocratized" lesbianism, attributing superior capacities of nurturance, sensitivity, empathy, warmth, and understanding to women, and by implication especially to women who loved women.[10] Lesbian relationships, many suggested, offered the best prospect for achieving equality and reciprocity—an idealization pivotal to lesbian feminist efforts to destigmatize lesbianism. But with time, many women came to question this formulation.

Looking at a lesbian feminist community in the Midwest in the mid- to late 1970s, sociologist Susan Krieger found that individuals frequently felt either overwhelmed or abandoned by the community. The merger of the individual and the community was something that many women sought, at least initially. But, in the end, it also led many individuals to experience a loss of self. All social groups confront their members with this kind of conflict, Krieger noted. But "in some groups," namely those in which the "desire for personal affirmation from the group is great, and the complementary desire for assertion of individuality is also strong," this experience is felt more intensely and seems to occur more frequently.[11]

As they reached their thirties and forties, several of my interviewees lamented, their involvements with other lesbians, as lovers, friends, or simply acquaintances, were often highly emotionally charged and even "merged."[12] As Cindy Ross told me,

> Often I felt these incredibly empowering feelings which allowed me to break out of my isolation, and see myself at one with those around me. It was exhilarating and empowering. A lot of the energy I felt for being a lesbian came from the feeling of being a part of community of other lesbians. But sometimes the shit hit the fan. People were hurt. It was difficult for us to say why we did certain things: were we doing them for ourselves, or for our friends? We couldn't tell the difference between the two sometimes.

The earlier tendency to idealize and aristocratize lesbianism had been transformed into a sense that lesbian relationships were *particularly* problematic. They offered the potential of an unparalleled degree of reciprocity and equality among partners—but sometimes *too* much of them. Cindy talked about her realization one day that "everyone in her circle had slept with everyone else." It was "fun, exhilarating at times, but also scary. We had lost a sense of ourselves." In the parlance of object relations psychoanalysis, this was a problem of merging: the loss of boundaries between self and other.

Karen Savo joked that when she became a lesbian, she first thought "everything was going to be so great. It was going to be tra-la-land—like you died and went to heaven. Women were going to be the answer to all my problems." She spoke of the way her idealism had faded as she had gotten older, referring in passing to her conflicts with an ex-lover. "But it was really only the beginning of my problems," she laughed. Sharon Lieberman recalled witnessing two women she knew in a "marital" quarrel. "I couldn't believe anyone would be involved with a woman if she was going to call you things you would never tolerate a man calling you. One was saying: you bitch. The other was saying: you asshole. To me, it was like: what's the big deal about lesbian relationships? They can be just as screwed up as any others—sometimes more so." Others spoke of the "trash-ings" that had taken place in many lesbian communities: the attacks meted upon women who slept with men, women who brought their boy children to all-women's events, middle-class women who failed to renounce their "class privileges," and others who dared to step out of line—however the "line" was configured at any particular place and time. Particularly after the mid-1970s, in many lesbian feminist communities separatists initiated border skirmishes, a series of acri-monious battles for inclusion and exclusion that led to frayed nerves and even more rigid community boundaries. As I have suggested, women of color were acutely aware of the limits of such a politics.

Though few of my interviewees mentioned these challenges spe-cifically, they clearly contributed to what I am here calling the "de-centering" of lesbian feminism. The brand of feminism that spoke of retrieving a lost sisterhood, which had animated many individuals' hopes and desires, was losing its clarity of vision. The fun and excite-ment women experienced during the initial period of lesbian feminist mobilization—posing challenges that had never before been articu-lated in public, building a new oppositional culture, and reshaping a sense of self—were dissipating.

Clearly, the terms by which sexual and close, nonintimate relations among lesbians were defined made them difficult to live up to. Be-cause the stakes were so high—not only were lesbian relationships highly stigmatized in the dominant culture, but they were also highly prized within the subculture—they were heavily charged in numer-ous ways. But how could any relationship be devoid of power and conflict? The "aristocratization" of lesbianism had so simplified and romanticized the realities of human existence that when such ten-sions finally appeared, they were often doubly disturbing, because of the great disparity between expectations and reality. As the "little disappointments" accumulated, the initial euphoria felt by many women in lesbian communities began to fade.

Many of my interviewees sought out therapy and self-help to assist them in describing and talking about a more autonomous self. They were not alone. "If we live any part of our lives in any 'woman's community' in this country," one observer wrote, "we know what therapy is. Almost everyone is either in therapy, going to therapy, thinking about going into therapy, or studying to become a therapist."[13] The very high proportion of therapists among my interviewees—twenty percent—testified to the appeal of therapeutic ideas and culture, particularly among middle-class members of the baby boom cohort. "I didn't have good boundaries and limits," said Cindy Ross, speaking of her experience in a lesbian feminist community in Chicago in the 1970s. She worked in the trades for fifteen years before going back to school in 1983 to become a therapist. This training led her to reevaluate her involvement with the lesbian community in psychological terms. "There were lots of unhealthy girls in the lesbian community. We were young, drank a lot. We thought that looking at our emotional problems would discredit lesbianism, and play into the notion of lesbians as sick."

In 1984, Cindy also began to attend a "twelve-step" group for "adult children of alcoholics." Through her participation in that group, she came to recognize that several members of her family were alcoholics and that her family was "dysfunctional." At the time, many of her friends were discovering the legacy of "alcoholism abuse" in their families. But she added: "All heterosexual families are dysfunctional for lesbians." The growing popularity of therapy and twelve-step groups, Cindy believed, was "a good thing." In many cities in the late 1980s, the number of gay and women's meetings offered by twelve-step groups was disproportionately large. In Boston, Alcoholics Anonymous offered twenty weekly gay meetings, one specifically for lesbians, and sixty meetings for women. Al-Anon (programs for family members and friends of alcoholics) offered meetings—ten gay, two lesbian, two women's, and one bisexual—with names like "Amazon Lesbians" and "Glitter and Be Gay."[14]

Part of the appeal of therapy lay in its affinity with feminism, which had politicized personal life and suggested that the self could be freed from oppressive patriarchal and heterosexist conditioning. The first statement of lesbian feminism, "The Woman Identified Woman," claimed that by throwing off the chains of heterosexuality, a woman could achieve her true essence as woman. She could overcome the sense of "being behind a locked window" and "get out what we know is inside."[15] bell hooks has argued that the recovery of a distinct feminist voice, language, and consciousness was the first step to becoming whole, to resisting the debilitating effects of the dominant culture. "Naming one's pain in relation to structures of dominance" was the beginning stage in the process of coming to political consciousness.[16]

Much as the search for an "authentic" self was an integral part of the coming out narrative guiding the individual on her path of lesbian self-discovery, so it underlay the rhetoric of therapy, which, rooted in ego psychology, promised to free her from unnecessary social constraints.[17] Therapy offered many of the same things that originally attracted women to feminism. But some feared that therapeutic practices had achieved a significance far beyond their relevant scope, that they were influencing all aspects of daily life. "Therapy used to name what happened between a therapist and 'client.' It now names, properly speaking, what happens between many women in daily interactions. We live at a time when therapy has become a way of life, when our language is suffering a profound change because of it, when the very way we *think* is affected by therapeutic practices."[18]

The growing influence of psychotherapeutic thought and practice in lesbian communities through the 1980s often posed a challenge to the dichotomous conceptualizations of gender—men and women as essentially different and politically opposed to one another—that had fueled many variants of lesbian feminism. Nina Samson had a revelation when she became a therapist and began to do couples therapy: "Men are the victims many times. Women are assholes too. I began to see the struggle much more as the dynamic between people, rather than between victim and oppressor. Having lived in a closed, rigid dogma for so long, I found that very liberating." Though it had once been viewed as a powerful transformative philosophy, some came to find lesbian feminism almost as restrictive as the patriarchal thinking from which women wished to flee. Cindy Ross recognized the limits of the lesbian transformative project: "We thought we had figured it all out. We thought we as women had a quality of being that was qualitatively different from men. We thought that hierarchy was patriarchal, and that racism and sexism flowed from it. But then we began to see those differences in us."

To critics of the growing popularity of therapeutic thinking and practice, women were reneging upon the original promise of feminism, abandoning the link between the personal and the political. Thus, bell hooks argued that feminism initially saw "the necessity for radicalizing consciousness in conjunction with collective political resistance," while therapy awakened women "to the need for change without providing substantive models and strategies for change."[19] It tended to seek individual not political solutions to the sense of powerlessness that many women faced. Similarly, Ellen Herman attacked the twelve-step program's core concept—"personal accountability for one's actions—[as] decidedly apolitical. The responsibility for both addiction and recovery rests squarely on the individual. . . . It turns the progressive political goal of empowerment on its head."[20]

Clearly, individualism and communal commitments coexisted uneasily among women of the baby boom, particularly those who were from the middle class, who felt an extraordinary degree of entitlement. They believed that they were entitled to control their own lives and to construct a sense of self that was as fulfilling as possible—not simply in sexual terms, but in all regards. Few working-class women and women of color harbored such grand hopes. Nonetheless, many looked to the feminist and gay liberation movements as offering the promise of collective self-realization. But by the 1980s, the collective dream of liberation was being modified, and individual sources of fulfillment and identification were coming to be more highly valued.

Choosing Children, Finding Work

Lesbians have always been mothers. According to some estimates, at least 10 percent of all women are lesbians and 20 to 30 percent of all lesbians have children—a figure that adds up to somewhere between two and a half and four million lesbian mothers in the United States today.[21] Many lesbians have children from previous heterosexual marriages. Others were single parents before they came out. From the mid-1970s and through the 1980s, the first postfeminist cohort reached their mid-twenties and early thirties, and they began to "choose children," intentionally parenting children outside of heterosexual marriages in what came to be known as the "lesbian baby boom."[22]

A newly sanctioned individualism encouraged an unprecedented move among these lesbians to construct familial structures that blended the traditional and nontraditional. Of the women in my baby boom cohort sample, five became mothers by their thirties. One had given birth to two boys before she became a lesbian. Two became "co-parents" of children born to their lesbian lovers. Two others became biological mothers after moving into heterosexual relationships, a phenomenon that we will examine in the next chapter. Beyond those who are centrally involved in parenting as either a biological parent or co-parent, about half of my interviewees reported having children in their lives.

Early second-wave feminists viewed women's mothering as contributing to male domination. They suggested that women free themselves from compulsory motherhood. But with time, many feminists came to affirm motherhood as a source of female difference and power. When members of this group of women who were in lesbian relationships began to bear children, they often did so in the belief that they could insulate their chosen families from the exigencies of heterosexual society.[23]

"In the early days," Naomi Kennedy told me, she and others believed that they could "choose children" exclusively within the confines of the women's community. In order to minimize male involvement in the process, many women used anonymous sperm donors. But this plan was foiled, at least in part, by the impossibility of choosing the sex of one's child. Anecdotal evidence suggests that a disproportionately high percentage of "turkey baster" babies, conceived through artificial insemination, were boys. While a small but very vocal separatist minority insisted upon collapsing the distinction between little boys and grown men, tarring both with the brush of patriarchy, having boy children prompted many women to question the previously unarticulated gender essentialism that sometimes motivated their political convictions. "How could I possibly see my son, this poor, defenseless creature, as the enemy of women?" asked Naomi, whose lover gave birth to a boy. In the early 1970s, debates about whether or not male children should be admitted to women's music festivals and other lesbian events divided her lesbian feminist community, leading Naomi to become very uncomfortable with women she had previously considered friends. "I found myself moving away from the women's community," she said, "toward a community comprised of other lesbian mothers."

When they had children, particularly older children who went to school, lesbian mothers were pulled by competing allegiances. There were PTA meetings to attend, baby-sitters to arrange, pediatricians to deal with. Naomi spoke of the exhilaration and confusion she faced when confronted with her maternal identity. "Was I a mother or a feminist lesbian? A lot of straight people, including my family, told me I couldn't do both: lesbians don't have children. A lot of lesbians told me I couldn't do both: children just get in the way, and what do you do with the boys? But we went ahead and had them anyway." When lesbians became mothers they did so primarily as women, and only secondarily as lesbians; in terms of the hierarchy of identity, here gender is generally much more salient than sexuality. The "heterosexual assumption," which assumes that individuals are straight "until proven gay," and the belief that lesbians and mothers are two mutually exclusive categories lead people to assume that mothers are heterosexual.

"Central to the definition of being a lesbian was not having children," Laura Stone said, explaining her experience as the nonbiological parent of a son, "unless you had a child from a previous heterosexual marriage." In her experience, heterosexuals who saw a lesbian accompanied by a child generally assumed she was straight and married. She had to keep telling them otherwise. This was particularly true of women who were the nonbiological parents of children: not only did they have to challenge the equation of motherhood and heterosexuality, but they also had to introduce to people the notion of nonbiological, or social, motherhood. "What we had to go through to break that barrier was inconceivable to people now. We screwed up everyone's stereotypes of what it meant to be a mother, and what it meant to be a lesbian."

Laura lived in a community in the Bay Area where there were a number of other lesbian mothers at her child's school, which helped matters and kept her from feeling isolated. But others experienced the process of "coming out" as lesbian mothers as painful at times. Sharon Lieberman, who lived in a suburb outside of San Francisco, described motherhood as a status that made her sexual identity practically invisible. "For the first time, I was acceptable, because I was a mother, not a lesbian. I often found myself playing along with it, and not revealing myself much, but I didn't take pride in it." This was even more difficult for her lover, who was made more invisible by Sharon's silence, which placed a great strain on their relationship.

Lesbian mothers, like single heterosexual mothers, often turned first to their nuclear families, especially their parents, for financial help, child care, and emotional support. Naomi Kennedy described how having given birth to a child changed her relationship with her mother.

> My mother and I were very close for many years—until I decided I was a lesbian. When I first came out to her, she was in shock. We rarely spoke for nearly two years. With time, things became more normalized, but still we were at a loss for things to talk about. I couldn't talk about my lover—she was too uncomfortable—in anything but the vaguest terms. When I had a child, that changed dramatically. Suddenly, I was asking her for advice about colds and flus and changing diapers. We had something in common again.

Ara Jones lamented never having had a child for very much these reasons.

> The saddest thing is that I don't have children. That is my main regret. The baby boom is so great, and the healthiest thing. It's very good for couples. When you're self-absorbed, and gay relationships can be self-absorbing, because of the way the world is, the more tradition is allowed in, the better. It often brings people closer to their families. . . . I used to think about being a single parent, but I never could afford day care. If I met a woman with children that would be great. . . . That's my one main regret. Which isn't to say I ever wanted to birth a baby. But I think it's great that when women come out now, it is a real possibility. That's new.

Though their lesbianism placed them at the social margin, motherhood moved some women back toward the center. It allowed many individuals to rejoin their natal families and the cultural mainstream. This was a mixed blessing. As anthropologist Ellen Lewin suggests, the growing number of women choosing to mother was an indication of social progress; but at the same time this development risked reinforcing in a new form the old idea that womanhood and motherhood go together "naturally."[24]

Considerations of work and career also contributed heavily to shifts in the meaning of lesbian identity. Many individuals had spent the 1970s piecing together odd jobs of various types; working for nonprofit organizations such as women's health collectives, bookstores, and child care agencies; searching for ways to make a living that would be true to their feminist and often socialist ideals. But by the end of the decade, the young women who had come of age in a milieu of social ferment could no longer survive within the counterculture. Sources of income once possible in the women's community—from bookstores, cafes, and other businesses that never paid much—dried up. The reasons ranged from mismanagement to lack of sustained interest to decreased public funding. Moreover, many individuals particularly those who had grown up with middle-class comforts, had tired of living on subsistence wages.

Some of those who had shunned the professions in favor of manual labor began to reconsider their choices. Such reflection led ten of the women I interviewed to seek advanced degrees. Two became nurses, one became a lawyer, and five became psychotherapists; others pursued careers as teachers, middle managers, and journalists. The remainder were evenly distributed among a variety of skilled and semi-skilled blue- and "pink"-collar occupations: gardener, graphic artist, technical writer, and health and social services administrator. Sally Kirk discussed her decision to go to law school when she was in her late twenties, at a time when "everyone seemed to be doing it." It challenged her loyalties to many of her lesbian friends, described by Sally as "rabidly downwardly mobile."

Reflecting on these developments, Julia Penelope and Susan Wolfe deplored careerism as a negative development, one which forced women to compromise their ideals:

The one sphere of our lives in which many Lesbians cannot avoid
having to deal with heterosexuals—men in particular—is work. Whatever kind of work Lesbians do, whether it's in a factory or in academia,
we do it because we know we must support ourselves; our work is not
a supplement to a man's earnings, and we enter our workplaces with
the consciousness that we are Lesbians working for a living. Although
most Lesbians work at the same kinds of jobs as heterosexuals and in
heterosexual contexts, we go home to our Lesbian dwellings and Lesbian contexts, to the lives we have constructed around our Lesbian
identities. We draw our strength from and establish our identities
through interaction with other Lesbians, both with individual Lesbians
and within our communities of Lesbians.[25]

This separatist response imagined a strict division between the heterosexual and the lesbian worlds, depicting the lesbian subculture as
a "haven in a heartless world," a defense against the incursions of the
world outside. While lesbian communities were in fact "cultures of
resistance," standing at least partially outside the mainstream and
offering support and nurturance, Penelope and Wolfe understate the
extent to which "mainstream" and "margin," "heterosexual" and "homosexual" worlds mutually interpenetrate. Especially for working-
class women and women of color, these boundaries were always permeable.

Irma Sands felt excluded by feminist conceptions of lesbianism
that presented it as a "master identity," separate from familial, work,
and other considerations: "I was working full-time, going to the bars
at night, and leaving my daughter with my mother, who wondered
where I was all that time. Lots of women saw me a Black woman
with a kid, and married and all, and wondered whether I was really
a lesbian." The crosscutting loyalties and influences experienced by
Irma and others made the goals of a movement dominated by white,
middle-class lesbian feminists seem unattainable at best, and racist
and exclusionary at worst. Poet and theorist Audre Lorde lamented:
"As a Black lesbian feminist comfortable with the many different in-
gredients of my identity, I find I am constantly being encouraged to
pluck out some one aspect of myself and present this as the meaningful whole, eclipsing or denying the other parts of myself."[26]

Women who became more involved with those outside their lesbian feminist communities found that they were changed by the experience, often in positive ways. After living on food stamps and money earned from odd jobs for many years, in the late 1970s Margaret Berg became a maternity nurse. Nursing allowed her to stay in a predominantly female world, but it also put her into contact with men for the first time in nearly ten years. Margaret recalls her surprise at what she found. "It was stunning to me that some men were nice to their wives during childbirth. I had been walking around with this ideology that men were totally incompetent." The "real" world was often not quite as stark in its contrasts. Nina Samson, who became a therapist in group practice with men, discovered that there were "certain men I liked and many that I didn't, but that the same was true of women—they weren't all saints."

As women entered the paid labor force, the responsibilities of work and family (or relationship) exerted twin pressures. Lesbians, like most women, found themselves faced with the difficult challenge of coping with both and trying to minimize what Arlie Hochschild has called the "second shift," the unpaid work that women do at home after they've worked a full day for pay.[27] Those who were in long-term stable relationships often found that partners tended to share the tasks of making a household and family, probably more so than did heterosexual couples.[28] However, the lack of institutional supports often worked against the pursuit of equality. In addition to the institutional constraints facing most families (inflexible work schedules, lack of parental leave, and so forth), lesbian families also grappled with institutionalized homophobia in the form of lack of legal recognition (which led employers to withhold spousal benefits such as health insurance and maternity and sick leave) and fears that they might lose custody of their children, particularly children from former heterosexual relationships.

Carrie Brown, who worked full-time as a nurse and was the mother of two adolescent boys, agreed to be interviewed only on the condition that the interview take place in the evening after work, while she folded her laundry and cleaned her house. Having children meant that she had to remove herself, in large part, from her friendship networks in the lesbian community. After her work and her children, she had little time for others. Like her straight friends, she said, she had become much more focused upon her work, her partner, and her kids. Sue Hammond, who remained single, and who did not parent a child, complained about the difficulty of maintaining contact with friends who had children: "Changing diapers, cleaning the house, and taking the kids to the doctor. For a while, it seemed that that's all my friend Sharon had time for. We used to spend lots of time together. But eventually, I had to take back seat to her 'primary' commitments—her kid and her lover."

But for others, children were a binding force, a way for friends and ex-lovers to maintain old ties and sometimes even compensate for the loss of romantic relationships. When Barb Herman was involved with Natalie, she helped to raise Natalie's child until their relationship ended, when the child was eight. It was a difficult breakup, and they were barely on speaking terms for many years. But Barb continued to see Natalie's child twice weekly because, she said, she "wanted to continue to be in her life": "It was much easier for me to maintain contact with [Natalie's child] than with Natalie herself. There was too much bad blood between us. But I had little of that baggage with her daughter. We were good friends as well as family." Over the years, Barb and Natalie have been able to make peace with each other—thanks, said Barb, to her continued connection with Natalie's daughter. So while motherhood drew some women away from old ties, often they found new lines of connection, through lesbian parenting groups, lesbian/gay religious organizations, and sometimes renewed links with old lovers and families of origin.

Cumulatively, the twin pulls toward motherhood and career reconfigured the meaning of lesbianism in the lives of the baby boom cohort, particularly among white middle-class women. But although these shifts in work and family commitments challenged the salience of lesbian identity, they often left the contours of the feminist critique intact. Women who went out into the workforce found that in many respects their feminism became even stronger than it had been before—if less connected to their lesbianism. Although Margaret Berg increasingly acknowledged that "men were not all jerks," she recognized that she was still living in a highly inegalitarian society, where many men grew up with a sense of power and entitlement that was virtually unknown to her. In the end, men were, after all, *men.* "I saw that some men could be wonderful in the labor room—but still be fucked up weeks later when it came to changing diapers."

Shifting Desires

The women of the baby boom are past the youthful stage of sexual experimentation; most say they have "settled into" what they believe to be permanent choices regarding their sexuality and lifestyle. Many women reported that their interest in sex had diminished over the years. Sue Hammond, for whom lesbianism was originally about sex first and foremost, described her evolution: "In the 1970s, I went through an intense period of hanging out in bars. I think that was probably in my sexual peak, when I was in my twenties, so that's where the action was. But with time I became less and less interested in sex. I became more interested in people that are creative and less interested in what their sexual orientation is." As she has reached her thirties, for Shirley Alvarez, too, sex has become less important.

> The sex thing is not everything. It used to be. I feel like that's changing with aging. Let me blame it on my hormones. I felt like a dog. There were times when I would hunt women down and never take no for an answer. It was kind of like this drug. Now I can see it was an ego thing more than anything. . . . I broke up with this woman who didn't give me enough. I spent days on end in bed. A lot of my time was spent doing it, or in pursuit of it. Doggin' on it somehow. Now, it's so what?

If the focus of a woman's lesbian identity was originally sexual and she ceases to be very interested in sex, then the meaning of her lesbianism necessarily shifts.

Several women reported that this declining interest in sex led to an identity crisis of sorts: the sense, in the words of Sunny Connelly, that "the rug was being pulled out from beneath me." It forced them to reevaluate the meaning of their lesbian identity. As Sunny said, "My whole sense of why am I here came up." Other women, however, found this diminished desire less significant and sometimes even liberating. For Shirley Alvarez, "The only thing I appreciate about aging is that sex doesn't control me now. Sex is not as key. The other things are just as important now. Before it was everything. I went through intense love and intense hate periods. Now I'm evening out. Sticking through things." Sue Hammond told me that in her eleven-year relationship, sex (particularly the frequency with which it occurred) was the major source of her conflicts with her lover. Her lover "always wanted more" than she did. But with time, as her lover's desires declined, their conflicts dissipated. For Sue, this was a welcome relief.

> Feminists have been saying all this time that lesbianism is about much more than sex but when it came down to it, there were lots of women I got involved with for whom sex was pretty important. For me, I could take it or leave it. To tell you the truth, I never really understood what all the fuss was about. Sex was all right, it was often good, but I didn't want to build my life around the search for it. If it was there, okay, but if not, that was okay too.

The diminished desires that many women experienced as they moved into their thirties and forties served to equalize the disparities between women for whom desire and sexual activity were central to their lesbian identification and those for whom they were not.

Only half of my interviewees are now in long-term, stable monogamous relationships, but virtually all of them wished to be, and they described their most pleasurable sexual experiences as being within the context of loving relationships. As sociologists Philip Blumstein and Pepper Schwartz point out, "It is difficult to translate the idea of tricking into the female idiom—either lesbian or heterosexual. While some may seek and enjoy one-night stands and even go through a period of having many sex partners, it is rare that a woman wants this to be a consistent part of her life. It is almost unheard of for a woman to have sex with someone whose name she does not know or whose face she has not seen."[29] Studying the relationships of over 12,000 people, Blumstein and Schwartz found that lesbian couples reported having sex less frequently than did married heterosexual, cohabiting heterosexual, or gay male couples. In 1988, JoAnn Loulan published the results of her interviews with over 1,500 lesbians and found a significant majority to have been celibate for some period of time. Some decried this development, labeling it "lesbian bed death" and warning of the threat it posed to long-term lesbian relationships. But others were more sanguine, suggesting that "romantic but asexual" couplings common within the context of long-term relationships were modern-day "Boston marriages."[30]

Paradoxically, as sexuality receded in importance for women of the baby boom, in many urban areas the public face of lesbianism was becoming increasingly sexualized. In San Francisco and other cities, a developing erotic literature drew upon the iconography of prefeminist lesbianism, gay male culture, and heterosexual porn to introduce a new vocabulary of lesbian desire, a world of dildoes and harnesses, butch and femme, tops and bottoms, lust and intrigue—symbols of a queer female culture recalling a world that, for all intents and purposes, had disappeared from public view by the lesbian feminist 1970s. A new playfulness about sexuality emerged, especially among younger lesbians, who welcomed dolled-up dyke fashion and new dance clubs that featured miniskirted go-go dancers and sleazy dancing. Mail-in orders for harnesses and dildoes skyrocketed, propelled by a new lesbian market. Sadomasochists and members of the "sexual fringe" became much more visible and vocal. Some proclaimed the arrival of a "lesbian sexual revolution." While it would be wrong to overstate the extent of these changes, which were as much (or more) about the *representation* of lesbian sexuality as about actual sexual practice, I wondered what my baby boom respondents made of all this new talk about sex.

Several wholeheartedly opposed what they saw as the emergence of a new sexual libertarianism, viewing it as a threat to communal norms. These were women for whom lesbianism was closely linked to radical feminist politics, who feared the loss of cohesion of lesbian culture if marginal sexualities such as sadomasochism were tolerated. Jackie Henry, a therapist, lamented the fact that lesbianism, in her words, "is no longer paired with radical feminism. A lesbian identity and an identity as a radical feminist were forged together. And that, at the time, meant certain kinds of behaviors. You did and didn't do certain kinds of things. . . . Today, anything goes: body piercing, sadomasochism, every fringe group. We don't dare criticize or pass judgments on certain behaviors within the lesbian community. . . . We have become a mush of liberalism." Jackie is a lifelong lesbian who does not see her sexual orientation as a matter of choice, yet she wholeheartedly embraces lesbian feminist ideology. Lesbianism, for her, is much more than a matter of sex. It is about a whole way of life, a whole system of values.

> I'm enough of an old school radical lesbian feminist that I still believe that the personal is political. I want myself as well as other members of this community, and the larger society, to take moral and ethical stands. Violence is one area in which we should be making moral judgments. To me, violence is bad. It damages people, it begets violence. Sadomasochism is not a normal variant of human sexuality. It is a perversion that comes out of the pairing of violence and sex.

She resists the most extreme "anything goes" position, valuing highly the relational model of sexuality embodied in lesbian feminist discourse and remaining unconvinced by "libertarian" claims that relational sexuality is inherently conservative and that it plays into traditional notions of women's sexual reticence. In contrast, Jackie maintained the feminist belief that a relational sexuality is less split off from the whole body and person, and therefore it is based on women's ideals rather than men's. For her, the "male model" of nonrelational sexuality failed to meet the needs of women, for whom erotic and relational needs were often fused.

But even if an emergent model of lesbian sexuality, emphasizing sex outside of relationships, held relatively little interest for them, most of my interviewees were willing to acknowledge that the growing discussion of sexual practice was having a beneficial, democratizing impact. They appropriated parts of the libertarian or "pro-sex" discourse, welcoming what they saw as a new tolerance for sexual difference—differences of desire, of sexual preferences, and of practices of all sorts.

Cindy Ross, who came out in Chicago in the early 1970s, recalled the handicap of sex being a taboo topic: "I found sex really scary. I was terrified. In 1975, we had a discussion group about sexual problems, but that was rare. None of us really knew what other people were doing. We had an image of making love with complete reciprocity, which is impossible. . . . Feminism, in a way, desexualized us. We were supposed to be the vanguard, but not be sexual, not be different from other women. We were afraid to show our sexual natures."

The new public discussions of lesbian sex that began in the 1980s, Cindy believes, are very liberating and long overdue. Several women welcomed the new willingness to talk about sex, while distancing themselves from the sex radical fringe. Judy Orr expressed disdain for sadomasochism and other expressions of power. "I hate to see women whipped. I hate pain. I wouldn't even like to be tied up with pink bows," she said. Yet she also complained that lesbians "don't talk enough about sexuality," because there are so many "taboos and embarrassments." Judy rejects the lesbian feminist's de-emphasis of sexual desire and practice, while retaining a belief that her relationships with women allow her to "subvert the dominance/submission issues" that she feels plague heterosexual relationships. When she seeks out sexual involvements, she usually expects that they will eventually lead to monogamous relationships.

When practitioners of sadomasochism became more visible in the early 1980s, Mary Lipton said that unlike most of her friends and her lover at the time, she "breathed a sigh of relief." Even though she "never closely identified with s/m women," she believed that their growing visibility opened up a space for freer sexual discussion. "They allowed me to do what I wanted to do and feel all right about it. They gave me permission to do things that I felt guilty about before." It led her to "soften" her assessment of straight women and bisexuals: "When I came out, I felt that I had crossed this line. I had little in the way of dealings with straight women. Now, in retrospect, I understand them a little better. I realize why some lesbians get so upset about bisexual women. Not everybody's a 6 on the Kinsey scale. It's threatening in that way. But I didn't have that perspective then." To some it seemed, paradoxically, that the further lesbians had moved from a sexual definition of themselves, the narrower was the range of possible ways of "being" a lesbian.

Feminists had expanded the meaning of lesbianism beyond what seemed to them a narrowly defined sexual emphasis. But this reframing had the unintended consequence of excluding women who never conformed to feminist, countercultural norms. Joan Bodewell grew up in the Midwest. In the late 1960s and early 1970s she was an ambitious drama student and a Christian, and passionately attracted to women. Yet she found herself alienated from the organized lesbian

movement at the time. "Women's consciousness-raising groups drew
the really ill-dressed, unclassy women, who regurgitated their personal feelings in small groups. If this was lesbianism, I wasn't interested. I had a career that had me doing that on stage—expressing
myself. And I knew that if I was going to go into the theater I had to
be very careful how I presented myself." Joan, who wished to "fit in"
with straight society, saw lesbian feminists as visible and uppity. She
felt that lesbian feminists tended to interpret every personal act as
either "patriarchal" or "lesbian feminist," taking literally the claim
that every such act is the creation and expression of one's politics.
For her, lesbianism was about "being sexual with other women." It
wasn't about "forming a whole life around that fact." Sometimes it
seemed as though the old prefeminist definitions of lesbianism,
which made desire central, were paradoxically more inclusive than
the new ones, which required a commitment to a whole way of life.
As Amanda Udis-Kessler noted, "If desire is the defining element,
any woman whose primary relationships or attractions involve women
could be called a lesbian. Lesbians, from this perspective, may wear
makeup, vote Republican, eat meat, hire maids, attempt to close
abortion clinics, and climb the corporate ladder."[31]

Fleeing from what they perceived as the "overpoliticization" of
lesbian identity, some looked to gay men, whose culture had always
been more overtly sexualized than that of lesbians, and who seemed
to be less interested in drawing boundaries that included some and
kept others out. Some women reported that by forming friendships
with gay men, they were able to remain involved in the gay community, but in a less demanding fashion. By the end of the 1970s, Mary
Lipton began to pursue her artistic interests, which had long lay dor-
mant. Partly as a result, she grew much closer to a group of gay men,
with whom, she said, it would not have been possible for her to be
involved ten years earlier, when lesbians and gay men were often
estranged from one another. "In the old days, at least in the lesbian
world I came out to, men were men and women were women, and
never the twain shall meet. But now many of my friends are men.
Men are much less intense about things. Because of this, I would
much rather be in a 'co-sexual' community." According to Mary, gay
men were less apt to say "who was gay and who wasn't" than were

lesbians. They "had a feeling of entitlement to their sexuality that I had never experienced."

Mary was living in California in 1977, when right-wing state senator John Briggs sponsored an initiative that would have deprived lesbian and gay men of basic civil rights. It prompted her to become involved with electoral politics, and with gay men: "It was exciting to me to be involved in politics that seemed very different from the kind of internalized identity politics that I had been involved in. It was really refreshing. I started to come alive again. And I liked working with gay men. I started to identify with the gay movement more and more." She was impressed by the ability of many gay men "to remain unabashedly erotic even as they battled a deadly sexually transmitted virus." In the 1970s, Mary lived and worked surrounded by women. But in the early 1980s in San Francisco, when the AIDS epidemic began to rage, through work and political affiliations she was brought into contact with many gay men. Prior to that moment she had some identification with the larger "gay community" but few close gay male friends. To her surprise, Mary found that her sense of lesbian identity was challenged by contact with this very different world. "They helped me to think about gayness as a proud, lustful identity."

In the mid-1980s, lesbians in many urban centers joined the ranks of such predominantly gay male organizations as ACT UP (AIDS Coalition to Unleash Power), which engaged in public actions to fight for a more effective response to the AIDS epidemic. Others attempted to construct sexualized subcultures that took their cue from an earlier era of gay male sexual abandon. The number of co-ed bars, social events, and institutions grew. The new identification between lesbians and gay men extended to personal style as well—clothing, music, and other forms of consumption. Not everyone welcomed efforts on the part of gay men and lesbians to reunite the two groups, however.

"I don't buy this stupid idea that lesbians are queer first and women second," said Robin Ward, a computer programmer. Lesbians and gay men, she said, continued to be divided by issues of power and privilege. Even Mary Lipton, who reveled in a newfound sense of connection to gay men, acknowledged, "There are times when I feel that I've been around gay men too much, when I need to be around lesbians." These comments suggest that while more women were choosing to form sexual identities that could not be assimilated into feminism, most refused to subsume gender under sexuality and collapse the differences between men and women.

Many of my interviewees strained to find a language suited to talk about their sexual relationships. Describing the sexual differences she had long experienced in her relationships, Judy Orr invoked the language of butch-femme roles, joking that her lover called her a "butchy femme." For the first time, thanks to the new license to talk about sex, she told me, she is able to name her own desires, and to ask for what she wants sexually. "I was almost always attracted to women who were more experienced, more butch. But the thought that I might be a femme was totally mortifying to me. . . . Eventually I started wearing makeup and dressing more femme at the bars. Now I have permission to do that." Similarly, Ara Jones told me that while she embraced the lesbian label, she always knew that it did not really do justice to the complexity of her own sexuality or that of many of her friends. When I asked whether she was always aware of this, she replied,

> No, I was not. I've only recently become aware of it. I was more vaguely aware of it and I was disappointed a lot in relationships with different people, because I expected them to be more like me. To me, I thought if somebody was a lesbian, there would be a certain sexual compatibility between me and that person. That's not necessarily so. I can call myself a lesbian, and have certain desires sexually. Another woman can call herself a lesbian and can be sexually very different— more into s/m, roles, into only the missionary position, perfectly happy to have sex only every six months. So I think within that category *lesbian,* the amount of sexual variation is infinite.

As these comments suggest, the notion of a singular sexual orientation is a reification. There is no such thing as "lesbian desire" per se. Just as heterosexuals have particular erotic desires and preferences, so do homosexuals. "The term *lesbian* implies that I am attracted to all women," said Joan Salton. "But I'm not. My attractions are specific. I like a certain type of woman: tall, dark skinned, with curly hair. My lovers all tend to fit this type." To paraphrase Nancy Chodorow's description of the complexity of heterosexual eroticism:

Some women find themselves repeatedly attracted to [wo]men who turn out to be depressed, others to [wo]men who are aggressive or violent, still others to narcissists. Some [wo]men are attracted to women who are chatty and flirtatious, others to those who are quiet and distant. Some choose lovers or spouses who are like a parent (and it can be either parent for either gender or a mixture of the two); others choose lovers or spouses as much unlike their parents as possible. . . . These choices have both cultural and individual psychological resonance.[32]

Earlier, lesbian feminists had embraced a politics of identity in which sexual behavior—"doing" lesbianism—was superseded by the identity of "being" a lesbian. With time, we see a reemphasis on sexual behavior and practices. Echoing theoretical debates on the political uses of essentialist identities, Ara Jones began to formulate a conception of the "strategic" uses of identity categories: "We need to talk about what people really do. Instead of trying to fit them into little labels: this one's gay, she's bisexual, and this one's straight. It doesn't really work with people who are our friends. . . . We should use the word against people like Pat Robertson, and throw it in his face. But when we're really thinking about sexuality we need to junk the category."[33] She and others came to realize that as a description of sexuality and selfhood in all their complexity, the label *lesbian* was somewhat limited.

Pluralism, Placelessness, and Ambivalence

In the early 1990s, Olivia Records, which had pioneered the production and distribution of "women's music," began to publish a glossy catalogue filled with small, clay goddess figurines and other "woman-identified" products. It most lucrative endeavor was Olivia Cruises, luxury women's excursions to the Caribbean, Greece, and other exotic locales. A full-page ad in a gay newspaper showed two women in a tropical setting—one black, one white, both with long hair—leaning against a palm tree and embracing another against the backdrop of a windswept beach. The text read:

Cruise with us to paradise: imagine a paradise where loving women is the norm and there is nothing to think about except relaxing and

having the time of your life in luxurious comfort and grand style. Par-
ties, dances, great entertainment . . romance with your true love or
find the woman of your dreams. And just when it seems like it couldn't
get any better, we'll take you to our own private island where your
visions of paradise will be totally fulfilled.[34]

Appealing to lesbian baby boomers with money, or who at least were
willing to save for months to find their island paradise, Olivia's business venture was a telling sign of the times.

The strength of lesbian feminism as a movement lay in its ability
to transform lesbianism into a normative identity, a total way of life,
which encompassed lifestyle, culture, and values and thus entailed
much more than simply eroticism. Though the dominant culture always remained a visible and in some respects threatening presence,
lesbian feminism was a centering paradigm, offering strength and
direction to those who were trying to construct a very different kind
of life. In the 1980s, with the rise of yuppies, a new entrepreneurialism, a lesbian baby boom, the feminist sex debates, and the self-
help movement, this vision was fading.

The politics of the nation as a whole was shifting to the right.
Touting supply-side economics and a pull-yourself-up-by-your-boot-
straps spirit, the Reagan administration worked to quell the collectivist ethos of progressive social movements. Rejecting the belief that
the state could be a vehicle of positive social change, laissez-faire
conservatives attacked the evils of government intrusion into individuals' lives. Social conservatives railed against so-called enemies of
"the family," directing much of their ire toward homosexuals. In this
din, it became more and more difficult to imagine the sort of radical
social transformation that had inspired lesbian feminists and other
radical social activists during the previous decades.

Few early lesbian feminists would have imagined that the movement they created would have spawned, a decade later, professional
groupings of lesbian "career women" who were eagerly integrating
themselves into the economic system rather than posing a radical
critique of its operations.[35] But all social movements arise in a particular context, reflecting both the grievances of the groups they mobilize and the larger society in which they operate. Lesbians have a

similarly dual existence, as they live in the dominant culture as well as in a lesbian culture. During much of the 1970s, the lesbian feminist movement provided an enormously powerful alternative way of looking at the world. But with the decentering of the movement in the 1980s, the dominant culture and its individualistic values became more appealing.

In a lesbian twist on critic Christopher Lasch's lamentation on the "me-ism" of modern culture, some warned of the coming of a lesbian culture of narcissism, disparaging the commodification of feminism's radical potential.[36] They looked around and saw women intent on shedding their anger and fitting in, on flaunting their sexuality and renouncing their faith in collective struggle. To some it seemed that lesbians were moving toward autonomous forms of identity in which the individual rather than the lesbian community was the primary basis for fashioning a sense of self. Yet radical individualism was rarely if ever an attractive alternative for my interviewees. As they moved into middle age and greater commitments to work, family, and elsewhere, they sought out forms of identification that were more autonomous, though often still connected to community.[37] They reconstituted lesbian identity and community in new, decentered ways.

Forty-four-year-old Judy Orr perceived the lesbian community as "a big thing in her life" when she was just coming out, in her twenties. Today, she says, she feels somewhat peripheral to the lesbian community, attributing this to "getting older" and to the fact that "it's not so hard to be a lesbian anymore." By the late 1970s, her locus of community had shifted: from centering on friends and attachments forged primarily among lesbians, it had grown to encompass a larger social world, one that involved not only lesbians but gay men, heterosexual friends, and families of origin and of choice. Judy described her life today:

> I play softball on a team comprised of lesbians and straight women. And through work and sports my circle of friends includes just about everyone. I do not live in an exclusively lesbian world. Partly that's a success, because it's easier these days to have straight friends who think: that's just another one of those things about this cool friend of ours. And they don't make a big deal of it. I think it's the women who are doing it a lot. I get a sense of women connecting with each other

more, regardless of sexual orientation. The feminist movement isn't new any more, and feminism isn't that big a deal.

As they entered their thirties and forties, lesbians of the baby boom searched for sources of attachment to replace those they had lost; they sought a lesbian identity that was less confining and demanding, that developed connections to the world beyond. They attempted to shape a new sense of identity and form new attachments that acknowledged *multiple* allegiances and the partial nature of lesbian identity.[38]

Women of color had been the first to articulate this emerging understanding.[39] While lesbian feminism often presented itself as a form of identification that would override differences of race, class, and ethnicity in posing a united front against patriarchal society, they questioned the viability of such a totalizing concept. Biddy Martin suggests that these critiques served as a

> provocation to white feminists to educate themselves about racism, about the material lives and realities of communities other than their own, about the relationship of the histories of their communities or growing-up places and those of people of color in the United States and elsewhere. [They also insisted] that we cease locating "race" in those individuals or groups in whom it is supposedly embodied, that we abandon the notion that to be "white" is to be unmarked by race. And further, [they were] a provocation to white feminists and lesbians to render their own histories, subjectivities, and writing complex by attending to their various implications in overlapping social/discursive divisions and histories.[40]

Living in San Francisco in the 1980s, I saw this changed consciousness at work at political meetings, where it became more common for people to preface their comments with statements that situated themselves ethnically and racially: for example, "As an African American woman," or, "As a white working-class lesbian, I believe that . . ." At around the same time, women of color became increasingly visible within the lesbian community. African American, Asian, and Latina lesbian feminist organizations marched at the annual gay pride parade. I myself became much more interested in exploring and practicing my own Jewishness, and occasionally went to services at a synagogue attended almost entirely by lesbians and gay men. I was drawn to consider the role that my background as a lower-middle-class Jew, and a child of Holocaust survivors, played in my own life and the particular cast it gave my lesbian identity. And I attempted to bridge the gap between my chosen family and my biological family, usually with mixed success. Many of my interviewees described similar experiences.

In lesbian feminist constructions of selfhood, upon "coming out" the individual is believed to be liberated from her former, "false" self. The process of becoming a lesbian consists of rebuilding a sense of self, anchored by a new, chosen community and constructed in opposition to the biological family, the site of "primary socialization." In the 1980s, the decentering of lesbian feminism, life cycle changes, and the critiques made by women of color worked together to call this model into question. Many individuals began to speak of themselves in terms of both an alternative community, which provides the locus of their identity without exclusively containing it, and the larger society, which provides another basis of identity.[41]

In the past, Sunny Connelly said, she had relied on the lesbian community as a mirror, as a reflection of herself. But now, she looks

> toward the world outside. I have my lesbian friends, and I have my lesbian family. But I have a solidness that I didn't have in my twenties. Confidence. I don't have to sing and dance to prove to other people what I am. If they can see it, fine. But I still have it, even if they don't see it. That took me a very long time to get. Because I was always using other people as a mirror. And if they didn't see what I was, I thought I wasn't that person. For some reason I do that less now.

Today, she says, she has a strong sense of herself as a lesbian, but increasingly she also sees herself operating within the context of the dominant heterosexual culture. She is helping to parent the child of an ex-girlfriend. She has become close friends with a heterosexual man who lives downstairs from her, and she considers him to be a part of her chosen family.

> The mirror is pointed in the other direction, so that I can always see myself. I'm not changing my identity to be heterosexual. I'm just using a heterosexual reflector. I am more and more concerned with who I

am in the big picture, in the universe . . . as part of the whole picture, including heterosexual culture. . . . I couldn't do that before. I had to keep being separate, and not be a part of the big picture. And that caused me a lot of pain. But it's interesting to see that pain turn into a kind of expansiveness today.

She continued to see herself in relation to others, but in a fashion that had become less demanding. The lesbian/gay community provided the values, ideals, and standards of conduct in whose terms her social identity is built. But the imagined perspective of the larger society, a much more abstract generalized other, provided an additional source of identification.

For lesbians of the baby boom, greater commitment to lesbian culture and values made sense during the early phases of the coming out process, when they needed to separate themselves from the dominant culture in order to develop strength and solidarity, to counter the stigma of the dominant culture. With time, as their certainty about their lesbian identity grew, they gained flexibility, responding to each situation by placing more or less emphasis on minority group identity as seemed best or most rewarding in that particular context. In the decentered community that developed, individuals shift easily from community to society, from social identity to personal identity, and back again. They feel "at home" in the community with which they mainly identify, but also in numerous other contexts in which they participate and with which they feel some sense of identification. They feel "like" a great many others rather than only a single category of others, capable of moving in several circles rather than one.[42]

Imagining a community that was more inclusive, less demanding, less confining, and more able to satisfy impulses toward choice and autonomy, women of the baby boom moved toward a more diffuse notion of power and resistance, one acknowledging that lesbians necessarily operate in a society marked by class and race, as well as by gender and sexuality. They forged a sense of attachment to a lesbian community that, while clearly important and central in the construction of a new system of personal meaning, was less dominant. The term *decentering* signifies this simultaneous sense of persistence and change, of commitment amid pluralism.[43]

But this decentering did not occur without costs. If the old "centered" lesbian community encouraged commitment to identity and provided a sense of relative security, its decentering fostered feelings of ambivalence. Members of a decentered community must juggle investments not only of time and energy but of self, of identification. As Alan Wolfe has noted about American institutions in general, "decentering involves powerful feelings of freedom, but, at the same time, scary visions of chaos."[44] If centering ensured commitment and stability, decentering called those commitments into question and opened up opportunities for individuals to exit.

Chapter Six

Sleeping with the Enemy?

Ex-Lesbians and the Reconstruction of Identity

At the Lesbian Herstory Archives in New York, I came upon a tattered piece of mimeograph paper. On it was a lesbian feminist song from 1970, sung to the tune of Burt Bacharach's "What Do You Get When You Fall in Love?"

> What do you get when you are straight?
> A guy with a pin to burst your bubble
> That's what you get for all your trouble
> I'll never be a straight again . . .

> Don't tell me what it's all about
> 'Cause I been straight and I'm glad I'm out
> Out of those chains, the chains that bind you
> That is why I'm here to remind you . . .

> I'll never be a straight again . . .

It was 1990, and this song caught my eye because the subject of lesbians "going straight" had just exploded in the pages of a national lesbian/gay quarterly, *Out/Look.*

Thirteen years after she had come out as a lesbian, Jan Clausen, a well-known lesbian feminist activist and author, proclaimed that she had become involved in a relationship with a man. In the early 1970s, Clausen believed that she was making a permanent choice to become a lesbian. Like many others who came out in the context of the feminist movement, she saw lesbianism as a political act, an act that implied consistency, stability, and long-term commitments. She be-

154

lieved that "our lesbian way of life was superior to the best of heterosexual arrangements." But by the late 1980s, she was not so sure: "For many if not all the years I spent as a technically irreproachable lesbian, I was perfectly well aware that I hadn't shed my potential for physical attraction to men. . . . It never seriously occurred to me that I would shortly find myself in a situation where this theoretical capacity would have practical implications."[1]

For Clausen, the promise that lesbianism would be a means to egalitarian relationships and sexual fulfillment was broken by the failure of a long-term relationship with a woman, and by a surprisingly satisfying relationship with a man. The taboo character of the heterosexual relationship, in the context of her lesbian feminist world, seemed to make her longing even more powerful. "I wonder about the astonishing malleability of my sexual inclinations," she mused. "Am I some sort of weirdo, or is it just that most people are a lot more complicated than the common wisdom of either gay or straight society encourages us to think?"

Out/Look, a magazine of which I was an editor, often courted controversy. It had published articles on sadomasochism, incest, racial and ethnic divisions within lesbian gay communities, and other highly charged issues, and its writers often took unpopular stands. But Clausen's story proved to be the magazine's single most divisive article ever, and three subsequent issues were filled with emotional letters to the editor. As one woman declared:

> For those of us who have known since childhood that we were same-sex identified and who struggled through the pain and fear of this in order to find our dignity and live our lives openly, articles like [this] are most disturbing, if not downright damaging. . . . The myth [is] that we're "recruited" or that we "choose" these sexual/emotional identities in order to "rebel" or "be different" when, in fact, for the greatest number of us, we have no choice.[2]

To this reader, Clausen's admission served as a lightning rod, igniting fears of community disintegration and decline. It also raised questions of authenticity. Clausen was never "really" a lesbian, she suggested, she was simply "passing" as one. Being a lesbian is not a matter of choice; it is a birthright.

For a second reader, however, Jan Clausen's story challenged the notion of lesbianism as essence, as irrevocable part of the self: "Thanks to [Clausen] for her courage to go public. . . . Lesbians are doing and talking about things we have never done or talked about before. We are moving beyond the realm of Sisterhood, into the world of the nasty, the tasty and the sexing . . . that the self-righteous atmosphere of political correctitude and erotophobia we called lesbian-feminism kept us from uttering; our new culture is actually producing new desires."[3] Decrying what she saw as feminist puritanism and rule making, this woman saw Clausen's declaration as a welcome relief, which voiced what many other women had not spoken publicly: that individual sexual identity is much more complicated than they had previously imagined. Clearly, this article touched a powerful chord.

Clausen was not, by any means, unique. In the 1980s many lesbians became aware of women who seemed to be "going straight." In the course of interviewing women who came out in the 1970s, I heard much discussion of those who "turned straight." Nearly every woman I spoke with of that generation knew one or more women who had done so. Most had known many more, sometimes including women with whom they had been romantically involved at some point. It was a highly emotional subject, perhaps even the most emotional subject of the interviews.

Individuals have always moved from heterosexuality to homosexuality and back again. Historically, we have evidence of the permeability of the boundary between heterosexuality and homosexuality, of "smashing" and of public school homosexuality among the middle and upper classes.[4] In Radclyffe Hall's 1928 novel *The Well of Loneliness,* Stephen, the butch protagonist, believing that she is making a noble sacrifice, drives her lover Mary back into the arms of a man so that Mary can lead a "normal" heterosexual life. In their landmark history of the Buffalo, New York, lesbian community, Elizabeth Kennedy and Madeline Davis tell of women who became lesbians during the 1940s, when their husbands were away at war, and then went back to their marriages when their husbands returned from military service.[5] In fictional and historical accounts, lesbianism is often the schoolgirl crush, the romantic interlude in preparation for the Main

Event—heterosexual marriage. With time, "immature" lesbian desires or experiences are expected to be forgotten.

However, while there have always been women who travel from homosexuality back to heterosexuality, in the 1980s this phenomenon seemed to achieve a qualitatively new character. The generation of women who had come out in the context of feminism turned the dominant narrative of sexual development on its head, contending both that progress from heterosexuality to homosexuality is healthy and that change in the opposite direction, from gay to straight, is defensive or regressive. They suggested that lesbianism, much more than being "just a phase," is a mature developmental achievement. Some went so far as to say that any woman is a potential lesbian—one simply had to declare oneself a lesbian and go through the process of coming out.[6] But by the 1980s, the ex-lesbian emerged as a veritable fly in the lesbian feminist ointment.

Was lesbianism so constructed by its historical context, I wondered, that in a period of relative conservatism, it was *deconstructing?* Or perhaps the opposite was the case. Did ex-lesbians prove the social constructionist argument wrong? Were they women who had been convinced by social constructionist arguments, only to find that they had taken on identities that were "untrue" to themselves?[7] A second set of questions also emerged: How did former lesbians adapt to their new circumstances and come to reconstruct a sense of self after they decided that a lesbian identity no longer suited them? Did they, true to society's dominant sexual binarism, repudiate their homosexual pasts in declaring their essential "heterosexuality"? Or did they attempt to forge a new category of identity, one that would acknowledge and affirm sexual boundary crossings and recognize the limitations of the heterosexual/heterosexual binarism?

Lesbians Who Sleep with Men

If heterosexual involvements by lesbian-identified women were once taboo, by 1990, the time of my interviews, a greater tolerance for slippages of identity seemed to be in evidence. Many women I spoke with, including some of the most politically engaged lesbian feminists, acknowledged that lesbians occasionally stray from homosexuality, and they felt this to be acceptable, as long as it didn't happen so often as to threaten their lesbian identities. They had come to believe that behavioral inconsistencies do not necessarily pose a threat to lesbian identity, that a lesbian could sleep with men and still be a lesbian. Many acknowledged that the dividing line between homosexuality and heterosexuality was highly variable and subjective, and that for some women a sexual involvement with a man could actually confirm their lesbian identity.

Several women reported to me that they had had affairs with men long after they had come out as lesbians, sometimes out of curiosity about heterosexuality. This was particularly true if they had come out very young, when they had little or no prior heterosexual experience. Meg Dunn came out in south Florida when she was seventeen, and she quickly became part of the lesbian subculture. Fifteen years later, when she was in her early thirties, she began to wonder, "What is all the fuss about men?" By that time, she felt freer to experiment. "It was interesting," she said of her affair with a man, even if it only served to affirm her sense of lesbian self. "I found that I can't get emotionally close to men. I can sleep with them and have an okay time, but not great, and I can be friends with them, but I can't get any closer."

Sometimes it was precisely this lack of connection, coupled with the fact that men were more sexually available, that made such affairs attractive. It was easier to meet men than women, several interviewees observed. Lesbians were, after all, women first, and thus treated as potential sexual partners by men, particularly by strangers who assumed they were heterosexual. As they aged, life cycle changes drew more and more women, even those who had lived their early adulthood in a largely homosexual world, into mixed settings at work and into heterosexual networks. Taking advantage of these networks, sometimes lesbians had affairs with men because potential lesbian partners were difficult to find.

"Lesbians don't know how to date," forty-year-old Muriel Pepper, an office administrator, complained. "They're either too scared of rejection, or they want to marry you right away." This attitude is captured in an often-repeated lesbian joke: "What does a lesbian bring on her first date?" Answer: "A U-Haul." Gay men commonly had little trouble finding casual sex, but found it difficult to establish intimacy and long-term relationships. Lesbians generally had the opposite problem: they reported having difficulties initiating relationships, particularly casual ones. But once established, such relationships became intimate very rapidly.[8] Indeed, lesbians who had affairs with men often reported that they found them enjoyable simply because they perceived them to be free of the emotional demands of relationships with women.

Meg Dunn told me that she often had short affairs with men— even at her "most extreme lesbian feminist stage," in the mid-1970s—simply because "they were quick and easy." Throughout her twenties and thirties, she met men at bars about once or twice a year, particularly if she was between lesbian relationships. It is difficult to know exactly who among my interviewees pursued such affairs; my sense is that only a small minority had. But in view of the stigma attached to such activities—even if now somewhat lessened—it is unclear how many would have admitted to similar affairs, despite my efforts to let them know that I would in no way condemn them for such a revelation. While several women described having affairs with men "for the sex," a few had a rather different experience: they had a connection with men that was emotional and indeed largely devoid of sexual pleasure.

Muriel Pepper recounted how she had recently rekindled a relationship with a fellow she had dated when she was in her twenties. When he visited from out of town, they ended up in bed together: "We didn't have intercourse, but we were kind of sexual with one another." Muriel was forced to reintegrate that experience into her sense of lesbian self. "I was totally flipped out for about a week after that. I felt that I had to turn my whole life around. I wondered, what does this mean? Does this mean I'm not a lesbian? It seemed to call into question who I was." But after a few days, Muriel said she began to realize that because they had known each other so long, and had gone through "so many changes" together, she and her friend had a "unique" relationship. The affair left her sexually dissatisfied but with deep emotional connections to him. Recognizing this, she "calmed down," because "it doesn't mean that you have to come out or go in or whatever." By thinking of a particular involvement as an aberration and labeling a particular man an "exception," some lesbians were able to integrate occasional involvements with men into their sense of lesbian self.

Though tolerating temporary violations of identity, most women I spoke with perceived a hierarchy of transgression; a high frequency of heterosexual involvements could threaten one's lesbian identity. When asked if women who sleep with men are in fact lesbians, Judy Orr responded, "It depends how many times. The people I knew did it once in ten years. If they're still relating to women, and they still feel very much inside that they're a woman's woman, then they're a lesbian. . . . In my heart of hearts, I'm a lesbian." For others, it was a matter of subjective experience. Sunny Connelly differentiated between her own experience of having occasional affairs with men and the experience of her ex-lover, who now identifies as a bisexual. Her ex-lover, she said, was "more open to her sexual feelings about men. . . . For me, being sexual with men is about having sex. I don't want to cook breakfast for them in the morning. And I don't want to go to the movies with them, and I don't want to know their whole life story. I just want sex. That's not true with [my ex-lover]. She wants the whole package." In this understanding, valuing a man as a "whole person" threatens one's lesbianism, while objectifying men does not. However, few women admitted to telling close lesbian friends about these affairs until after they were over, a reticence that reveals the extent to which, among many lesbians, such behaviors continued to be stigmatized. Heterosexual involvements that happened suddenly and unexpectedly were more tolerated than those that resulted after women "went out looking for it." A particular spontaneous affair could be attributed to an attraction to a particular man or could be written off as situational, as "experimentation." But a prolonged affair with a particular man or discussions about attractions to men were viewed as more serious, as posing a possible threat to identity.

Can a lesbian sleep with men and still be a lesbian? By the late 1980s, the answer seemed to be a qualified "yes." Several women managed to embrace a certain degree of inconsistency between sexual identification and behavior, if one or more of the following conditions were met: (1) such affairs were kept private, (2) they were isolated occurrences and not long-term liaisons, and (3) it was understood that individuals were "in it for the sex" only—and not emotionally attached. However, if those whose behavior demonstrated such occasional lapses were often tolerated, women who had a prolonged relationship with a man were generally not.

Fakers, Turncoats, and Seekers

Very few of those couples had stayed together. Of course, that could really be said about anyone who fell in love idealistically. Love with political implications had always interested her from a distance.

Sarah Schulman,
People in Trouble (1990)

Among lesbian-identified women, views of the "ex-lesbian," generally defined as a woman who had a "primary" or prolonged relationship with a man (or men), varied widely. Some women saw ex-lesbians as having been inauthentic or "fake" lesbians. Others imagined that they were once "real" lesbians but had abandoned lesbianism for an easier life and for the privileges heterosexuality affords. A third group believed that they were sexual seekers whose desires had simply shifted over time.

The first group mobilized an essentialist argument, suggesting that ex-lesbians were *fakers.* Contrasting their experiences with her own, Shirley Alvarez told me, "I've known since childhood that I was a lesbian and I struggled through the pain and fear of this in order to find my dignity and to live my life openly. The greatest number of us have no choice." In her view, the only "true" lesbian is the woman who experiences her sexuality as involuntary, as beyond "choice." It was not at all surprising that many feminists had reneged upon their lesbian identities—they were never "real" lesbians to begin with. Many were "really" bisexual.

Some were quick to note the high percentage of former separatists among the group of women who "turned straight." As Shirley told me, "The women who were the biggest manhaters, the women who would have nothing to do with men for years—those were the women who went straight. It was true every single time. Nearly every single time. They were the ones that raised the biggest fuss about men. The harder they come, the harder they fall." Other women agreed that many of the women who had been the most adamant ideologues were now with men. In the course of my interviews, I heard numerous similar stories. In view of the attractiveness of separatist ideologies to many formerly heterosexual women who had "become" lesbians, this account is somewhat plausible. The embrace of separatist ideas, and the concomitant exclusion of men from one's life, as we saw in chapter 4, was a form of identity work, a way to reshape the self and consolidate a lesbian identity. As such, it was a stage.

Whether or not the interviewees' perceptions were accurate is less important than what their comments seem to suggest: real lesbians did not become lesbians for political purposes; their feminist politics did not predate their lesbian desires. Real lesbians did not have to engage in identity work to "become" lesbians—they simply had to be "true to themselves." In this formulation, the "ex-lesbian" becomes a kind of contradiction in terms. Former lesbians had never "really" been lesbians; they were "straight women masquerading as lesbians," as Sue Hammond put it (see chapter 4). Their lesbian experiences are instances of "dabbling," of heterosexual "tourism," or ideological "play." The belief that feminist ideology produced "fake" lesbians implies an essentialist understanding of lesbianism, which declares that the only "true" lesbian is the lifelong lesbian who never strays, the woman for whom desires, behavior, and identity are perfectly congruent.

In contrast, a second group of women were resolute social constructionists. They believed that ex-lesbians were no different from currently identified lesbians, except that they were *turncoats*—they had "gone back into the closet" and renounced their lesbian commitments. In the most extreme formulation of this view, ex-lesbians were seen as sellouts, defectors from the ranks, women who "got going once the going got tough." They embodied a metaphor of disintegration, a testament to the difficulties of maintaining a lesbian identity over time. Margaret Berg told me that in the late 1970s she had heard of a woman who, upon hearing of several women who had "gone straight," characterized them as "rats leaving a sinking ship."

Another woman had once lit a *yahrzeit* candle, a Jewish memorial ritual, in memory of a formerly lesbian woman she had been close to. In her view, leaving the lesbian community was a kind of symbolic death, and her actions mirrored those of orthodox Jews who mourn the death of a child who "marries out" of the Jewish community.[9] This mode of explanation was most popular among women who attributed their own coming out to feminism. Having framed the coming out process as a "progress narrative," as a challenge to patriarchal norms, they viewed those who left the lesbian community as turncoats or, as a contributor to one feminist periodical put it, "hasbians."[10] Only the strongest, most politically committed women were able to resist the allure of familial approval, material benefits, and other privileges that accrue to heterosexuals, they believed.

These two ways of framing the ex-lesbian—as faker or as turncoat—rest on two very different explanations for why women might move from homosexuality to heterosexuality. Both assume a binary conception of sexual identity, the belief that individuals must forever and always be *either* homosexual or heterosexual. And both assume that lesbian identities are not to be taken lightly, that they entail important commitments—personal, political, or both. The first mode of explanation stresses personal commitments and the importance of authenticity, of being "true to oneself." The second emphasizes the importance of collective, political commitments and the belief that lesbians, as an oppressed group, should "stick together" and make common cause against the dominant heterosexual society.

However, a third group of interviewees saw former lesbians as sexual *seekers;* these women acknowledged the possibility of sexual fluidity and inconsistency, as well as the limits of sexual binarism. They imagined that there may be inconsistencies among sexual desires, identities, and practices, and that one's identity—the way one presents oneself to others—may not always perfectly reflect one's desires. As one reader of *Out/Look* observed, "The fact is that many lesbian-identified women do sleep with men. Some of us identify as bisexual, and many others as lesbian. We are by no means a homogeneous community."[11] Those who embraced this position saw sexual categories as partial, individual lives as complex. Some suggested that desires may change over time: sexuality might be experienced at an earlier age as essentially fixed—that is, invariably focused on women—but later in one's development as more fluid.[12] Sometimes, such fluidity was the result of specific conditions and events, as Joan Salton's comments suggest: "I think that what happened was that a lot of women opened up to the possibility of sexual relations with other women. And some of them found that they were really happy that way. Others found that it just didn't work for them because they were more sexually driven toward relations with men. Like anything else, some people are happy with it, some got burned, hurt pretty badly." Insofar as it affirms the importance of individual choice, the move away from lesbianism is in this view analogous to the process of coming out as a lesbian.

Having heard how women currently self-identified as lesbians talked about ex-lesbians, I became interested in the ways in which ex-lesbians saw themselves. It seemed likely that they would depict their situation and their choices differently, more sympathetically. What, I wondered, might their experiences tell us about lesbian identities and about the formation of sexual identity more generally? I decided to seek out women who came out in the 1970s but who have since decided that the label *lesbian* may not fully describe their sense of self.

Becoming an Ex

Should I stay or should I go?
If I go, there will be trouble.
If I stay, it will be double.
    The Clash,
    "Should I Stay or Should I Go?"

If this study had been a cohort analysis that traced individual identities over time, chances are good that a number of women who originally identified as lesbians would have, over time, given up that label. Because my study instead focused upon those who currently identified as lesbians, I needed to locate some former lesbians.

Finding them through word of mouth, I interviewed ten women, ranging in age from thirty-four to forty-six, who came out in the 1970s but who, for any number of reasons, no longer consider themselves to be lesbians. Five were interviewed individually, five more as a group. All were white; six out of the ten had at least attended college; several held professional degrees, and the greatest number worked in psychotherapy and social services. On the whole, they were a better educated and more homogeneous group than my larger sample of current lesbians. They were also far more articulate and self-conscious about their sexual choices than the other groups of women in my study, at least in part because of their high levels of education and their training in psychology, which led them to value introspection and self-analysis.

All had identified strongly with the ideas of lesbian feminism. They were somewhat more likely to identify themselves as originally bisexual or heterosexual than were the lesbian-identified women whom I interviewed. But they were not merely "political lesbians," if that label signifies women who took on the lesbian label without engaging in lesbian activity or fully claiming a lesbian identity. Most *believed* they were lesbians, and they lived as such for anywhere from eight to fifteen years (the average was ten years). Half said that they had experienced their lesbianism as wholly authentic; the other half reported that they had sometimes secretly wondered if they were "really" lesbians. However, this sense of "role distance" was not in itself an accurate predictor of eventual heterosexuality. Many women in my larger sample who reported that they sometimes questioned whether they were "real" lesbians lived successfully with this sense of ambivalence; for others, this ambivalence receded with time.

Forty-one-year-old Laura Stone, whom we met in chapter 3, was perhaps typical of this group of women. Laura was of middle-class origin and worked as a therapist. She had come out as a lesbian in the early 1970s. For Laura, becoming a lesbian was not, as she put it, a "coming home" experience. Before the women's movement, she felt that she was "completely straight." But as she spent more time around women, her desires for women strengthened. With time, Laura believed that she had firmly established an authentic lesbian identity. She raised a child in a lesbian relationship and was part of a lesbian community in California for fifteen years. But in the early 1980s, she had, in her words, "gone straight." She settled down with a man, married him, and had her first biological child. Today she thinks of her lesbianism as a thing of the past, yet she does not deny its authenticity. She says she was once a lesbian, and now she is heterosexual.

Laura didn't simply wake up one day and discover that she was heterosexual. Rather, she, like the other women who moved from lesbian to heterosexual identities, proceeded through what I call the "ex-lesbian trajectory," a process that was roughly the opposite of coming out. In sociological terms, it was a type of "role exit," a highly patterned process that occurred over time—not unlike the experiences of former nuns described by sociologist Helen Ebaugh, herself an ex-nun. Like devotees who move away from the Catholic Church, lesbians, particularly those heavily influenced by feminist ideology, disengaged from a role that was "central to their self-identity" and reestablished an identity "in a new role that takes into account one's ex-role."[13]

Laura welcomed me into her home and was eager to speak with me about her life, particularly her "transition away from lesbianism," as she put it. Indeed, to my surprise, most of the former lesbians I contacted enthusiastically shared their stories with me. Many of them were very self-aware of how they had disengaged from a lesbian identity and established a new identity. Coming out had been a highly reflexive process for many women who first identified as lesbians in the 1970s, and so too was the process of "becoming an ex." For Laura and other women, the transitions both to and away from homosexuality were highly self-conscious. As Laura put it, "I was a lesbian who thought a lot about lesbianism. Now I'm a straight woman who thinks a lot about heterosexuality. I processed everything. I still do. But I have to tell you that the end of the story is that I have no idea of this stuff at all any more." In the dominant culture, heterosexuality operates as a social norm, the unmarked category against the pathologized, homosexuality. Though acutely aware of the difficulties involved in *being* heterosexual, and maintaining relationships with men, straight women tend to be less self-reflexive than lesbians about the "constructedness" of sexual categories—including their own heterosexuality.[14] Former lesbians, even those who came to call themselves heterosexual, were an exception to the rule.

Laura said she started having "first doubts" about her lesbianism in the early 1980s. She and her partner were not getting along well, and she was not getting along with their child, her lover's biological offspring. She described herself as being "kind of dead" in the relationship. For many women, this questioning of a particular relationship would have simply resulted in a new lesbian relationship, not a wholesale change in sexual object choice and identity. But in becoming disillusioned with her life, Laura also became disillusioned with her lesbianism. This is at least partly because her lesbianism figured so prominently in her life. Most of her friends were lesbians; her political involvements were generally feminist, and largely lesbian; she worked mainly with feminists and with lesbians.

> I remember saying to other people, saying that if I wasn't with Vicki, I don't know if I would be with a woman. So I knew the question was up. But I also knew that there was no way I was going to find out the answer to that question, given that my life was entirely involved with women. I worked with women, played with women, everything. I was completely in the women's community. I had maintained some relations with the left, the straight left, but minimal.

With time, the lesbian community had begun to feel "very stifling" to her. Lesbian feminism had idealized women's relationships, and while she acknowledged that they were often much more egalitarian than heterosexual relationships, "they were certainly not as egalitarian as the feminist vision had promised."

> There were moments when I hated the lesbian community and hated lesbian relationships, so I became less "we're all superior to those straight couples and straight people" and more feeling that there were advantages and disadvantages to straight relationships. I began to wonder whether I needed the straight kind more than I needed the gay kind. I was feeling very distraught. I had a kid, I was working my ass off, she was depressed, she couldn't get a job. I never thought I could get out of the relationship. But divorce was not part of my repertoire.

Former lesbians often framed their emergent heterosexuality in the language of desire, longing, and "internal" selves, contrasting this newer understanding of themselves with that of their former, lesbian self, which had been forged within a lesbian subculture.[15] Some saw heterosexuality as providing a release from the intimate demands of relationships with women. Toby Miller spoke of having a couple of brief affairs with men "to test the waters": "I was at the point of breaking up with my [female] ex, a long-term relationship. It was a little step into the sexual twilight zone. Emotionally, there was nothing in it. It took my mind off a relationship where there was a lot of emotion going on. It was some kind of weird escape." The libertarian "pro-sex" discourse that emerged among some feminists in the 1980s publicly sanctioned the pursuit of pleasure. Though unaware of these "sex debates," as they had come to be called, Laura recalled her realization at the time that "maybe penises weren't so bad after all." The fact that heterosexual love was so forbidden in her friendship circle made it even more powerful. When she eventually became involved with a man, it had "some of the flavor" of her first relationship with a woman—precisely because "it was so not right": "It had the power that I realize was the power that lesbians had when they came out. That's what I think is so frightening to me. It's that here I had come into the situation thinking: I want to try this and see. I expected the same thing to happen to me when I tried women. But instead what happened was this incredibly powerful falling-in-love experience that I didn't know how to interpret." The taboo aspects of that longing made it even more attractive, rekindling a passion that had been missing from her lesbian relationship after the initial few years. "I knew that it might mean that I was straight," she laughed. "I don't think I expected that experience."

But, ultimately, there was much more at stake than simply erotic pleasures. When discussing their relationships with women, many former lesbians mentioned that the differences that once elicited desire had proved to be problematic in the long run.[16] Some ex-lesbians described a dynamic of having been drawn to female lovers who were very different from themselves in terms of class, race, gendered roles, and so forth. As we saw in chapter 3, Sally Kirk found that in her relationships with women, she "always had to be attracted to people who were really different." But over time, "it was too hard to sustain a relationship" with a woman who was "so different" from herself. In a striking reversal of feminist ideology, which claimed that lesbian relationships offered an intimacy founded upon the pairing of equals, Sally came to believe that a male lover could provide a "better mix" of qualities than a female lover. Her description of her current male partner illustrates her point:

> The thing that feels great about being with him, and that's related to his being a man, is that he's so much like me. The thing that is really great about being with Henry is that he's interested in all the same things. So there is a lot of it that is very validating, but it doesn't feel like I'm relating to myself because he has this penis. It makes him different enough, that there's this dynamic. His being a man enables me to be with him for a long time in terms of our values and our worldview, which is so much more similar.

By becoming involved with a man, according to Sally, she has been able to find a good mix of "sameness and difference" in a partner.

Toby Miller told a similar story. She met a man who, like her, "is very gay-identified": "He identifies as bisexual but he's really more gay than straight. He's primarily had relationships with men and has really been entrenched in gay culture. He's really into drag and stuff. He told me he had crushes on me when he was in total drag. There's actually a picture of him in drag, you can see . . . the odd couple. He told me that he had a crush on me. Anyway, I said that's nice but I'm a lesbian. But we eventually fell in love." While heterosexual, Toby described her relationship as affording an extraordinary reversal of roles. "We're not your average straight couple. . . . With Sandy, I'm the man. He's much more in touch with how he feels at any minute, at every second. He's an unusual man. He's also very good when I have feelings. It's more balanced than many of my other relationships. [My woman lover] could hear me only after huge, dramatic, gigantic fights. Sandy and I never get that far."

Many women spoke of life cycle changes, which also introduced the question of children. In the 1980s some lesbians of the baby boom came to raise children within lesbian relationships, but others doubted that these couples could provide the sort of security and stability they believed was necessary to raise a child. Lacking strong cultural and institutional supports, lesbian relationships were in flux, perhaps more than heterosexual ones (which were by no means terribly stable). More important, perhaps, was the continuing appeal of respectability and social legitimacy, or "heterosexual privilege":

having a child with a partner of the opposite sex linked one to the larger heterosexual society and fulfilled romantic dreams of reproducing life with one's lover.

I heard about one woman who very much wanted to have a child after having engaged in serial monogamy for many years with women. This woman, I was told, was bisexual, but always "much more attracted to women." She was nearing her mid-thirties and had not found a woman to "settle down" with. A former lover, a woman, introduced her to a heterosexual man who also wanted children, but who was not in a long-term relationship. They embarked upon an informal arrangement to parent a child together, outside of a relationship, initially through donor insemination. Facing the added difficulties of that procedure, they decided to have sexual intercourse, and physical intimacy led to emotional closeness. They eventually married, parenting four children together.

A friend of the woman in question told me this story, as if to suggest that "external" identities do not always do justice to "internal" realities. The woman was someone who was deeply committed to other women and who continues to be attracted to women, even if, on the surface, her life is quite conventionally heterosexual. But this story reveals much about the attractions of parenting in a heterosexual context. For one thing, from a purely technical standpoint, it was easier to "do it" with a man who was one's regular sexual partner. One did not have such worries as coordinating monthly cycles to ensure fertility, as did women who used artificial insemination. Some women went to great lengths in their attempts to conceive a child through donor insemination, only to fail. Moreover, for many women for whom lesbianism was at least partially a matter of choice, women who were always bisexual in terms of desire, the allure of heterosexual romantic love and partnership, sanctified and idealized by the dominant culture, was powerful.

Coming Out—Again

Once they decided to follow their heterosexual longings, ex-lesbians began to signal those around them of possible changes, evaluating their responses.[17] Becoming "heterosexual" was much more than an individual act: it involved an audience.

One way they made known these shifts was by changing their self-presentation. In chapter 3, we saw how in the process of becoming lesbians, many women had earlier engaged in "identity work," becoming more masculinized, "butchier," modeling themselves on the way they believed the "typical" lesbian looked. In a reversal of this process, in their transition to heterosexuality, many women refashioned themselves as more feminine. During the last few years of her lesbian relationship, Laura Stone began to dress differently. "I hadn't worn a dress in eons. I began to get more comfortable with my femme identity, and when I did, I began to get more in touch with desire in general. I began to fantasize about men again." This reformulation of self-presentation anticipated her reentry into the heterosexual world. Eventually, she began to date men, and after several "false starts"—falling in love with men who were not in love with her—she found someone who returned her love.

But disclosure was often very difficult. Laura told me that among her close friends, "there was some relief" on their part that she was "feeling happy, and that [her] relationship was a good one." Her close friends understood her decision to "go heterosexual," because they cared about her "as a person," quite apart from her social identity as a lesbian. More difficult were her initial interactions with casual friends and acquaintances, as well as with family. Carrie Brown told me of going to a clinic to get birth control and being served by a lesbian. She felt that the women knew that she was an impostor, a "fake" straight woman, and "really a lesbian." But the hardest part about "coming out" as straight was telling her parents—"they were delighted."

Several women spoke about how publicly touching or showing affection to a man they were dating was a cause for self-scrutiny. Laura said that she was "terrified" of running into people, either alone or with her male partner, who were simply acquaintances. "My friend Marian, my closest friend, she understood me well, and knew what was best for me. But for many of my second-tier friends, and acquaintances, I was a traitor. Or at least I felt that way a lot. Maybe some of it was my own personal stuff. But I felt terrified of bumping into them." Former lesbians often felt divided between their loyalty to other lesbians and their own yearnings. They were often highly aware of "heterosexual privilege," recognizing that the greater the number of individuals who came out as lesbians, the more powerful and less stigmatized lesbians in general would be. This understanding made them uncomfortable, a discomfort manifest in their interactions with others in public. "Deep down," Laura said, "I understood why some women were mad at me. I knew how difficult it was to be a lesbian."

The decision to marry was especially hard. To many, marrying was equivalent to publicly flaunting their newly acquired heterosexual privilege and denying their homosexual pasts. Toby was married to a man the year before I interviewed her; it was a large family wedding, replete with religious ritual and the exchange of traditional vows. They got married, she said, because "both of us wanted it": "Both of our parents had cancer and were going to die, and so we were going to do it sooner rather than later, and traditional rather than not, because why not, if that makes them happy. We didn't necessarily want to have legal and traditional, but we wanted to have something, and it wasn't hard to do that for our parents." Despite their new status, she and many other former lesbians did not wholly reject their lesbian pasts; instead, they struggled to understand how those pasts informed and defined their current perceptions and self-presentations. At the same time, most were firmly committed to binary identity categories: they believed that the world was divided into two groups, homosexual and heterosexual.

Some former lesbians came to interpret their lesbian identity as being circumstantial, as being a "phase." Sharon Lieberman said she always felt a certain degree of "identity distance"; she never felt that her lesbian "performances" were successful. Sharon described herself as first having consolidated a heterosexual identity, and then becoming a lesbian. She had engaged in quite a lot of identity work of various kinds to establish that sense of self, navigating the various stages of the "gay trajectory" to claim a lesbian identity. She viewed herself as "naturally" heterosexual and her lesbianism as a historical accident. When asked whether she was ever "really" a lesbian, she replied: "I don't know. I think you'll have to come up with your own definition of lesbian. I was never a lesbian the way [my lover] was a lesbian. But I was in love with the woman, I was identifying with the politics of the lesbian community, all my friends were lesbians, I had a kid in a lesbian relationship, I was in a lesbian mothers group. I lived like a lesbian. But I wasn't one really." Sharon questions whether she would have chosen lesbianism had a movement not come along to make that choice easier and indeed, in some quarters, even desirable. For her, becoming a lesbian was a product of being young and open to new experiences. She attributed her lesbian past to the convergence of lesbian feminist politics and her stage of life:

> If I was ten years older I would have been married and had a kid, and I might not have ever gotten involved in the kind of women's community that encouraged coming out. . . . I think it has to do a lot with life cycle. We were at this point in developing our adult identities, and this was like another transitional world that we entered in which to do that. If I had been older and my adult identity had been more firmly established, I would never have been as open to all that was happening.

Certainly it is true the young have a sense of self more open to reinterpretation and change. But the implication that lesbianism is somehow "immature" is rather conservative. Lesbianism becomes once again a "stage" that is transcended in order to become "adult." While acknowledging the malleability of sexuality during the early stages of development, this view naturalizes the heterosexual/homosexual dichotomy in adulthood.

While some ex-lesbians I spoke with interpreted their lesbianism as false or immature, women of the baby boom more often were ambivalent about denying the authenticity of their past and thereby reproducing the heterosexual/homosexual binary. Initially, Laura Stone felt that she "was naturally bisexual, had been socialized to be straight." But through the women's movement, in her words, "I resocialized myself essentially to be gay." She experienced her sexuality as fluid: "I have never thought of myself as being in the same place the whole time," she says. After her initial feelings of alienation, and her sense that she was "a straight woman masquerading as a lesbian," she became involved in a serious relationship with another woman, parented a child with her, and lived primarily within the boundaries of the lesbian community.

In reflecting upon her life, Laura became conscious of having rein-terpreted her past and essentialized her lesbian identity while coming out. She remembered that while she had "pretty good experiences with men compared to other lesbians," at the time she "didn't trea-sure that knowledge," instead viewing it as evidence of the vestiges of her own internalized homophobia. Laura recalled:

> When I was recasting my past, these were the things that I began to reconstruct . . . and then I had this best friend who I was totally in love with. In recasting my past, I thought this was interesting—because we were split up by the school. The word to me was that she was too dependent on me. But when I was in my recasting period, I thought: oh my God, they must have thought this was a lesbian relationship, and split us up. It was the only trauma of my early childhood. And so these were all pieces of evidence, that maybe I was in fact more gay than I thought. I wasn't this straight woman.

Terms like "recasting the past," which had, by the 1980s, trickled into the lexicon of therapy, reflected the psychology-imbued underpin-nings of Laura's self-consciousness. In retrospect, she came to see her earlier identity account as a narrative construction that had become normative in her social world, and she came to question whether *any* identity is more authentic or unmediated than any other. "I can talk about two points when I had clarity of what my sexual identity was. Now I don't know what the fuck sexual identity really is. I have some spot opinions, but they often contradict each other."

Unlike Sharon, Laura resisted the tendency to dismiss her past and deny the authenticity of her lesbianism. When she "went back to men," she said, "everybody around me, especially my lesbian friends, and my mother felt like: ah, I was always straight, and I was one of these political lesbians who had come out." Yet that assessment rings false: "I lived as a lesbian for fifteen years, more than a third of my life, parented a child in a lesbian relationship, and spent my formative years in a lesbian community. The term 'heterosexual' does not accu-rately describe my life experience." Laura resisted the temptation to recast her past a second time to reveal a continuous "true heterosexuality" and "false homosexuality." Like many of the ex-lesbians I interviewed, she tried to fit her lesbian past into her present identity.

Yet as she moved away from her lesbian community and into a heterosexual world, Laura described a "vacuum experience" of living in two different worlds—having left the old, yet not yet a part of the new—and her feelings of being "identityless." This phase was very isolating. When she came out as a lesbian, in the context of the women's movement, she found much social support for claiming a lesbian identity. But when she "went straight" there was, at least initially, no parallel community to back her. To be sure, she received support from her family and from the culture at large, but she was nonetheless very conscious of and reluctant to claim "heterosexual privilege."

Should her marriage end, she believes it unlikely that she would become involved with a man again. Depending on how old she was, she said, "I think it would be more likely that I would get involved with a woman." Carrie Brown, who is now married and has two children, told me that shortly after our interview, she had a sexual dream about a woman, acknowledging that "if anything happened to my husband, I'd be with a woman." Many ex-lesbians made similar comments to me. Sarah Hart did in fact begin a relationship with a woman about a year after I had originally interviewed her, when she had told me that she was more interested in becoming involved with a man. I never spoke with her directly about her decision, but a woman who knew her explained to me that after months of dating men, and forming unsuccessful relationships, she fell in love with an older woman who had pursued her affections. Sarah's experience suggests that situational factors are often as important as sexual desires in determining sexual identity.

As ex-lesbians attempt to incorporate aspects of their lesbian identities into a reconstituted self-concept, they struggle with the general perception in the dominant culture that homosexuality and heterosexuality are radically opposed and mutually exclusive categories. The experience of women such as Carrie Brown was indicative: "I was almost a separatist, and now I have two sons and a husband! If I could have seen myself then, I would never have believed it. I don't want to lose that part of myself. I still resent that I have to call myself one or the other. I will never again call myself a lesbian, or a heterosexual." Her feeling—of operating in both heterosexual and homosexual worlds while fitting into neither—was common.[18] And yet most ex-lesbians were themselves committed to binary categories. Even though the label "bisexual" seems, for many ex-lesbians, to be an adequate description of sexual *orientation,* many resist adopting it as a sexual *identity.*

Laura admitted that early on she thought of herself as bisexual, but qualified her statement: "Almost from the moment I was with a man I called myself straight. I never called myself bisexual." Yet she acknowledges today that "every once in a while I'm beginning to feel that I'm probably bisexual." Many women who came out through feminism believed that everyone was naturally bisexual in terms of their potential sexual attraction to both men and women, but that it was the political responsibility of women to channel their desires toward other women. Laura explained,

> Bisexuality had such a negative connotation to me as a lesbian . . . when people were coming out they thought of themselves as bisexual—it was an immature thing. Or the bisexual movement in the city, which was very much in my mind a sexual liberation, nonmonogamous scene which I didn't relate to. It's not that I didn't think they brought some interesting consciousness to the discourse, but I just never had very positive feelings about people who called themselves bisexual. And I thought the essential categories were the ones set down by society.

She described her lesbianism as at least partly an "external" process, motivated by political loyalties and by the historical context provided by feminism. As we saw in chapter 3, for some women, becoming a lesbian was a "coming home" experience, allowing them to express their deeply felt desires; others, like Laura, who were more bisexual or heterosexual in orientation, found that becoming a lesbian entailed identity work and a considerable amount of conscious effort.

But by the late 1980s, sexual differences among women could no longer be concealed by talk of lesbian community and solidarity, and many came to realize that some women within the lesbian community were more bisexual than others. Yet the taboo against bisexuality persisted. For Laura, in an ideal society bisexuality would be the norm; but she suggested that in the present heterosexist society, bisexuality is politically ineffectual.[19] While several of my interviewees told me privately that they consider themselves to be bisexual in terms of desire, they were not comfortable with the label. Some felt that *bisexual* implied an equal attraction or involvement with men and women in the present, which did not fit their reality. Though uncomfortable with calling themselves heterosexuals, none of the women I interviewed claimed "bisexual" as a public identity, despite efforts on the part of a burgeoning bisexual movement to popularize the term.[20]

A few women tried to resolve this conflict by continuing to identify as lesbians even as they maintained primary relationships with men.[21] Toby Miller, now married to a man, told me that she still thought of herself as a lesbian, though she had come to define her lesbianism as a "cultural" rather than a "sexual" identity. For her, being a lesbian while married to a man is "a lot like being a nonpracticing Catholic." When asked why she did not call herself bisexual, she said it was because bisexuality "was more of a sexual identity than a cultural identity," and that she feels that having been a lesbian for more than eighteen years—half her life—she is "more culturally akin to the gay/lesbian community."

> There's always a big uproar when you say you're a lesbian. People want to know what you do in bed. And I always said: that's not what it's about, that's not the whole story. And now it seems that it is the whole story. Being a lesbian used to be a lot more than just about sex. And now it's just about sex. Now that I'm with a man, that's all that people see, that I'm having sex with a man. . . . But I'm still attracted to women, I still have dreams, I still think about it. I still have those feelings. I'm very ambivalent about being monogamous with a man for the rest of my life. But I've made a commitment and I've made choices about what I want in my life, and I don't want tons of drama. I've done that, I'm not cut out for that.

As Toby suggests, being a lesbian, according to lesbian feminist ideology, was about "a lot more than just sex." Lesbian feminism had reconceptualized sexuality and, by implication, lesbianism. It had expanded the definition beyond the narrowly genital meanings, which focused on sexual object choice. It turned lesbianism into a way of being, encompassing an oppositional worldview.

In the 1980s, the feminist sex debates and the sexualization of

lesbianism challenged the normative view underlying this conception. But the emergence of visible sexual diversity within the lesbian
community was not welcomed by all. For Toby, paradoxically, the
sexualization of lesbianism meant that she felt increasingly marginalized. In the 1970s the virtual lack of discussion about lesbian sexual
practices meant that identity claims had primacy over desires; when
desire once again became a badge of lesbian identification in the
1980s, women like her, for whom lesbianism had become a matter of
identification rather than sexual practice, found themselves without
a supportive subculture.

Yet many former lesbians talked about the binary conceptions of
sexuality that cause lesbians and heterosexual women to reside in two
different worlds. Unable to fit into either category, many ex-lesbians,
at least initially, constitute an identifiable group unto themselves.
Sarah Hart said: "When I'm with my straight friends there's this part
of me that feels deviant, and with my lesbian friends there's this part
of me that feels deviant. With other former lesbians, I can be all of
who I am." As a testament to this, five ex-lesbians whom I interviewed collectively found the experience of meeting together so affirming that they continued to meet as an ongoing monthly support
group for over a year afterward.

Making Sense of the Ex

Nothing so unsettles us, men women children I mean the
lot, as our own precarious sexual identity. And there you
are blowing the lid by calling it all into question.
                                   Kate Millett, *Flying* (1974)

Did ex-lesbians prove the social constructionist argument wrong?
Were they women who had been convinced by social constructionist
arguments, only to find that they had taken on identities that were
"untrue" to themselves?

Let us consider the dominant explanation, that Laura and other
ex-lesbians were never "really" lesbians. It is true that ex-lesbians
were more likely than most to have experienced themselves as bisexual or heterosexual prior to coming out. They were also more likely

than the rest of the interview sample to have engaged in a great deal of "identity work" to consolidate a sense of lesbian identity. A few of these women reported experiencing a sense of "identity dissonance": they never felt that they were primarily attracted to women, though they called themselves lesbians. Some of them, as we have seen, went on to renounce their lesbianism. Yet to say that ex-lesbians were never "authentic" lesbians suggests a narrow definition of lesbianism, one that mandates congruence among desires, identities, and practices—a congruence that may not exist for some women. It also discounts the self-reports of women like Laura, who say that their lesbianism *felt* authentic.[22]

Though it avoids the assumption that ex-lesbians are "really" heterosexual, the second position—that ex-lesbians are "turncoats," women who chose heterosexuality because it is an easier option—is also problematic. Certainly there are many advantages to being a member of the dominant culture, including the dominant sexual culture; the ex-lesbians I interviewed were well aware of them. Some expressed despair at their feelings of marginality as the pressures they faced as lesbians became too great, the benefits too few. Still, it seems to me that the movement of women away from lesbianism cannot be explained in terms of a search for heterosexual privilege alone, particularly given the disapproval many ex-lesbians encountered from their friends, their discomfort with such privilege, and their feelings of loss of community when making the transition away from homosexuality.

In the end, neither of these two explanations—ex-lesbians were either fakers or turncoats—adequately conveys the complexities at hand. The first suggests a narrow essentialism that fails to explain how social and historical contexts may shape women's sexual options. The second suggests a radical constructionism that fails to account for individual differences, and the ways in which desire may not always be malleable. Both positions maintain a conception of sexuality that promotes a heterosexual/homosexual binarism and downplays what psychologist Carla Golden has called "the diversity and variability of female sexuality."[23]

But what of the third, more libertarian explanation, that former lesbians were sexual seekers who were simply following their desires, and that these desires had changed? Laura and other ex-lesbians tended themselves to favor this view. It is the position that seems most sympathetic to their situation, acknowledging the authenticity of both their lesbianism and their heterosexuality. But this interpretation too is flawed, I believe. Certainly it's true that some women experience their sexual desires as fluid and changing. It is conceivable that they may have felt themselves to be authentically heterosexual, then authentically homosexual, and then heterosexual again. But this explanation assumes a rather undersocialized conception of the individual, one that fails to recognize that desires are at least in part socially determined.

That the movement away from lesbianism among many women occurred at a particular historical moment, for example, cannot be considered incidental. In the early 1980s, when most members of my ex-lesbian sample began to have doubts about their lesbianism, the feminist communities that had provided a context for identity formation were becoming increasingly fragmented and decentered. As we saw in chapter 5, lesbian feminism was losing its strength as a unifying and centering ideology. These challenges weakened the commitment to lesbianism that some women had previously felt. Yet the transition of some women away from lesbianism is related but not solely attributable to their newly unfettered desires for men.

Thus I found each of these three positions to be flawed in different ways. To fully account for individuals' choices, we must consider the interaction of factors—internal and external, personal and cultural. As Nancy Chodorow suggests, "we need a cultural and individual development story to account for [particular sexual] choices."[24] Toward this end, I propose an alternative story, one that tries to capture some of this complexity.

Lesbian feminists had created a culture that helped to reconstitute desire, countering a normative heterosexuality that idealized heterosexual romantic love and establishing a subculture that both idealized women and affirmed love between women. Some individuals were able to "reinvent" themselves as lesbians, and it was in this context that many former lesbians first were attracted to women and consolidated lesbian identities. Through the various performances of identity work, many felt that they had successfully "become" lesbians.

I suggested in chapter 3 that becoming involved with a woman experienced as "other," whose otherness was often defined in terms of greater experience with and commitment to lesbianism, aided many women—particularly those whose lesbianism was less highly driven—in forming a lesbian identity. Despite the feminist rhetoric of equality and egalitarianism, many women felt that attraction between women depended upon maintaining difference in a relationship. But often those very differences became problematic, making it difficult to sustain relationships that did not enjoy heterosexual respectability and social approval. Those who had early homosexual desires or experiences seemed to have a more deeply felt sense of lesbian identity than individuals who did not. These early impressions were reinforced by "significant others"—families, friends, and lovers—who seemed to have an investment in the "perduring self-images," in preserving that self.[25]

As the cohort of women at the core of lesbian feminism aged and progressed through life cycle changes, the communities that earlier had provided support began to endure outside threats. As the nation lurched to the right, many community institutions coped with diminished sources of funding. At the same time, a revolt emerged from within, as women of color, working-class women, and sexual minorities of various sorts within lesbian communities questioned the boundaries that lesbian feminism had constructed: the result was the decentering of lesbian feminism.

By the 1980s, as the supportive culture and community had been transformed and as sexual desire became more central to lesbian identity (at least in many parts of the country), many women began to question their lesbian identities. Those who had been somewhat ambivalent about their lesbianism found that when their relationships became more difficult to sustain, and when living on the social margins appeared less attractive, then their desire for women began to wane. Women whose sexual desires tended to be fluid were more susceptible to "external" social forces than were women who experienced their lesbianism as a given; the former were more likely to become ex-lesbians. The very same impulses that drew many women into lesbianism—the longing for authenticity and self-expression—eventually challenged the collective definition of lesbian identity.

I do not wish to imply that this process was somehow mechanical or unavoidable, or even that all women underwent it in the manner described here. However, in order to fully understand the ex-lesbian, we have to explore how the connections among identity, desire, and difference were constituted at a particular historical moment. No process of identification is simply a matter of conforming to external social roles or enacting a performance. Nor is it a matter of discovering or reclaiming something "inside," something seeking to break through. Rather, identity formation involves an interplay of internal and external selves. Culture shapes individual lives, providing narrative templates for individual development and self-formation. All who take on a lesbian identity conform, to a greater or lesser extent, to the norms of lesbian communities and to expectations of what a lesbian "is." They "perform" identities. But individuals "choose from, react to, ignore, interpret, and modify culture."[26] They often have a long-term investment in a particular self-conception. They search for congruence and consistency between their emergent social identity as a lesbian and a preexistent subjective sense of self.

The story of the ex-lesbian reveals the contradictory ways in which feminists reconceptualized lesbianism in the 1970s. They downplayed desire in the interest of political identity, while making sexual consistency and commitment a test of membership. They conceived of lesbianism as an identity that transcended sexuality and, at the same time, defined women according to their sexual relationships. They challenged compulsory heterosexuality but remained firmly invested in binary identity categories and in strong group boundaries. But the story of the ex-lesbian highlights not only these contradictions but also our problematic understanding of sexual identities in general—in binary terms, as either heterosexual or homosexual. This schema understates the diversity that exists within each category and refuses to acknowledge that the boundaries between them are frequently uncertain.

In the 1980s, the emergence of the "ex-lesbian" called into question the naturalness of these boundaries. And it revealed that for some women, lesbianism *is* a phase, albeit one that is far from inconsequential; whatever their future identities, some find lesbianism to be a viable option, at least for a time. It also made clear that as long as we live in a society in which homosexuality remains highly stigmatized, there will be prohibitions against moving in and out of the lesbian category—prohibitions imposed by homosexuals and heterosexuals alike.

Chapter Seven

Seventies Questions for
Nineties Women

In 1991 news circulated in San Francisco that Amelia's, a lesbian bar which had been located on a busy street in the Mission District for thirteen years, was preparing to close. Bars had come and gone before, reflecting shifts in sexual politics and population. Maud's, the city's longest-running lesbian bar, had closed down two years earlier in the Haight District on the other side of town. Amelia's was the last lesbian bar in San Francisco, so its closure seemed particularly poignant. It marked, some suggested, the end of an era, the end of a time when the community possessed a spatial center. "In the old days," Robin Ward told me, referring to the 1970s, "one could go to a particular place"—a cafe, women's center, or bar—"to find the lesbian community." Fifteen years later, when she broke up with a longtime lover, she went out searching for that community and couldn't find it.

Yet even while Robin and others lamented what they saw as the loss of a "home base" for lesbians, women continued to pour into San Francisco and other cities and towns in search of sexual freedom and community. A columnist in the *San Francisco Examiner* observed that "more lesbians than ever live in San Francisco but the last lesbian bar is set to close." Some explained this in economic terms: unlike gay men, they suggested, lesbians lacked the capital necessary to support a commercial infrastructure. But the owner of Amelia's, a longtime participant in San Francisco's lesbian scene, put it best: "It's a victim of the lesbian community becoming more diverse," she said. "There is an absence of a lesbian community in the presence of a million lesbians." [1] Paradoxically, it was the growth and diversification of lesbian communities, rather than their decline, that destroyed the neighborhood bar.

In the early 1990s, in major urban centers across the nation one could find lesbian parenting groups, support groups for women with cancer and other life-threatening diseases, lesbian sex magazines, organizations for lesbian "career women" and lesbians of color, and mixed organizations in which out lesbians played visible roles. Gay/lesbian newspapers contained notices advertising hiking clubs for lesbians and their dogs, support groups for adult children of alcoholics, "leather and lace" motorcycle clubs, groups for lesbian-identified transsexuals, and many others. A multiplicity of lesbian groupings emerged, each representing a smaller subculture and special interest. There was no longer any hegemonic logic or center; lesbian culture seemed *placeless*. It had become more and more difficult to speak of "lesbian" identity, community, culture, politics, or even sexuality in singular terms. "I don't think there is one lesbian community," said Sunny Connelly, reflecting on nearly twenty years of change. "The community is getting bigger and smaller. Some of the infrastructure is going, bars are closing. In that way it's getting smaller. In the sense that more women are able to feel good about leading lesbian lives, it's getting bigger. But it's spreading out and becoming decentralized, which is good and bad."

Laments about the loss of lesbian community spoke to the loss of a center, of a sense of certainty and unity. For a brief period in the early 1970s, there was a burst of extraordinary solidarity, a feeling that lesbians shared a common oppression and a collective sense of identity. Lesbianism seemed to offer a settled, stable source of identification, affording membership in a bounded group with a common history, which offered both a refuge in a male and heterosexual world and a base for political action against male domination and compulsory heterosexuality. Lesbians were thought to possess one shared culture, "one true self," which was hidden inside a multiplicity of more superficial or artificially imposed "selves." Their common historical experiences and shared cultural codes were believed to provide them, as "one people," with unchanging frames of reference and meaning that continued beneath the vicissitudes of their actual history. This "oneness," underlying all other, more superficial differences, was thought to be the truth, the essence.[2]

But as the lives of the baby boom cohort became more settled, a younger cohort of women emerged, stamping their own generational sensibility upon the contours of lesbian culture and calling into question these earlier notions of collective identity. Like those before them, they constructed their lesbian identities in opposition as much to their lesbian predecessors as to the dominant heterosexual culture. Unlike their older sisters, however, who believed that together they could forge a unified sense of what it meant to be "a lesbian," young women coming of age in the 1990s had to establish lesbian identities at a time when many of the apparent certainties of the past had disappeared.

Questions of Identity Revisited

As a 1970s-influenced feminist studying women psychoanalysts from the 1930s, Nancy Chodorow found that a lack of attunement to gender characterized her interviewees' interpretation of their professional lives. Early women psychoanalysts were highly accomplished individuals who defied standard expectations of women. They had, it seemed, every reason to be conscious of themselves as women. But they were not. This indicates, observes Chodorow, the "variable and situated quality of gender."[3] For some women, and at some historical moments, consciousness of oneself as having a "gender" is more central than for other women at other times.

As a 1980s-influenced researcher looking at the experience of baby boom lesbians, who came of age in the 1970s, I was struck by how salient were their gender and sexual identities. Could the same be said of women coming out today? How, I wondered, do "nineties women"—young lesbians coming of age now—make sense of "seventies questions"? How do they understand their sexual identities, and does this understanding vary significantly from that of their baby boom predecessors? With these broad queries in mind, I interviewed ten lesbian-identified women, ranging in age from nineteen to twenty-nine, whose median year of birth was 1967, asking many of the same questions I had posed to women of the baby boom.

I imagined that I would find that for these younger women, sexual identifications do not play as central a role as they did for the older cohort. Twenty years of feminism, I surmised, had to some extent normalized lesbianism, making it less stigmatized and therefore less central to their lives. However, with some qualifications, I did not find this to be the case. Though the small number of interviews makes any claims speculative, it appears that among those coming out as lesbians today, as for their predecessors, sexuality is typically a highly salient, central aspect of the self. Becoming a lesbian entails placing oneself outside the dominant heterosexual culture, and all that that implies. Young women in particular, who must construct a sense of personhood as they establish a sexual understanding of themselves, face a complicated and frequently difficult task.

However, while the *salience* of lesbian identification among younger women did not seem significantly different from that of baby boomers at the same age, the *meaning* of this identification did. For example, among baby boomers, talk of "community" embodied the belief that lesbians all shared some basic common ground: a common marginality and a shared project of liberation. They believed that out of the diversity of women's lives and experiences they could construct a collective sense of what it meant to be a lesbian, developing subcultures that could nurture that vision. In contrast, when asked whether they considered themselves members of a "lesbian community," most of the younger women equated the idea of "community" with the imposition of "rules" and with the construction of idealized conceptions of lesbianism with which they could not fully identify.

Speaking of her knowledge of feminist theory and culture, twenty-four-year-old Lucia Hicks told me,

> I went through a period where I identified with "sisterhood is powerful" and all. I learned about it in school. I think that there are some really positive things I can take from that. But as I get older, I think that that whole era was simplistic in a lot of ways. There are a lot of rules. When you read the literature from that period there are a lot of ways of being in the world, and not being in the world. And you fit that picture, or you don't. And that's a little too simplistic for me.

Though criticizing feminism for its alleged simplicity, Lucia is quick to acknowledge that the existence of lesbian feminist culture—books,

ideas, music, and simply lesbian visibility—made her own coming out
much easier. "I have to attribute my coming out in part to getting a
grasp on feminism," she said. While keeping their distance from lesbian feminism, she and other younger women have also been profoundly influenced by it. "My sense is that a lot of younger dykes
don't reject lesbian feminism, but they do take it for granted, not in
a bad way. They just don't have to particularly announce it," said
Lucia. "They just live it." This sensibility is evident in *Go Fish*, a 1994
film about a circle of lesbian friends in Chicago, which enjoyed mass
distribution. The story starts from the assumption of an inherent acceptability, and even respectability, of lesbian lives. There are no
painful coming out stories, the hallmark of lesbian narratives of the
1970s and 1980s. There are no painstaking justifications for lesbianism. It is the perspective of filmmakers who are in their twenties
today, who have come of age two decades after Stonewall.

Nineties women have little hope of constructing a unified, collective sense of what it means to be a lesbian or a feminist. They are
leery of attempts to define the "lesbian community," doubting if any
one image could possibly represent the complexity of lesbian experiences. Twenty-five-year-old Judy Thomas told me, "What I am is in
many ways contradictory. . . . I feel that I'm postfeminist, which isn't
to say that I don't think we live in a male-dominated world. I just
don't know whether the way to undermine it is to establish new expectations of what we should be. Everything is out there to be sliced
and diced and put under the fine microscope." Judy's sense of indeterminacy and contradiction is related to shifts in the relationship
between margin and mainstream. To become a lesbian in the 1970s
was to stand outside the dominant culture. To affirm and celebrate
lesbian lives, feminists were compelled to create an alternative culture. Lesbians of the baby boom went outside the music industry to
make a women's music defined against commercial imperatives and
"cock rock." They produced films, literature, and theories to make
sense of their lives, to make themselves visible. Thanks to these efforts, nineties women have greater access than any previous generation to cultural images, narratives, and other resources that mirror
their desires. Today, young women can learn about lesbian lives in
women's studies courses, feminist fiction, and, increasingly, in mass-

produced popular culture, such as the television show *Roseanne,* or the music of k. d. lang.

Because of these expanded opportunities, women of the postfeminist generation do not feel as strong a sense of loyalty to "feminist" or "women's" culture. They believe that they should be represented in mainstream culture, and they long for that representation. When I asked her what types of music she listened to, nineteen-year-old Ann Carlson answered, "I like 'cock rock' and women's music. I like both. But I like mainstream women's music the best." Rather than listen to "out" lesbian musicians recording on alternative women's music labels, "I like music that speaks to women but isn't only about women. . . . Tracy Chapman, Melissa Etheridge, Michelle Shocked. They don't use pronouns, proper nouns. To us that's cool. And we notice that men don't listen to that music." Ann subverts the feminist critique of masculinist music by embracing cock rock as a symbol of power *and* women's music as a reminder of her feminist roots. At the same time, however, she prefers "mainstream women's music": women musicians who employ lesbian and feminist imagery but perform for a mass audience. These performers' sexual ambiguity allows for the double appeal of the music—to the subculture, as well as to the mass audience. It permits audience members such as Ann to listen to music they consider to be "lesbian" and know that millions of other people are also listening to it. For her, the ambiguity is part of the appeal.[4] But the pluralization and "mainstreaming" of lesbian images are themselves ambiguous signs of progress: the increasing importance of mass-produced lesbian culture means that while lesbian images are much more plentiful than they ever were before, their production is much more reliant upon the whims of Hollywood and the culture industries, and thus lesbian lives are being commodified.[5] Nonetheless, many younger lesbians welcome this mainstreaming.

Other important differences between the seventies and nineties cohorts concern their views of the sexualization of women's bodies. While the older women claimed power by renouncing lipstick, coquettishness, and sexually explicit representations and by opposing the commercialization of beauty and sex, by 1990 many younger lesbians were asserting their sexual power by reclaiming these practices

and withholding access from the conventional male beholder. As the
decade wore on, the debates that emerged in bars, in coffee houses,
and in the pages of community newspapers often appeared as a generational clash: Were the full-color spreads, in the glossy fashion
magazines from *Elle* to *Vanity Fair,* that touted the joys of "lesbian
chic" furthering lesbian visibility, or were they creating new, idealized, airbrushed versions of a genteel sapphism? Were younger
women, who were pioneering a new roving club scene and unabashedly embracing sexual imagery, the rightful heirs of lesbian feminism
or evidence of its demise?

When I first arrived in the Bay Area in 1981, lesbian bars, clubs,
and social events were frequented by women who embraced lesbian
feminist antistyle—workshirts, jeans, and "sensible shoes." But
through the next few years, many lesbians began to dress up. In night
clubs and on the street it was not unusual to see younger women
flaunt high heels, short skirts, and other trappings of femininity, often
consciously evoking the butch-femme codes of the 1950s. Twenty-
eight-year-old Jill Dinkins wears her "butch" identity proudly. Whenever she goes out with her girlfriend, they adopt sharply differentiated gender styles. Jill wears leather jackets, short-cropped hair, and
men's vests; her girlfriend has long hair and wears makeup and skirts.

As Jill describes these forms of self-presentation, they sound very
different from the butch-femme roles practiced by earlier working-
class lesbians. For her, adopting a role is more a matter of play than
necessity. "I like to play with power and sexuality. It's all a game." She
and other nineties women selectively and self-consciously take on
elements of butch-femme style. Some interpret the roles in a essentialized way, as showing their "true" nature and refusing the constraints of straight society, but for many these roles are more ambiguous and less naturalized than in the past. They are an aesthetic
practice, a self-reflexive performance.[6]

This commitment to individual choice often also extends to sexual
practices. Members of the nineties cohort tend to be much more
tolerant of "slippages" of identity in general—of inconsistencies
among identity, desires, and sexual practices—than their baby boom
predecessors. Judy Thomas, who felt attracted to women and girls at
a very early age, and who calls herself a "lesbian virgin" because she

has never had a heterosexual experience, told me that she was toying with the idea of sleeping with a man, "just for the experience," and that she did not see this as a threat to her lesbian identity. She related a story about her best friend, a lesbian, who recently told her that she was having an affair with a man, fearing Judy's response. She reassured her friend that this news was not a threat to their friendship. "I was so shocked that she even asked me," she said. If there is a greater tolerance for inconsistencies of identity, this may be related to the greater propensity of younger lesbians to speak openly about their sexual practices.

Certainly, the sexual practices and politics of feminist lesbians were more diverse in private than was publicly admitted. As my interviewees suggested, frank sexual talk was muted in the interest of constructing lesbian solidarity. Recall Cindy Ross's description of lesbian sexuality in the 1970s: "Nobody knew what anyone else was doing." For nineties women, particularly members of urban lesbian subcultures, the gap between theorizing and practicing sexuality has seemingly narrowed. The belief that lesbian sexuality is radically different from and superior to other forms of sexuality, and that sexuality and desire are only peripheral aspects of the lesbian experience, is no longer widely held. As Jill Dinkins told me, "I've heard many conversations about sex recently in social settings. Not necessarily in a lovey-dovey manner, or in a clinical manner, but in an experimental sense. That's what a lot of young women are going through right now. They're not modeling themselves after older women." Nineties women were more likely to know about different types of sexual practices and to be aware of sexual and relational problems such as "lesbian bed death," the tendency for long-term lovers' sexual interests to wane. They are also far more likely than their baby boom predecessors to consider sexual fringe groups, such as sadomasochists, to be a legitimate part of the lesbian community. Most striking, perhaps, is the tolerance for—and even celebration of—bisexuality.

Women of the baby boom, I have argued, often suppressed their bisexuality in the interest of identifying as lesbian and challenging compulsory heterosexuality. Today, anecdotal evidence suggests that many young women, particularly on college campuses, have come to openly identify as bisexual rather than exclusively lesbian.

Twenty-two-year-old Cindy Yerkovich explained that while she is attracted to men, she feels most comfortable with and sexually fulfilled
by women. The label that best expresses who she is is "bi-dyke,"
signifying that her "sexual orientation is bisexual but [her] identity
is lesbian." Cindy, who has long hair and a traditionally feminine
appearance, said that she fights against the tendency to place her and
others "in boxes": "A lot of stuff that has come down on me has been
really looksist. People will call me bisexual not knowing whether
I've ever slept with a man. Just because I have long hair. It bugs me
that people assume I'm bisexual just because I pass. Gay people assume that I'm bisexual, if they don't assume that I'm straight." When
I asked my younger interviewees if they were currently friends with
or would choose to be friends with a bisexual woman, or how they
would feel if a lesbian friend decided to become involved with a man
on either a short-term or long-term basis, their responses tended,
on the whole, to be quite positive. Some even suggested that lesbians
and bisexual women have much in common by virtue of their
"queerness."

Sometimes Cindy calls herself "queer," signifying a fluid sense of
sexual orientation and a refusal to fully embrace the term "lesbian."
For her, the term signifies a loose but distinguishable set of political
and intellectual movements that are quite distinct from an "ethnic"
style of lesbian/gay identity politics. *Queer* signifies the possibility
of constructing a nonnormative sexuality that includes all who feel
disenfranchised by dominant sexual norms.[7] Thus, on the Kinsey
scale, Cindy says, "queer means anything that is not a 1 or completely
heterosexual. . . . I think that 1s are just as abnormal as 6s, whatever
abnormal means. Queer implies ambiguity. It implies that you can't
define things in terms of us and them—it's not that easy. I don't want
to define my identity in terms of exclusion." She and others who have
been influenced by the queer critique insist that the refusal of les-
bian/gay identity, rather than its affirmation, is the radical act. "We
have a lesbian identity, a lesbian culture now. It's established. We
don't have to fight to establish it. Now's the time to question what
we've taken for granted." The presence of people with ambiguous
sexual desires, such as bisexuals, challenges the faith in sexual object
choice as a master category of sexual and social identity and offers the

greatest potential to disrupt the normative heterosexual/homosexual binary.[8]

Armed with poststructuralist and postmodern theories of gender and sexuality, some also suggest that cross-gender practices such as butch-femme and drag are subversive acts that undermine the illusion of a coherently gendered self, therefore providing an alternative to a politics grounded in identity. They quote Judith Butler's claim: gender identities are "performative acts" that are always on uncertain ground.[9] The lengths to which we must go, through dress, demeanor, and all manner of social practices, to prove our masculinity or femininity attest to their tenuousness. Once differences *within* the categories—"woman" and "man," "heterosexual" and "homosexual"—are exposed, the old dichotomous conceptions are called into question.

In major cities, young "queers" infiltrated straight bars, carrying on "kiss-ins" designed to upset "normal" heterosexuality. Relying largely on the decentralized, cultural activism of street posturing, their styles and tactics were a pastiche of images and elements from popular culture, communities of color, AIDS activism, hippies, MTV, feminism, and early gay liberation.[10] At the 1993 march on Washington, marchers chanted in front of the White House: "We're here; we're gay; can Bill come out and play?"[11] Queer activists traveled to shopping malls, proclaiming, "We're here, we're queer, and we're not going shopping." They rejected civil rights strategies in favor of a politics of carnival, transgression, and antiassimilation, blending the in-your-face stance of gay liberationists with a parodic sense of the limits of identity politics.

Describing a short-lived but influential organization that embodied these ideas, one analyst wrote: "In its resistance to social codes (sexual, gender, race, class) that impose unitary identities, in rebelling against forces imposing a repressive coherence and order, Queer Nation affirms an abstract unity of differences without wishing to fix and name these."[12] In other words, the preference for the label *queer* represents "an aggressive impulse of generalization; it rejects a minoritizing logic of toleration or simple political interest-representation in favor of a more thorough resistance to regimes of the normal." Such generalization "suggests the difficulty in defining the population whose interests are at stake in queer politics."[13]

My conversations with young lesbians indicate that while relatively few—only the most highly educated and theory-savvy—claim the term *queer* wholeheartedly, many more, if not most, identify with the indeterminacy and irony at the heart of the queer project. They oppose the construction of an identity founded upon exclusions and are uncertain about the content of the category *lesbian.* Yet they tend to qualify their allegiance to "queerness" by retaining a critique of gender inequality. Judy Thomas, who works for a predominantly gay male organization in San Francisco, cautioned that among the men she works with "there is a complete lack of knowledge about lesbians."

> I don't think straight men know us, or gay men. . . . There is a very profound fear or kind of terror toward women that have any kind of sense of self, and there is a terrible resistance on the part of men to look at their own sexism. Some of my friends say that there's not a whole lot of common ground [between gay men and lesbians]. I don't really believe that, actually. But I do know that sexism is alive and well and living in gay male communities, just the same as racism is alive and well and living in my life, and my friends' lives.

Judy and her peers inherit a world in which women still lag far behind men with respect to all common measures of structural equality—pay equity, child care provisions, and the like—while at the same time feminist ideas have made considerable cultural headway. They were far from convinced that their loyalties stood with men. Indeed, among political activists in San Francisco and other cities, gay men and women often coexisted uneasily: ACT UP and Queer Nation chapters in many cities were marred by gender (and racial) conflicts.[14] The new "co-sexual" queer culture could not compensate for real, persistent, structural differences in style, ideology, and access to resources among men and women. This recurrent problem underscored that while the new queer politics asserted the sexual difference that could not be assimilated into feminism, gender, too, resisted being completely subsumed within sexuality.

Even as they integrate feminism into their daily lives, young lesbians seem to reject the view that lesbianism is *the* feminist act and the belief that any sexual identity is more authentic and unmediated than any other. Talk of "lesbian community," "lesbian identity," or "women's culture" and the global theories that underlie such language hold little appeal. When asked whether she identifies as a member of a lesbian community, Jill Dinkins replied: "I feel a sense of community with my friends who are lesbians. But I don't feel a sense of community with all lesbians. We agree on some things: that we love women, and that we want to live our lives as openly as we can. But we disagree on a lot of things: worldviews, political concerns, you name it." Jill spoke of refusing ghettoization, of acknowledging internal group differences, and of affirming individual choice of style and political and sexual expression. In this sense, she is "postfeminist," if that term describes women and men who, while holding their distance from feminist identities or politics, have been profoundly influenced by them.[15] She and other nineties women simultaneously locate themselves inside and outside the dominant culture, and they feel a loyalty to a multiplicity of different projects—some of them feminist oriented, others more queer identified. They recognize that while marginalized groups construct symbolic fictions of their experience as a means of self-validation, and thus compulsory heterosexuality necessitates the construction of lesbian/gay identities, nevertheless such identities are constraining as well as enabling.

Necessary Fictions

> *Thre is no doubt in my mind that the feminist movement has radically changed, in an important way, everybody's concept of lesbianism, straight or gay. There's not a dyke in the world today (in or out of the bars) who can have the same conversation that she could have had ten years ago. It seeps through the water system, you know?*
>
> Amber Hollibaugh, in Hollibaugh and Moraga, "What We're Rollin' Around in Bed With" (1981)

A veteran activist and early gay liberationist told me a story about going on a shopping expedition with several older relatives to a suburban mall outside of San Francisco. The year was 1990. When they arrived at the mall, she and her relatives encountered some young "queers," dressed in ripped t-shirts and buzz-cut hairdos: they were chanting and holding a "kiss-in," an action designed to break the calm of compulsory heterosexuality and generally cause a stir. She looked at the young queer activists and saw her younger self. "I've always felt stifled by people who want to put me into a kind of strait jacket. There's a part of me that always wants to throw things in for shock value and stir them up a bit."[16]

Twenty years earlier, she had joined gay liberation and feminism out of a similar impulse to "smash the categories" and deconstruct reified notions of gender and sexuality. She judges her generation's efforts to be a qualified success: "We made homosexuality much more visible, we created a presence for gay life in this country. But we were young, naive, and very bold." Though they problematized heterosexuality, activists of her generation failed to problematize the constructed, indeed fragile, nature of their own collective self-concepts. "We wanted to turn everything upside down. Sometimes we failed to see that we were very much a part of the system we were trying to change. Sometimes we asked for too much. We ended up demanding too much of people."

Lesbians of the baby boom passionately affirmed their sexual identities, insisting, at least initially, that such identities are open-ended, evolving, and often situational. They found inadequate the conventional view that sexual identity is, for all intents and purposes, consolidated early in life. It could not account for the experiences of housewives who had never harbored desires for women, but who in the boundary-breaking times of the 1960s and 1970s left their husbands and took up with women. As Jeffrey Weeks put it, sexuality is "provisional, even precarious, dependent upon, and constantly challenged by an unstable relation of unconscious forces, changing social and personal meanings, and historical contingencies."[17]

Having revealed the contingent character of sexuality, however, many women of this generation, particularly those who had been touched by feminist ideas, began to seek stability, closure, and certainty, keeping a watchful eye on the boundaries of the "lesbian community." Over time, the impulse toward consistency won out. They sought congruence between individual and collective identities, even while placing great value upon achieving authenticity, being "true" to oneself. They believed that by achieving a stable sense of identity, they could maintain a sense of coherence and commitment despite external flux, instability, and change and their own passage through different periods of life. They downplayed internal differences: different desires, different self-conceptions, and different varieties of lesbian identification.

By externalizing difference and developing a gender separatism that policed the boundaries around the lesbian group, lesbian feminists came to reinforce the differences—between insider and outsider, normal and abnormal, male and female, heterosexual and homosexual—that they had originally sought to erase. This had the unintended effect of strengthening the notion of sexual minorities as "other," which left the "center"—heterosexuality—intact. The problem with this "ethnic" conception of homosexuality, writes Barbara Ehrenreich, is that "it denies the true plasticity of human sexuality and, in so doing, helps heterosexuals evade what they fear. And what heterosexuals really fear is not that 'they'—an alien subgroup with perverse tastes in bedfellows—are getting an undue share of power and attention, but that 'they' might well be us." [18]

Perhaps the eventual resurgence of essentialism and sexual binaries, both of which lesbian feminists had initially attacked, was inevitable, given the contradictions within feminists' reconceptualizing of lesbianism in the 1970s. They downplayed desire in the interest of political identity, while making sexual consistency and commitment a test of membership. They imagined lesbianism as an identification that transcended sexuality and, at the same time, defined women according to their sexual relationships. They tried both to undo the old categories and to form stable, consistent sexual identities, to embrace a universalizing conception of identity and unify lesbians as a minority group. But ultimately, they failed to escape dominant conceptions that saw sexuality in binary terms, as either heterosexual *or* homosexual, thus neglecting the diversity within each category and the variability of the boundaries separating them.

It appears that social movements organized around sexual identities are caught in a troubling paradox. "We are," observes Jeffrey Weeks, "increasingly aware that sexuality is about flux and change, that what we call 'sexual' is as much a product of language and culture as of nature. But we earnestly strive to fix it, stabilize it, say who we are by telling of our sex."[19] Perhaps stability and predictability are basic human needs, particularly for those of us living through rapid social transformations, whose identities are accordingly under great pressure to change. Yet the effort spent on keeping collective sexual identities intact may do no more than expose their ultimate instability and impermanence.

The history of lesbianism is the history of the progressive growth of knowledge, reflexivity, and group self-consciousness. Whereas knowledge accumulated about sexuality, as about human life in general, was once believed to clarify our understanding of the world, we have found instead that this knowledge has actually come to undermine our sense of certainty. The more we know, the less we can take for granted. Our capacity to reflect upon everything around us now actually threatens the stability of our institutions, and the resulting uncertainty has become a constituent element of modern institutions.[20] In particular, the more we know, the more we've come to see sexuality as fleeting, unstable, and up for grabs. Queer politics and poststructuralist-inspired queer theory may represent the latest stage in the development of greater and greater reflexivity and indeterminacy.

Today's queer activists enact a new universalizing move, a new attempt to smash the categories; while not unlike the early lesbian/gay liberation impulse, theirs seems more keenly aware of the provisional nature of *all* identities. As they wrestle with the tensions between identity and difference, they too have had heated boundary disputes. "They are trying to combine contradictory impulses: to bring together people who have been made to feel perverse, queer, odd, outcast, different, and deviant, and to affirm sameness by defining a common identity on the fringes," two veteran gay liberation activists note.[21] But at least these young activists seem to be highly sensitive to the contradictory nature of their project. Problematizing homosexuality along with heterosexuality, they are wary of engaging in fights over who belongs in the lesbian/gay/queer community and skeptical about "the possibility and desirability of a clear criterion of belonging."[22]

So while the contested nature of lesbianism is familiar, there is also something new; in Biddy Martin's words, "the irreducibly complex and contested status of identity has itself been made more visible."[23] This is deeply troubling to many women, particularly those who once held out the hope of constructing a unified lesbian feminist movement. The element of uncertainty here is bound to be unsettling: in contrast, carving out a sense of space, forming a community, and drawing boundaries, however precarious they may be, promote a sense of security. Indeed, the persistence of institutionalized and culturally reproduced normative heterosexuality, as well as the heterosexism that accompanies it, makes it necessary to continue the construction of a sense of difference based on (homo)sexual object choice.

As long as individuals are defined as different and inferior on the basis of their sexual desires or practices, they will need to develop a sense of collective identity and maintain institutions that counter stigma. This seems particularly true today, as a powerful and well-organized right wing in the United States mobilizes to deny lesbian and gay rights, along with the economic and political rights of other marginalized groups.[24] Without an organized and self-conscious movement, these rights cannot be defended. A collective identity requires that boundaries be established by setting forth at least minimal criteria for claiming that identity. The alternative is a vague pluralism that speaks only of "difference" and views all differences as equal and good. This "hundred lifestyles" strategy, which calls for "a pluralism of sexual choice," as Margaret Cerullo says, "doesn't represent an adequate response to the one lifestyle that has all the power"—heterosexuality.[25]

Today many of us, queer and not-so-queer, are searching for a way of talking about (and acting on) sexual identities and politics that avoids the twin pitfalls: an identity politics that refuses difference or a politics of difference without collective identity.[26] As individuals we are members of social groups yet remain ultimately irreducible to categories. "We are," writes Shane Phelan, "specific individuals as well as members of multiple groups."[27] As lesbians, we share differences *and* commonalities. We need to affirm what we share in common without feeling compelled to deny what makes each of us unique.

Individual differences will always exist. We have seen that even
among self-identified lesbians, sexualities vary widely. For example,
for some women, sexual object choice is open to choice and change.
Others experience their sexual desires as relatively fixed. As long as
we live in a society in which heterosexuality is normative, women
who have early homosexual desires or experiences will develop a
more deeply felt sense of difference than those who do not. But this
difference is not of paramount significance and should not be used
to determine who does and does not belong in our communities.
Instead, we need to tolerate ambiguity. We need to question assumptions about who and what constitutes the lesbian community, deliberately courting greater uncertainty rather than seeking closure. This
politics is already emerging in practice.

I have described how women of the baby boom, as they enter
middle age, are combining commitment to lesbian communities with
a greater sense of individualism. They are reconstituting lesbian identity in new, decentered ways as their responsibilities to work and
family increase. Many younger women coming of age and coming
out today are also reconstituting lesbian identity, in ways that tolerate
inconsistency and ambiguity. They simultaneously locate themselves
inside and outside the dominant culture as they pursue a wide range
of projects. Their strategic deployment of lesbian/gay identities is balanced against their recognition of the limits of such identities.

In the decentered conception of identity that is emerging, individuals are comfortable in multiple contexts. They embody what Kathy
Ferguson calls "mobile subjectivities," which are temporal, always in
motion, and contingent. Identities, she suggests, are "deceptive ho-
mogenizations" that always conceal "some turbulence." If we simply
identify on the basis of race, class, or sexuality, we cannot make sense
of the used-to-be-working-class-now-professional, the woman of
mixed race parentage who appears white, the divorced-mother-now-
lesbian, or the former-lesbian-turned-straight. Many of us experience
ourselves *between* rather than *within* existing categories of identification.

As part of this process, "coming out" may be losing its appeal as
the guiding narrative of lesbian self-development. The coming out
story may no longer be the central narrative of lesbian existence.

Bonnie Zimmerman notes that lesbian writers today, as opposed to twenty years ago, have a different focus: "How I came out—how I discovered my real self—no longer engages our attention. We are out, and it's time to get on with our lives."[28] Coming out was once seen as a linear, developmental, goal-driven process, but today it is more likely to be conceptualized as an ongoing, dynamic social interaction, a process of self-creation that is both collective and individual, a "be-coming" rather than a "coming out."[29] This decentered model of identity formation mirrors the decentering of lesbian culture and communities, making it possible for us to imagine lesbian identities and communities that are more inclusive, less demanding, less confining, and more able to satisfy our desires for choice and autonomy.

If we understand the permanently unsettled nature of identities and group boundaries, we will be less apt to see this decentering as a sign that the lesbian feminist project has failed. Indeed, it may present new democratic potential. Many women who felt excluded by totalizing conceptions of lesbian identity may find that they can finally participate on their own terms. For example, those who experience their sexuality as fluid may claim lesbian identifications or not, as they find such identifications useful. Women who choose to move from homosexuality to heterosexuality (and back again, perhaps) may not experience that move as quite so threatening to their sense of self.

Sexual identities are fictions. But they are, as Jeffrey Weeks puts it, "necessary fictions." Lesbianism is now conceived as a collective and increasingly public basis of identity. Today, its emerging forms are broadening the range of possibilities for women. The future will undoubtedly bring yet new and different possibilities.

Methodological Notes

Narrating the Self

As I conducted the interviews, I was aware that while interactionist approaches such as the life history method lead one to seek out the diversity, ambiguity, and negotiation in the construction of an individual's life, such approaches may encourage one to find ambiguity, flux, contradictions, and diversity where little exist. The very act of allowing a subject to talk at length about her life will confirm the tenets of interactionist theory about the rambling and negotiable aspects of life.[1]

But there is an opposing tendency: individuals "recast the past," emphasizing consistencies of biography and minimizing inconsistencies. Such coherence is highly valued in our culture, particularly among the middle classes, who prize careerism and individual self-cultivation. Those who change, who move from job to job and partner to partner, who switch hobbies and fail to plan methodically for the future, are often seen as dilettantes who can't "make up their minds," shiftless characters who can't fully be trusted. Likewise, those who change sexual identities are seen as dabblers, untrustworthy people who lack a strong sense of self—and such judgments are particularly likely, I have argued, in the context of a social movement that sought to politicize sexuality and to mobilize individuals. Symbolic interactionists tell us that when people talk about their lives, they actively frame their experience to suit their own needs, filtering their descriptions of actual events and behaviors through narrative.

The tendency of the life history method to produce accounts that stress ambiguity and flux may be balanced by the social pressures to recast one's past to highlight biographical consistency. Hence, I paid attention to consistency and singularity in these self stories, as well as inconsistency and multiplicity. Though I assumed that these retrospective accounts reflect how the interviewees in fact feel and felt, the interview data say less about the

concrete details of individuals' lives in some objective sense than about how
they framed their stories, emphasizing some aspects of their lives and de-
emphasizing others.

As the preceding suggests, I embarked on this study with a sense of skepticism about "mainstream" social science methods. Social science research
requires that the researcher separate her- or himself from the "object" of
study in order to produce "objective generalizations."[2] Generalizations are
made possible, according to the standard approach, by decontextualizing all
human characteristics, values, interests, experiences, and emotions. Historically, much sex research has operated within this positivistic model. Sexologists have conducted detailed case studies of sexual variations, from "acquired sexual inversion" to "zoophilia"; their studies aimed to explain the
properties of sexuality by reference to an inner truth or essence—a uniform
pattern ordained by nature, not connected to values and emotions.[3] However useful quantitative approaches may be in gathering aggregate data,
helpful for drawing preliminary links between sex and social structure, they
rarely forge connections between sexuality and the self. Sexual activity is
most often reduced to a "summation of orgasms."[4]

In contrast, social constructionists suggest that the very notion that an
individual's homosexuality can be causally explained is itself a social construction. In this view, homosexuality is above all a social category, a cogni-
tive tool created to organize perception and experience; as new understandings make possible new experiences, the existence of homosexuality cannot
be separated from knowledge of it. Positivistic approaches fail to reckon
with the human capacity for self-reflection, which plays a powerful role in
shaping the expression of seemingly physical drives.

Qualitative research methods, because they emphasize *Verstehen,* or interpretive understanding, which is based on the researcher's need to live
through or recreate the experiences of others, can get "closer" to these questions. In the process of doing research, the researcher is an active participant in shaping the world she or he is observing. Qualitative methodologists
understand that it is vital to delve both into how the researcher's personal
and social world lead to these constructed understandings and into how
such constructions are subsequently used in the social world. We must keep
in mind the truism that issues of personal experience, social morality, and
public politics are always present in research and need to be directly confronted.[5]

In recent years, feminist and racial/ethnic minority epistemologies have
consciously rejected the traditional, narrow definitions of sociology, as well
as its positivistic claims to truth. They have redefined "objectivity," recognizing that truth is partial, contextual, and subjective and that researchers, like

all subjects, are socially located. A growing literature has documented how the social researcher is not a mere conduit through which "truth" is revealed; he or she can also be seen as a "constructor" of "knowledge," which is no longer assumed to be absolute.[6] Feminist researchers have often chosen methods that emphasize women as people in their own right rather than methods that view women as the "other" and take men to be the norm. Renate Klein explains why this concern is so important for feminist research: "A methodology that allows for women studying women in an interactive process without the artificial object/subject split between researcher and researched (which is by definition inherent in any approach to knowledge that praises its 'neutrality' and 'objectivity') will end the exploitation of women as research objects."[7] All research, regardless of the sex of research and researched, is fraught with power—we must recognize the importance of these dynamics and of the object/subject split. How could our historical, intellectual, and personal location *not* shape the questions we ask, how we ask them, and how we interpret the responses we get?

I knew that my study was motivated and indeed shaped by the fact that I identify as a lesbian. In relation to the group of women I interviewed, I was in many respects an "insider." As a lesbian studying other lesbian women, I shared an "intimate identity stake" with my subjects.[8] But I was an outsider of sorts, as well. While possessing a common identification with a marginalized group, we often did not agree on the meaning we attributed to lesbianism. For example, while many of my interviewees saw their lesbianism as absolutely key to understanding who they are, I have often felt that my sexuality only partially explains who I "am." Indeed, this tension was at the heart of the project—a tension, it soon became clear, that created certain dynamics within the interviews themselves.

I was made aware of my role in shaping interactions at many points during the research. Like Susan Krieger, who was also a lesbian studying lesbians, I discovered myself hoping that my interviewees would "help me solve the problem of who I was."[9] I often found myself looking up to women whose lives I respected, as well as feeling an extraordinary amount of pity for older women whose lives seemed unfulfilled. I responded to an interview with one woman with such intense identification and fear that I bolted out of the house. I later wrote in my interview notes: "She looked a lot older than her years. Illness had aged her. I looked at her premature old face and saw a reflection of how beautiful she once was. I thought of my own aging, and that of my mother, only a few years older than she. I thought of being old and sick and alone. I won't be like that, I reassured myself, I have [my lover]. She'll be there for me." Though positivist methodologists recommend that the interviewer neutralize what has been termed "interviewer effect," I reject their notion that research can ever be objective, rational, detached, and value-free. Accordingly, I've been conscious of the importance to the interview process of "bringing the interviewer back in," of acknowledging that every interview is a social interaction. Being conscious of these dynamics did not stop me from sometimes identifying (and sometimes overidentifying) with my interviewees, but at least it helped me to recognize the pattern and struggle to "separate out" a sense of myself when I analyzed these interviews.[10]

The method of "separating out" was particularly useful in interviewing women with whom I had much in common, when boundaries between self and other sometimes seemed blurred. To a certain degree, my identification and involvement with my interviewees were exaggerated by our common situation as women who are members of a marginalized sexual minority. But other factors often undermined this commonality. I found that I was less likely to overidentify with women who were noticeably different from me in terms of age, race/ethnicity, or class than I was with women who were similar—either Jewish, or in their early to mid-thirties, or from a lower-middle-class background.

As I interviewed individuals who differed from myself in some marked way, other challenges presented themselves. Should I make a particular point of discussing racial difference with an African American woman, or should I let her bring it up, if it bears upon the interview? I found that if I did not bring up the question of race, the interviewee who was African American, Latina, Asian, or from a mixed race background did not tend to do so herself. But once I asked, she was typically eager to talk about race and its relationship to her lesbianism. I also knew that to bring up race only with women of color is to deny that white women are also "raced," which perpetuates white hegemony.[11] Selves are multiply situated. Just as feminist researchers are coming to recognize that "gender is not enough"—class, race, and other divisions can have as much (or more) bearing upon how women organize their lives—so too sharing a stigmatized sexual preference does not override other life contexts.[12]

The Sample

As I pointed out in the introduction, some have suggested that a gay generation is defined in terms of when one comes out, or identifies as lesbian or gay; they differentiate between age and identification, allowing for the fact that many people come out relatively late in life.[13] While agreeing that sex-

ual desire or behavior is not equivalent to sexual identification, I chose to
designate my cohorts by age, hypothesizing that early homosexual desires
often create a sense of personal difference that is significant even before the
moment of coming out. Hence, I designated my baby boom cohort by year
of birth, selecting lesbian-identified women who were born between the
years 1945 and 1961; individuals in the post–baby boom cohort were born
between 1961 and 1971 (see table 1).

My sample is somewhat skewed against mothers. Although some 20 to
30 percent of all lesbians have children,[14] only 20 percent of my baby boom
sample are mothers. This is a relatively small proportion, perhaps because
lesbian mothers, particularly those with small children, were less likely to
agree to be interviewed. Indeed, the only women who turned me down
when I requested an interview were four mothers who cited their lack of
time and energy.

An additional factor that may "bias" this study in certain respects is its
location: all of the interviews were conducted in the San Francisco Bay Area,
an area known for its tolerance for homosexuality and for the large, lively,
and relatively powerful lesbian and gay communities that have made their
home there during the last several decades. Few of the women I interviewed
were "natives"; nearly all had been drawn there in search of work or by the
Bay Area's reputation for tolerance. One might wonder whether my sample
therefore emphasized women for whom lesbianism is both more highly salient and less stigmatized. This is quite possibly the case.

Cities such as San Francisco, New York, Chicago, or Boston, which serve
as "gay magnets," include a critical mass of like-minded individuals and a
lively lesbian/gay economic and cultural infrastructure—featuring gay-
friendly businesses, theaters, newspapers, and political clubs. Urban communities in the United States are laboratories for experiments in lesbian/gay
culture and identity. There the debates erupt and the trends emerge that
eventually affect less urbanized communities, as well as isolated individuals
who identify as homosexual. I would speculate that rather than being anom-
alous, the San Francisco Bay Area is a trendsetter for lesbian/gay life in this
country, and therefore my findings are generalizable to other parts of the
country—at least to other urban areas. Individuals living in such areas may
well have a more strongly developed conception of homosexuality as a *cultural* identity that transcends sexuality than do those who are more isolated.
But while produced in cities, lesbian/gay culture tends to "trickle down"
throughout the country. To a large extent, as San Francisco goes, so goes the
Lesbian Nation—if not immediately, then several years later. Thus Verta
Taylor and Leila Rupp describe a lesbian community in a midwestern city:
"Columbus [Ohio] is a noncoastal but urban community where develop-

TABLE 1. Interview Sample

Name (Pseudonym)	Age (In 1990)	Race/Ethnicity	Class Background	Occupation
		Baby Boom Cohort		
Shirley Alvarez	34	Latina	Working	Gardener
Margaret Berg	44	White/Jewish	Middle/Working	Student
Sue Bergez	40	African American	Working	Tech writer
Joan Bodewell	44	White	Middle	Administrator
Carrie Brown	38	African American	Middle	Nurse
Andrea Brum	38	White	Working	Writer
Sunny Connelly	45	White	Working	Caterer
Meg Dunn	37	White	Working	Sales
Linda Gomez	37	White	Working	Teacher
Sue Hammond	44	White	Working	Tech writer
Sarah Hart	36	White/Jewish	Middle	Therapist
Jackie Henry	42	White	Middle	Therapist
Barb Herman	42	White	Working	Programmer
Dale Hoshiko	34	Asian American	Working	Graphic artist
Ara Jones	40	African American	Working	Social services
Naomi Kennedy	40	White	Working	Teacher
Sally Kirk	40	White/Jewish	Middle	Lawyer
Sharon Lieberman	43	White/Jewish	Middle	Therapist
Mary Lipton	42	White	Middle	Teacher
Sarah Marcus	44	White/Jewish	Middle	Professor
Toby Miller	36	White	Middle	Nurse
Judy Orr	44	White	Middle	Social services
Muriel Pepper	40	White	Middle	Advertising
Cindy Ross	44	White	Middle	Therapist
Joan Salton	45	White	Working	Social services
Nina Samson	37	White	Middle	Therapist
Irma Sands	45	African American	Working	Secretary
Karen Savo	32	Mixed	Middle	Teacher
Carol Solberg	33	White/Jewish	Middle	Activist
Laura Stone	41	White/Jewish	Middle	Therapist
Robin Ward	40	White	Middle	Programmer
		Post–Baby Boom Cohort		
Name (Pseudonym)	Age	Race/Ethnicity	Class Background (In 1990)	Occupation
Ann Carlson	19	Mixed	Working	Student
Jill Dinkins	28	White	Middle	Social services
Laurie Gambone	28	White	Middle	Administrator
Lucia Hicks	24	African American	Working	Student

TABLE 1. *(continued)*

Name (Pseudonym)	Age (In 1990)	Race/Ethnicity	Class Background	Occupation
Joan Jesky	19	White	Working	Student
Carla Jimenez	26	Latina	Working	Social services
Sarah Margolis	19	White	Middle	Student
Judy Thomas	25	White	Upper	Editor
Karen Turley	29	White	Working	Nurse
Cindy Yerkovich	22	White	Middle	Student

ments in New York, Washington, D.C., Boston, San Francisco, and Los Angeles are played out later and on a smaller scale. In that sense, Columbus both reflects national trends and typifies smaller communities that have been less studied by feminist scholars."[15] Debates about lesbianism—for example, the explosive "sex debates" that erupted in the early 1980s in San Francisco and New York around pornography, sadomasochism, and other marginalized sexualities—have, over the past several years, found their way into regional music festivals, homegrown periodicals, and less cosmopolitan areas.

In short, the reader should approach this book keeping in mind the historical, cultural, and geographic context in which it was researched and written. We must remember that all social science research is partial, tentative, and evolving.

Sample Interview "Schedule"

A. Background Information
   Age
   Marital status
   Education
   Religious/ethnic background
   Occupation
   Father's occupation; education
   Mother's occupation; education
B. Sexual Identity
1. How would you describe your sexual identity?
2. What does that word mean to you?
3. Have you always been a lesbian?
4. When did you come to call yourself that?

5. What was it like for you to come out?
6. Can you recall what your earliest feelings about lesbianism were?
7. What was your knowledge of lesbianism before you came out?
   –did you know any lesbians?
   –what were your images of lesbianism before?
8. Why do you think you are a lesbian?
9. How important do you think your lesbianism is to the way you see the world? Has that changed over time?
10. Is being a lesbian a political act for you? Has it ever been?
11. Is being a lesbian a choice for you?
12. Do you think that all women are potential lesbians?
13. Have you ever doubted your lesbianism?
14. Have you ever been involved with men sexually?
15. Would you say that you have found men attractive?
16. Would you say that you have ever been in a fulfilling relationship with a man? Could you imagine being in one in the future?
17. If you could rate yourself on Kinsey scale, where 1 is completely homosexual and 6 is completely heterosexual, where would you place yourself in terms of sexual attractions?
18. According to that same scale, where would you place yourself in terms of actual sexual experience?
19. Do your sexual attractions/interests vary over time?
20. Can one be a lesbian and still sleep with men?
21. How do you feel about bisexuality?
22. Do you tend to be attracted to women who are like you? Unlike you? In what ways?
23. What does the term *butch-femme* mean to you?
24. Do you identify as either butch or femme? On a scale of 1 to 6, where 1 is butch and 6 is femme, where would you place yourself?
25. Are you involved in a relationship now? If so, for how long?
26. Do your feelings about your lesbian identity change when you're in a relationship?
27. Would you say that you are part of a lesbian community?
28. If so, what does that community look like?
29. How has that community changed over time?
30. Are you out to all significant persons in your life?
31. If not, who are you not out to?
32. Would you say that you identify with all lesbians (bisexuals)?
33. What do you share with them in common?
34. Do you know many older lesbians? Do they seem at all different from you and your friends? How so?

35. Do you know many younger lesbians? Do they seem at all different from you and your friends? How so?
36. Do you see yourself as a "typical" lesbian?
37. Would you say that your sense of your lesbianism has changed over time? If so, how has it changed?

Notes

Introduction

1. Raymond 1989, 149. In a similar vein, see Jeffreys 1994.
2. Yvonne Zylan, letter to the editor, *Out/Look,* Spring 1990, p. 4.
3. Barbara Ehrenreich, quoted by Echols 1989, 281.
4. See, for example, Rubin 1984; Phelan 1989.
5. Though the term "identity" has come into general use only recently, it has been used by sociologists since the 1920s. For an overview of the social science literature on identity, see Weigert, Teitge, and Teitge 1986. On the reflexive character of identity under modernity, see Giddens 1991. Identity is rooted in "identification," defined as "an attitude in which a person experiences what happens to another person as if it had happened to himself" (R. Turner 1970, 66). In this book, I use the term *identity* to refer to a socialized sense of individuality, an internal organization of self-perceptions concerning one's relationship to social categories, that also incorporates views of the self perceived to be held by others.

To understand the differences that exist "within" homosexual identities, it may be necessary to draw some conceptual distinctions. Steven Epstein defines the term *sexual orientation* as what psychoanalysts have traditionally called "object choice," namely whether the gender of one's partner (or one's fantasized partner) is the same as, or different from, one's own. Beyond this, sexual preference/orientation can be extended to include other characteristics (physical, emotional, behavioral) that one consistently feels compelled to seek in a partner. Epstein draws a distinction between sexual orientation/preference and two related concepts: the first is *sexual identity* (the conscious identification of self with social sexual typologies, or the failure to do so). In modern Western societies, this means the adoption (or nonadoption)

of labels such as homosexual, gay, lesbian, heterosexual, bisexual, exhibition-
ist, sadomasochist, and so on. These self-identifications might or might not
correspond to sexual preference/orientation; for example, a woman might
consistently have fantasies about, or sex with, other women and still consider
herself to be a heterosexual. The second concept is *erotic role identity*,
which includes "what you like to do": for example, "active" and "passive"
roles, or various sexual practices that have been consolidated into one's sexual routines (Epstein 1991, 827–28). This typology suggests that (1) sexual
orientation/preference, (2) erotic role identities, and (3) sexual self-
identifications are relatively autonomous characteristics and processes that
may or may not vary together, distinctions that can help us to make sense of
the differences *within* lesbian identities.

6. Simon and Gagnon 1987, 371.

7. Bauman 1991; Plummer 1995; Giddens 1991. The portrait of the dis-
ciplinary and regulatory society painted by Foucault 1978 may understate
these reflexive elements.

8. On the problem of obtaining representative samples of lesbians and
gay men, see Weston 1991.

9. Weston 1991.

10. See Whisman 1996.

11. Denzin 1989 gives as an example of a self story the comments of a
recovering alcoholic on his "using days." In contrast to self stories, "life stories" examine a life, or a segment of a life, as reported by the individual
in question. Personal experience narratives are more likely to be based on
anecdotal, everyday, commonplace experiences, while self stories involve
pivotal, often critical life experiences. Plummer 1983 calls this the "limited
life document" because it does not aim to grasp the fullness of a person's
life but instead confronts a particular issue (108).

12. Denzin 1989, 73.

13. Gagnon and Simon 1973; Weeks 1985.

14. David Gelman, "Born or Bred?" *Newsweek*, February 24, 1992, 46–
53. See LeVay 1993, the latest in a century-long obsession with linking homosexuality with particular genes and chromosomes.

15. For social psychological literature on "coming out" as lesbian and
gay, see Coleman 1981–82; Gramick 1984; Cass 1979.

16. Berger and Luckmann 1966, 181.

17. There is a growing tradition of research on the anthropology of homosexualities. For a review of the relevant literature, see Weston 1993b.

18. Kinsey, Pomeroy, and Martin 1948.

19. Bell and Weinberg 1978.

20. The earliest "constructionist" studies were conducted by young

American and British radical scholars who challenged the very categories in question, locating "deviance"—not deviants—within frameworks of power. At around the same time, sociologists William Simon and John Gagnon (1967) began to bring matters of meaning, gender, and social organization to the fore. Important later studies in this tradition include Warren 1974 and Plummer 1975.

21. See, for example, Smith-Rosenberg 1975; Faderman 1981.

22. An important early study of lesbians also placed gender at the center of analysis (Simon and Gagnon 1967).

23. Krieger 1982, 227.

24. Richardson 1984, 83.

25. Krieger 1982, 225.

26. See, for example, Kennedy and Davis 1993; Newton 1993; Bérubé 1990; D'Emilio 1983. For a collection of important historical essays whose topics span several centuries and continents, see Duberman, Vicinus, and Chauncey 1989.

27. Katz 1976, 7.

28. On the relationship between individual development and social events, see Mannheim [1928] 1952; Stewart 1994. On the relationship between cohort and sexual identity, see Herdt 1992.

29. See Evans 1979; Echols 1989; Taylor and Whittier 1992.

30. Mannheim [1928] 1952 is the seminal work on the generational concept. Beth Schneider has applied the concept of "political generations" to feminism (1988).

31. A "decisive generation" is one that "for the first time thinks new thoughts with full clarity and with complete possession of their meaning, a generation that is neither still a precursor nor any longer bound by the past" (Marias 1968, 100).

32. On the problems of periodization and of writing feminist "history," see King 1994.

33. See, for example, Fuss 1991; de Lauretis 1991; Lorde 1984.

34. On butch-femme roles and "lesbian gender" before the 1960s, see Nestle 1987, 1992; Kennedy and Davis 1993. On the recent resurgence of butch and femme, see Stein 1992a; Weston 1993. For theoretical analyses of lesbian "gender," see Butler 1990, 1991; Rubin 1992.

35. Ponse 1978. B. Vance and Green 1984 interviewed forty-three self-identified lesbians and found that age of first homosexual experience was key in separating "exclusive" and "bisexual" lesbians. Those who engaged in homosexuality before age seventeen were more sexually active at an early age, saw themselves as having more stereotypic masculine traits, and were exclusively homosexual. Those who did not engage in same-sex relations

until after age twenty, and who were heterosexually involved before, were more likely to engage in more bisexual activity.

36. Burch 1993 draws upon these distinctions to suggest that the pairing of women with these differing sexual histories is common. She speculates that lesbians with different sexual histories see things differently and, at the same time, project their fantasies, fears, and desires onto each other, so entering into an eroticized identification with one another. Lesbian relationships are pursued unconsciously through these fantasies, through projective identifications, as each tries on the other's experiences.

The "bisexual" (or "elective") lesbian may actively question her lover about her relationships with other women, about early lesbian experiences, about the world of lesbians. The "primary" lesbian, in turn, might inquire about her partner's past experiences with men. The lifelong lesbian seeks a greater understanding of women's sexual and emotional intimacy with men; the elective lesbian is attempting to understand the sense of self of a woman attracted exclusively to other women.

37. Kennedy and Davis 1993, 326.

38. Kennedy and Davis 1993, 336.

39. A notable exception is Krieger 1983, who utilized object relations psychoanalytic theory to study the "dilemmas of identity" in a lesbian community. Yet Krieger may understate the extent to which individuals resist collective identifications.

40. Hewitt 1989, 179. Plath 1980 uses the term "perduring self-images" to refer to the "sense of self one uses as major guides by which one steers one's personal course" (15). They are, he says, the core images of self that hold together a person's portfolio of identities, persisting from one interaction to the next (223). Often these early impressions are reinforced by "significant others," by families, friends, and lovers, who tend to have an investment in the longer-run "preservations" of that self. For a similar argument in relation to gender, see Chodorow 1994.

Chapter One

1. Nagel 1994, 152–76. See also J. Gerson and Peiss 1985. On the power of naming and the importance of symbolic struggles, see Bourdieu 1991; 1987, 13. See also Sandra Harding's (1990) discussion of epistemologies as "justificatory strategies."

2. As Giddens 1984 suggests, "experts" help create social groups that, in turn, develop a radical skepticism toward the institutional discourses that created them.

3. On social movements' framing practices, see Snow and Benford 1988. On the importance of cultural representations to "new social movements," see Melucci 1989.

4. Breines 1992, 87.

5. Breines 1992, 87; May 1988, 136; Ehrenreich and English 1978, 217–22.

6. Writing in the years before Stonewall, Mary McIntosh (1968) applied labeling theory to the "homosexual role." Earlier, K. Erikson 1964 understood deviance to be a definer of norms. The deviant is "the other" against which the norm is measured and determined. For a historical argument about the parallels between lesbians and prostitutes in the postwar era, see Penn 1994.

7. See Chauncey 1982, 118.

8. Chauncey 1982, 143–44. On the medicalization of lesbianism, also see Faderman 1981; Terry 1991; Newton 1984.

9. Though Freud recognized human sexual variation as somewhat benign, he believed nonetheless that lesbianism represented an "oedipal failure," which was attributed variously to fixation on the mother, presence of some congenital factor, narcissism and castration anxiety, or failure to resolve a "masculinity complex." After his death, Freud's American followers succeeded in establishing the view that homosexuality was a psychopathology. See Caprio 1954, 303–7; cited by Penn 1994, 367. See also Freedman 1987, also cited by Penn. For a generally sympathetic portrait of Freud's thinking on homosexuality, see Abelove 1993.

10. For a history of this period, see D'Emilio 1983.

11. Penn 1994, 359.

12. Martha Shelley, interview by author, 1990.

13. See Kennedy and Davis 1993.

14. Bérubé 1990; Kennedy and Davis 1993.

15. Faderman 1991; Lorde 1982; Duberman, Vicinus, and Chauncey 1989; Newton 1993.

16. Lorde 1982, 225.

17. Martha Shelley, interview.

18. Nestle 1987, 104.

19. Nestle 1981.

20. Ann Bannon's novels have been republished by Naiad Press.

21. Nestle 1981, 21–22.

22. Feinberg 1993; Kennedy and Davis 1993.

23. However, Esterberg 1990 notes that in 1960, several women wrote to the lesbian publication *The Ladder* that they were lesbians by choice and, at least in part, as a response to male domination (71–72). Furthermore,

there have always been women who have had sexual/emotional relationships with other women without calling themselves lesbians.

24. Martha Shelley, interview.

25. Sociologists of Jewish ethnicity draw a similar distinction between a "core" and "enlarged" Jewish population. The "core" consists of people who consider themselves Jewish, while the "enlarged population" include also people who previously considered themselves Jewish, other persons of recent Jewish descent, and non-Jewish household members associated with any of these categories. In other words, the boundaries around the group of people called "Jews" are highly variable, subject to fluctuation, and can be defined in a narrow or a loose sense. See DellaPergola 1994.

26. J. Johnston 1973, 58.

27. Shelley [1969] 1970, 310.

28. For accounts of the Stonewall rebellion, see Duberman 1993; Adam 1987. The rebellion was partially rooted in the civil rights struggles of the early civil rights groups, the Mattachine Society, and the Daughters of Bilitis (D'Emilio 1983). McAdam 1994 points to the civil rights movement as providing the "master protest frame" that was appropriated by the women's liberation, gay rights, American Indian, and other movements of the late 1960s and early 1970s. On the centrality of the notion of "ethnicity" in lesbian/gay movement politics, see Epstein 1987.

29. Weitz 1984 argues that lesbian feminists were able to become "radical deviants" once the feminist movement enabled them to define their behavior as consciously chosen. According to D'Emilio 1983, one of the great contributions of the movement was to construct a culture that transcended sexuality.

30. "Notes of an 'Old Gay,'" 53. Anonymous author. Mimeograph from the private collection of Ruth Mahaney, San Francisco.

31. Wittman [1970] 1972.

32. The social science literature on lesbianism reflected this intellectual shift: etiology, or explanation of the "causes" of homosexuality, ceased to dominate the discussion, replaced by studies of behaviors and perceptions of experience (Krieger 1982). See also Stein and Plummer 1994.

33. Faderman 1991, 201.

34. Phelps 1976, 161. See also the discussion of the early women's liberation groups—Cell 16, the Feminists, and Redstockings—in Echols 1989.

35. Shelley [1969] 1970, 307.

36. Shelley [1969] 1970, 307.

37. On the splits among liberal feminists regarding the issue of lesbi-

anism in the movement, see Abbott and Love 1972; Jay and Young 1979; Myron and Bunch 1975; Gornick 1978.

38. Radicalesbians [1970] 1988, 21.

39. Radicalesbians [1970] 1988, 18.

40. Radicalesbians [1970] 1988, 18.

41. Abbott and Love 1972, 124.

42. "A Lesbian Feminist Statement," *The Other Woman* (Toronto), September–October 1973, p. 25.

43. Brown 1976, 76.

44. Quoted by Charlotte Bunch, "Learning from Lesbian Separatism," *Ms.*, November 1976, p. 61.

45. Grahn 1970.

46. A. Rich 1980, 648.

47. Sedgwick 1990, 36. Earlier, a tension between two conceptions of gender was often evident. The first saw lesbians as the embodiment of the androgynous ideal of a world without gender. In the late 1960s and early 1970s, "androgyny" was the cultural ideal. Feminists minimized the difference between women and men, and embraced an antinatalist, antihousewifery politics that placed lesbians in a "cross-gender" position (see Abbott and Love 1972, 173). But with time, lesbians became the embodiment of a redefined femininity.

48. Echols 1989, 239.

49. On female bonding as nascent lesbianism, see Faderman 1981; Smith-Rosenberg 1975.

50. Faderman 1991 draws a distinction between "essentialist" and "existentialist" lesbians.

51. Laporte 1976, 218. See also "Notes of an 'Old Gay.'"

52. Brown [1973] 1988, 155–56. Describing the impact of the new political definitions upon lesbian novelists of the 1970s, such as Brown, Zimmerman 1990 writes that they are "much more likely to propose the born-again or elective model" and to "reject the 'born-lesbian' argument—at least in public" (54).

53. Ponse 1978, 162.

54. See, for example, Phelan 1989.

55. Faderman 1991, 207.

56. "Notes of an 'Old Gay.'"

57. "Notes of an 'Old Gay.'"

58. Joanne Cordova, "Ticket to Lesbos: Who Qualifies?" *Lesbian Tide*, May–June 1978, p.19.

59. Sidney Abbott, "Lesbians and the Women's Movement," in Vida 1978.

60. Robin Morgan, "Lesbianism and Feminism: Synonyms or Contradictions?" *Amazon Quarterly,* May 1973, p. 19.

61. Brown 1976, 114.

62. On political lesbians, see Gay Revolutionary Party Women's Caucus [1972] 1977.

63. Martha Shelley, interview.

64. Debbie Lempke, "Gay and Proud," *Berkeley Women's Music Collective,* 1976, Olivia Records HAB1.B1.

65. Rita Goldberger, "On Straight-Gay Dialogue," *Lesbian Tide,* March 1972, p. 5.

66. See Kennedy and Davis 1993, chap. 8.

67. Abbott and Love 1972, 153. For a later examination of the problems of subsuming lesbianism into feminism, see MacCowan 1984.

Chapter Two

1. Plummer 1981 calls the dominant account the "orientation" model and the emergent account the "identity construct" model. They have also been referred to as "essentialist" and "constructionist" conceptions.

2. In its most radical form, the discourse of coming out suggested that all women were "naturally" lesbians who had become alienated from their authentic selves through a process of gender/sexual socialization that operated in the service of compulsory heterosexuality. A milder version suggested that many more women were "potential" lesbians, but that the taint of stigma kept the numbers of self-identified lesbians artificially low.

3. Many of my interviewees spoke about their lives in terms that sharply divided the period "before I came out" from that "after I came out," conveying the impression that coming out was a signal event. This event featured an epiphany or "defining moment" that altered the individual and allowed her to see the world differently, changing the fundamental structures of meaning in her life. See Denzin 1989 for a discussion of the role of the "epiphany" in a self story.

4. On the coming out narrative in lesbian fiction, see Zimmerman 1990. For an examination of the notion of the closet, see Sedgwick 1990; for the foundational sociological study of stigma, deviance, and identity "management," see Goffman 1963.

5. I am certainly not the first to note variations among women who self-identify as lesbian. See Ponse 1978; Faderman 1991; B. Vance and Green 1984. Here I have refrained from labeling different "types" to avoid reifying them.

6. Zemsky 1991 cites studies indicating that the mean age at which women recognize and pronounce (at least to themselves) that this sense of difference and disquiet has something to do with lesbianism is approximately fourteen. See also Tolman 1991. Herdt and Boxer 1993 found a disparity between male and female homosexual experiences. For males, first homoerotic sex typically preceded first heteroerotic sex. For girls, however, the average age of same-sex experience is later than the average age of first sex with a male.

7. For a sense of how dominant cultural norms shaped the lives of teenage girls in the 1950s, and how girls resisted these norms, see Breines 1992.

8. A. Rich 1980 and Kitzinger 1987 question whether lesbianism can ever really be a free "choice" or individual sexual "preference" under a system of normative heterosexuality.

9. Faderman 1981, 18.

10. As Weston 1991 suggests in a similar context, "To treat each individual as a representative of his or her race, for example, would be a form of tokenism that glosses over the differences of gender, class, age, national origin, language, religion, and ability which crosscut race and ethnicity" (11).

11. The historical moment shaping the culture when key transitional points occur is what Karl Mannheim [1928] 1952 calls "fresh contact" (148).

12. See Ann Swidler's (1986) conception of culture as a toolbox.

13. This term is R. W. Connell's (1987).

14. Plummer 1975, 148.

15. In this sense, I depart from the tradition of interactionist studies exemplified by Ponse 1978, in which the role of bodily experience is discounted. See Herdt and Boxer 1993 for a fuller explanation of the interplay between cultural and developmental factors in the sexual development of gay youth. During postpuberty, social desires and adjustments match social selves to real-life worlds, a process that is heavily influenced by social norms and cultural symbols and concepts, such as the relative invisibility or accessibility of homosexual persons or cultures.

16. My interviews suggest that stereotypic "butch" or more masculine-identified lesbians were less likely to see their sexual identities as being chosen than were feminine-identified women, though most of the women I interviewed refused such labels as "butch" and "femme." The reasons for this are unclear. Is it because "mannish" lesbians were more "essentially" lesbian in orientation? Or is it because butches were the most identifiable lesbian figures since they stood out, often from an early age, and were more apt to be called lesbian by family members and other authority figures?

17. Burch 1993, 121.

18. Lancaster 1992, 270. This claim is now being contested by a new wave of genetic and other biological explanations for homosexuality, most notably by LeVay 1993.

19. Biddy Martin, quoted in Jay and Glasgow 1990, 6.

Chapter Three

1. Recent literature has argued that emotional experience, including the physiological, is essential to the authenticating process as a clue to self-knowledge/self-identity (see Ellis 1991). This emotional experience was often linked to physiological sexual response, a relationship that is difficult to ascertain from my interviews, but one worth probing in a future study.

2. Zimmerman 1990, 34–75.

3. Phelan 1993, 774. For Butler 1991, the performance of sexuality, like the performance of gender, is an act of resistance waged by actors who are situated to see through the illusion of gender and sexuality as coherent, core identities. See also Fuss 1991. For a cogent, grounded critique of performative theory, see Weston 1993a. For an earlier, seminal treatment of identity work undertaken by an "intersexed" person, see Garfinkel 1967.

4. Ponse 1978, 91.

5. Goffman 1959 distinguishes between use of symbols to denote prestige and stigma. A prestige symbol serves to "establish a special claim to prestige, honor, or desirable class position," while a stigma symbol "draw[s] atttention to a debasing identity discrepancy" (43–44). But a symbol that denotes stigma to society at large may well serve as a prestige symbol within a subculture. Such a symbol "adds another layer of complexity to the act of managing information in self-presentation" (Kraus 1990, 4).

6. Here "the actor does not try to seem happy or sad but rather expresses spontaneously" (Hochschild 1983, 35).

7. Hochschild 1992; quoted in Kraus 1990, 4–8.

8. Plummer 1995 situates the confessional mode of sexual storytelling in late modernity. The coming out story is one among many types of sexual stories that have come to be told in the late modern world.

9. Popkin 1979, 212.

10. Abbott and Love 1972, 223.

11. Esther Newton, quoted in Abbott and Love 1972, 218.

12. For examples of this "development myth," see Stanley and Wolfe 1980. For a critical review of this literature, see Zimmerman 1990. On the importance of authenticity and expressive individualism in American culture, see Bellah et al. 1985.

13. Hewitt 1989, 167.

14. Butler 1991, 18.

15. Ponse 1978, 125.

16. Berger and Luckmann 1967; Ponse 1978.

17. *Lesbian Connection,* September 1975, p. 4.

18. Epstein 1991.

19. Ponse 1978.

20. Gagnon and Simon 1973 conceptualized the "sexual script" as a counterpoint to "drive theory," suggesting that sexual behavior is, for the most part, a simple, everyday occurrence that is constructed from variable social motives and settings. Also see Plummer 1982.

21. *Lesbian Connection,* June–July 1984, p. 15.

22. *Lesbian Connection,* August–September 1984, p. 11.

23. See Segal 1983.

24. *Lesbian Connection,* August–September 1984, p. 11.

25. Toder 1978, 96.

26. Ponse 1978, 184.

27. Ponse 1978, 189–92.

28. Risman and Schwartz 1988 suggest that lesbians' "transformation of sexual orientation to suit political beliefs deserves more analytical attention" (138).

29. Nestle 1992, 14–15.

30. Nestle 1981, 21.

31. D. Gerson 1995, 3.

32. Abbott and Love 1972, 173.

33. Abbott and Love 1972, 35–36.

34. Connell 1987.

35. On subcultural style as resistance, and punk subcultures in particular, see Hebdige 1988.

36. As D. Gerson 1995 notes, what was burned "was not the literal bra but the social bra, the political bra; the brassiere as symbol and practice of the exploited breast, the controlled breast, the subordinated, domesticated, playboy breast, the imperfect if not perfect breast, the man's breast" (18–19).

37. Wolf 1980, 85–86.

38. Stein 1992a.

39. Rubin 1992, 468.

40. See Lorde 1984 for a holistic definition of lesbian eroticism.

41. Reback and Loulan 1988, i. In a positive assessment of this dynamic, they have written of the significance of these differences in relation to a first lesbian experience.

42. This complementarity, according to Burch 1993, may be pursued

unconsciously through these fantasies, through projective identifications. The lifelong lesbian seeks a greater understanding of women's sexual and emotional intimacy with men; the elective lesbian is attempting to understand the sense of self of a woman attracted exclusively to other women. Such claims, rooted in unconscious desires, are difficult if not impossible to verify, but they do convey a sense of why these sorts of differences appear to be a consistent feature of many lesbian relationships, and why they appear to play an important role in the "deep identity work" undertaken by "elective" lesbians.

43. Lindenbaum 1985, 88. Also see Burch 1987.
44. On the "paradox of performativity," see Butler 1993, 241.
45. Hochschild 1983, 36.
46. Weston 1993a, 13.

Chapter Four

1. E. Erikson 1959, 102, 89. See also Habermas 1979, 85.
2. Plummer 1975.
3. Kanter 1972, 65.
4. This example is not meant to present ethnic identities as more "natural"; but because ethnic identifications are learned in the family, they tend to be associated with a greater sense of permanence and tradition.
5. Havelock Ellis is quoted by Whisman 1996, 28. See also Chauncey 1982.
6. The term "intermittent lesbians" is used by Leila Rupp, in Rupp 1989.
7. Whisman 1996. See also Kennedy and Davis 1993.
8. On these differences among lesbians, see Ponse 1978; Burch 1993.
9. Burch 1993.
10. Hewitt 1989, 77.
11. Quoted in Brody 1985, 13.
12. Brody 1985, 51.
13. *Lavender Woman,* June 1974, p. 2.
14. D. Cartier, "A Dyke's Manifesto," *Lesbian Tide,* February 1973, p. 13.
15. Old gays' use of the term "queer" should be distinguished from the term's contemporary uses by a younger generation, whose members appear to be more self-consciously political and to be motivated by a "reverse affirmation" of queer as a marginal, despised category.
16. Jeanne Cordova, "What's a Woman to Do?" *Lesbian Tide,* April 1974, p. 10.
17. Berger and Kellner 1964, 180.

18. Giddens 1991, 92.

19. Rosalie Nichols, "Defining Lesbianism," *Lesbian Voices,* Winter 1975–76, p. 6.

20. Mimi Brown, "Is a Lesbian Born or Made?" *Leaping Lesbian,* June 1977, pp. 4–5.

21. Rubin 1992, 467.

22. Kennedy and Davis 1993.

23. Ponse 1978.

24. Jeanne Cordova, "Radical Feminism? Dyke Separatism?" *Lesbian Tide,* May–June 1973, p. 27.

25. Ann Forfreedom, "Lesbos Arise!" *Lesbian Tide,* May–June 1973, p. 5.

26. Echols 1989, 6.

27. They were inspired by influential books such as Adrienne Rich's *Of Woman Born* (1976), Nancy Chodorow's *Reproduction of Mothering* (1978), and Carol Gilligan's *In a Different Voice* (1982), which sparked reassessments of traditional female cultures.

28. See A. Rich 1980. In this sense, cultural feminism may be an archetypal "new" social movement. In many "new" social movements, the purposive and expressive disclosure of one's subjective feelings, desires, and experiences—or identity—to others, whether verbally or through the embrace of a common lifestyle and worldview, is taken as equivalent to collective action (Melucci 1989).

29. On the relationship between cultural feminism and feminist institution building, see Echols 1989.

30. Bourdieu 1991. For a survey of the different institutional and cultural components of lesbian feminism, see Taylor and Whittier 1992.

31. Holly Near is quoted in Gaar 1992, 154.

32. Karen Durbin, "Can a Feminist Love the World's Greatest Rock and Roll Band?" *Ms.,* October 1974, pp. 24–27.

33. In the late 1970s, a latin rock album by the band Be Be K'Roche and albums by Black artists Mary Watkins and Linda Tillery sold little; a 1978 tour, "The Varied Voices of Black Women," featuring Tillery, Watkins, and poets Pat Parker and Gwen Avery, was sparsely attended.

34. On lesbian community, see Wolf 1980; Krieger 1983; Julia Penelope, "Lesbian Relationships and the Vision of Community," *Feminary,* 1978, p. 5; Taylor and Rupp 1993. For critiques of this model of community, see Young 1990; Phelan 1989.

35. Alison Bechdel is quoted in Udis-Kessler 1990, 1.

36. Megan Adams, "Thoughts on Separatism and Lesbian Identity," *Leaping Lesbian,* Spring 1979, p. 5.

37. J. Johnston 1973.

38. Adams, "Thoughts on Separatism and Lesbian Identity," p. 5.

39. Charlotte Bunch, "Learning from Lesbian Separatism," *Ms.*, November 1976, p. 60.

40. Bunch, "Learning from Lesbian Separatism," p. 100. In a much-quoted historical argument in favor of separatism as strategy, Freedman 1979 invokes the experiences of the first wave of feminists. She argues that separatism emerged from women's private networks in the culture in the nineteenth century and helped build a base for women's entry into the public, political sphere in the twentieth century. The decline of feminism after 1920 may be attributed in part to the decline of separatist politics, a lesson that, Freedman suggests, "may be crucial for the women's movement today" (524).

41. As V. Turner 1969 suggests, all rites of passage or transition are marked by three phases: separation, margin (or limen), and aggregation. The first phase of separation comprises symbolic behavior signifying the detachment of the individual or group from an earlier fixed point in the social structure.

42. "A rigid assertion of difference," Nancy Chodorow has argued with respect to gender, "reflects a defensive need to separate: it stems from anxieties about one's sense of self that are manifested in a refusal to recognize the other also as a self—as an active subject" ("Gender, Relation, and Difference, in Psychoanalytic Perspective," in Chodorow 1989, 110). In this psychodynamic view, essentialist constructions of identity, which draw rigid boundaries between the straight and gay worlds, are the product of inadequate individuation. Individuals who feel secure in their sense of self are less likely to feel the need to assert their individuality by separating from others. In contrast, rigid, essentialist constructions of lesbian identity, in both an individual and collective sense, are a defensive reaction, a compensation for the failure to individuate and to be recognized by others.

43. On essentialism as a strategy of legitimation, see Fuss 1989; Harding 1990.

44. Penelope 1988, 510. For an analysis of lesbian separatism that places it at the core of lesbian feminist activism, see Frye [1978] 1993.

45. Nichols, "Defining Lesbianism," p. 5.

46. Echols 1989, 65.

47. One could argue that separatism broadly defined—the tendency to form groups based on likeness—is an impulse that lies at the very heart of American culture: Fitzgerald 1986; Varenne 1977. See also Bourdieu 1991; Taylor and Whittier 1992, 11.

48. At "Twenty Years After," a lesbian separatist forum in Oakland, California, that I attended in March 1989, many of the themes of separatist

politics were still in evidence: the lament that separatists were an embattled minority among lesbian feminists and were the only truly committed lesbians, along with radically essentialist conceptions of gender that vilified men. "Pricks have privilege when they're born," one woman proclaimed, to a sea of affirmative nods. Indeed, it seemed, paradoxically, that men were the primary topic of discussion.

49. Melucci 1989, 209, xv. Phelan 1989 makes a similar argument. Women of color were also very vocal critics of separatism and cultural feminism on the grounds that it failed to acknowledge crosscutting allegiances and loyalties. See, for example, Audre Lorde's "Letter to Mary Daly" in Lorde 1984, 66–71.

50. Quoted in Abbott and Love 1972, 124.

51. For this insight I am grateful to Elizabeth Lapovsky Kennedy.

52. On the emergence of an "ethnic" model of homosexuality among lesbians and gay men, see Epstein 1987.

53. Epstein 1987, 254.

Chapter Five

1. Abbott and Love 1972, 232.

2. Miller 1989, 108.

3. Plummer 1975 calls this the "subculturation" phase.

4. For a chronology of the feminist "sex debates," see R. Rich 1986; C. Vance 1984; Phelan 1989.

5. Susie Bright, interview by author, October 1989.

6. See Rubin 1984; English, Hollibaugh, and Rubin 1981; Nestle 1981; Cindy Patton, "Brave New Lesbians," *Village Voice,* 2 July 1985, pp. 23–25.

7. "The Combahee River Collective Statement" [1974] 1994, 29–30.

8. Preface, Moraga and Anzaldúa 1981, xiv.

9. Another early anthology that collected critiques of lesbian/feminist identity politics by women of color was Smith 1983. Beck 1982 made a similar argument about lesbian feminism and Jewish ethnicity. For a more recent analysis of race/ethnicity and the limitations of lesbian identity politics, see L. Hall 1993.

10. Ponse 1978 uses the term "aristocratization" to describe the tendency within lesbian communities to idealize lesbian life.

11. Krieger 1983, xv.

12. On the problem of merger, see Lindenbaum 1985; Vargo 1987.

13. Bonnie Mann, "Validation or Liberation? A Critical Look at Therapy and the Women's Movement," *Trivia* 10 (Spring 1987), p. 45.

14. In 1981, there were only fourteen adult child of alcoholic groups

registered in the United States. In 1988, there were more than 1,100 such groups, which typically hold meetings once a week. In a parallel trend, Alcoholics Anonymous membership in 1988 reached 750,000, up from 550,000 in 1983. At the same time, dozens of groups came to apply the principles of Alcoholics Anonymous to other human problems—groups like Debtors Anonymous, Overeaters Anonymous, Sex and Love Addicts Anonymous, Cocaine Anonymous, Smokers Anonymous, Incest Survivors Anonymous, and Narcotics Anonymous (Lily Collett, "Step by Step: A Skeptic's Encounter with the Twelve-Step Program," *Utne Reader,* November–December 1988, pp. 69–76); see Herman 1988, 12.

15. "Woman Identified Woman" [1970] 1988, 21.

16. bell hooks, "On Self Recovery," in hooks 1989, 32.

17. For an example of how this language has permeated lesbian popular psychology, see Loulan 1987. My essay "The Year of the Lustful Lesbian" (Stein 1993b) attempts to contextualize this development.

18. Mann, "Validation or Liberation?" p. 45.

19. hooks 1989, 33.

20. Herman 1988, 18. For an analysis of the relationship of women to self-help culture, see Simonds 1992. For a more general critique of self-help culture, see Kaminer 1992.

21. Herman 1992, 12.

22. On the "lesbian baby boom," see Weston 1991; E. Lewin 1993. Also see Burke 1993; Pollack and Vaughn 1987.

23. Wolf 1980, 150–51.

24. E. Lewin 1993, 192.

25. From Penelope and Wolfe 1993, 3.

26. Audre Lorde, "Age, Race, Class, and Sex: Women Redefining Difference," in Lorde 1984, 120.

27. Hochschild 1989.

28. Blumstein and Schwartz 1983.

29. Blumstein and Schwartz 1983, 297. For a critique of lesbians' reluctance toward sex outside committed relationships, see Nichols 1987.

30. Rothblum and Brehony 1993, 4; Blumstein and Schwartz 1983; Loulan 1987.

31. Udis-Kessler 1990, 1.

32. Chodorow 1994, 38. Also see hooks 1984; Fuss 1989; Sedgwick 1990.

33. In the pages of *On Our Backs,* a lesbian porn magazine, pro-sex activist Susie Bright exhorted her readers to "start talking about *what we do* instead of who we supposedly *are.* Don't say 'I'm an s/m lesbian' when you could be saying, 'I fantasize about eating out my manicurist on the bathroom floor' " ("Toys for Us," *On Our Backs,* September–October 1989, p. 9). See Stein 1993b.

34. Advertisement in *San Francisco Bay Times,* August 1989, p. 21.

35. On the relationship of cultural feminism to feminist entrepreneurialism, see Echols 1989.

36. Raymond 1989; Lasch 1978. See also Jeffreys 1994. Echols 1989 is similarly critical of a retreat to "lifestyle," but she defines the term differently and locates its emergence in an earlier period. Hewitt 1989, 216, and Bellah et al. 1985 locate careerism, entrepreneurship, and the quest for celebrity and status, as well as some aspects of psychological self-realization and therapeutic culture, in the American middle classes.

37. For an analysis of 1960s radicals that draws similar conclusions, see Flacks and Whalen 1989.

38. On the shifting salience and situated character of identities, see Stryker 1987; Nancy Chodorow, "Seventies Questions for Thirties Women," in Chodorow 1989; M. Lewin 1976.

39. African American theorist W. E. B. Du Bois wrote of the "double consciousness" that shapes the experience of African Americans who live in two worlds: members of a marginalized racial group and members of the dominant culture. For a compelling recent reading of Du Bois's notion of double consciousness, see Gilroy 1993. For a related discussion in terms of lesbian feminist culture, see Lugones 1994.

40. Martin 1993, 282.

41. On lesbian feminist self-construction as a voyage of discovery, as reflected in fictional works, see Zimmerman 1990. For a critique of the politics of identity and community implicit in this model, see Young 1990.

42. Cf. Hewitt 1989, 216. What Goffman 1961 calls the "multiplicity of selves," Coser 1991 terms "role segmentation," which she defines as individuals' ability to "alter behavior according to the situational context and with a repertoire of alternatives that has been learned through multirelational synchronization" (21). For poststructuralist approaches to identity which resemble these, see de Lauretis 1990; Haraway [1985] 1991; Marcus 1992.

43. Taylor and Whittier 1992 find a greater degree of persistence of lesbian feminist community and culture through the 1980s. While I agree that reports of the death of lesbian feminism are greatly exaggerated, I place more emphasis on the shifting terrain of lesbian identities and cultures.

44. Wolfe 1991, 46

Chapter Six

1. Clausen 1990, 12. Singer-songwriter Holly Near is another important figure who has faced difficulties in conforming to the heterosexual/homosexual binary, as her autobiography, *Fire in the Rain* (1990), attests. Filmmaker Maria Maggenti, from a slightly younger cohort, is a recent example

of someone who publicly identifies as a lesbian but who is involved in a primary relationship with a man. In many respects her essay, "The Man I Love" (*Village Voice*, 27 June 1995, pp. 16–17), resembles Clausen's earlier article.

2. Tish Perlman, letter to the editor, *Out/Look*, Summer 1990, p. 78.

3. Yvonne Zylan, letter to the editor, *Out/Look*, Spring 1990, p. 4.

4. Vicinus 1989; Rupp 1989; Sahli 1979.

5. Kennedy and Davis 1993, 343.

6. Plummer 1975.

7. Ponse 1978, 185, notes that "a systematic study of the identity resolutions of women formerly identified as lesbian awaits another investigator."

8. Psychodynamic explanations rooted in object relations psychoanalysis suggest that lesbians, like women in general, are better suited to relationality than to sexual individualism. But there may also be an economic structural reason for lesbians' dating patterns. Gay male communities tend to be relatively wealthy, and their members have had more access to wealth and have invested more heavily in sex-related commerce—bars, clubs, and the like—than have lesbians.

9. Hillary Freeman, "Tears at the Wedding," *Guardian* (U.K.), 26 July 1994, p. 19.

10. Patricia Roth Schwartz, "On the Hasbian Phenomenon," *off our backs*, June 1989, p. 11.

11. Robyn Ochs, letter to the editor, *Out/Look*, Summer 1990, p. 78.

12. In an informal survey conducted among undergraduates, Carla Golden (1987) interviewed lesbians in their late twenties, thirties, and forties who described shifts in their thinking about the nature of their lesbianism. See also Kinsey, Pomeroy, and Martin 1948; Kinsey et al. 1953.

13. Ebaugh 1988, 1. However, like all stage theories (including those that focus on coming out) the "role exit" notion tends to overstate the extent to which the phenomenon is sequentially patterned and to understate the effect of cohort and individual influences.

14. Several years ago, in an undergraduate seminar on the sociology of sexuality at the University of California, Berkeley, I asked students to write a personal narrative about the formation of their sexual identities. The lesbian and bisexual students found the essay relatively easy to write, as they had struggled with their homosexuality and had access to the cultural template of the "coming out" story. But most of the heterosexual students had difficulty understanding the assignment, and a few were unable to complete it.

A small but growing number of heterosexual feminists are beginning to theorize heterosexuality as a social construction. See, for example, Chodorow 1994; Segal 1994; and many of the essays contained in Wilkinson and Kitzinger 1993. For a historical look at of the emergence of "heterosexuality," see Katz 1990.

15. As Hewitt 1989 points out, "social and personal identity are fundamentally different, and in some sense opposite modes of personal organization." While one is always conscious of oneself as an individual, as a separate person, "social identity becomes something of which the individual is conscious only when it is somewhat problematic" (17).

16. Despite the ostensible sameness of two women in love, differences among women were a salient part of many relationships, as I noted in chapter 4. Butch-femme role identification, sexual orientation, class, race, and ethnicity were all pervasive differences that were eroticized in lesbian relationships. At the same time, lesbian relationships tended to entail varying degrees of merger, as individual differences were muted and partners became similar to one another in various respects. Difference and sameness could each be seen as pleasurable or threatening, depending upon the particular experience of the individuals involved.

17. Ebaugh 1988 calls this "cuing behavior."

18. So Clausen 1990, 17: "I amuse myself by inventing ironic self-descriptions, metaphors for my non-identity: Stateless Person of the Sexual World. Tragic Mulatto of the Sexual World. Lesbian-Feminist Emeritus. Twilight Girl."

19. See Ara Wilson, "Just Add Water," *Out/Look,* Spring 1992, pp. 22–28.

20. Many leaders of an emerging bisexual movement are former lesbians. In addition, a growing number of women are publicly embracing both their bisexual and lesbian identities, sometimes calling themselves "bidykes." See Weise 1992; Hutchins and Kaahumanu 1990. Anecdotal evidence suggests that this may be particularly true among younger women.

21. Pauline Bart reports a similar finding, leading her to pronounce the "tenaciousness of lesbian identity"; see Bart 1993, 250.

22. A hallmark of much feminist research has been to "take women at their word," though in recent years this has been complicated by the turn to postmodern textual and linguistic analysis.

23. Golden 1987, 267.

24. Chodorow 1994, 37.

25. As Mannheim [1928] 1952 suggests, early impressions "tend to coalesce into a natural view of the world," in which later experiences come to be superimposed upon earlier ones (298).

26. Chodorow 1994, 72.

Chapter Seven

1. Rob Morse, editorial, *San Francisco Examiner,* 12 November 1991, p. A3. For similar trends in other cities, see Kelly Harmon and Cindy Kirschman, "Women Behind Bars: Lesbians Lock Horns over the Changing Generational Face of the Lesbian Bar Business," *Advocate,* 31 December 1991, pp. 36–38.

2. This derives from Stuart Hall's work on Black identities (1989).

3. Nancy Chodorow, "Seventies Questions for Thirties Women," in Chodorow 1989, 217.

4. In the early 1990s, a few women were able to "cross over" and achieve mainstream success as out lesbians, integrating their sexuality into their art without allowing it to become either *the* salient fact or else barely acknowledged. k. d. lang and Melissa Etheridge, who had previously coded their sexuality as "androgyny," came out as lesbians, to great fanfare within lesbian/gay circles and to even greater commercial success. On the phenomenon of the "crossover" artist in popular music, see my "Crossover Dreams: Lesbianism and Popular Music since the 1970s" (Stein 1994).

5. For a more detailed explanation of the political implications of this mainstreaming, see Stein 1994. On the recent commodification of lesbian culture, see Clark 1993.

6. For a longer version of this argument, see Stein 1992a.

7. On queer theory and politics, see Allan Bérubé and Jeffrey Escoffier, "Queer/Nation," *Outlook,* Winter 1991, pp. 12–14; Duggan 1992; Fuss 1991; Hark 1994.

8. Seidman 1993, 122.

9. Butler 1990.

10. Gamson 1995.

11. Phelan 1994, 153.

12. Seidman 1993, 133.

13. Warner 1991, 16.

14. On the checkered history of recent queer organizing, see Dan Levy, "Queer Nation in S.F. Suspends Activities," *San Francisco Chronicle,* 27 December 1991, p. 21; Michele DeRanleau, "How the Conscience of an Epidemic Unraveled," *San Francisco Examiner,* 1 October 1990, p. 24.

15. For a discussion of postfeminism that articulates this sense of continuity along with change, see Stacey 1990. As Mannheim [1928] 1952 suggests, the transition from one generation to another takes place continuously, through interaction between the two.

16. Martha Shelley, interview with author, 1990.

17. Weeks 1985, 186.

18. Barbara Ehrenreich, quoted in the *Guardian* (U.K.), 4 May 1993, p. 5. See also de Lauretis 1991.

19. Weeks 1985, 186.

20. Giddens 1991.

21. Bérubé and Escoffier, "Queer/Nation," p. 14.

22. Gamson 1995, 20.

23. Martin 1992, 100.

24. On recent right-wing challenges to lesbian/gay rights, see Patton 1993; S. Johnston 1994.

25. Cerullo 1987, 71.

26. This is close to Stuart Hall's (1989) conception. Similarly, North American feminists have drawn upon the vocabulary of poststructuralism to problematize any simple notion of the category "woman" or "woman's experience" as the point of departure for late-twentieth-century sexual politics. See, for example, Scott 1989; Butler 1990.

27. Phelan 1994, 11.

28. Zimmerman 1990, 210.

29. Phelan 1994. Perhaps what is needed, as Rust 1993 suggests, is a social constructionism that "allows for the possibility that individuals who are creating their identities will introduce their own goals" (71). Identity is here conceptualized as more open-ended and evolving, not as "what is, only what is becoming," and often as situational (Cass 1984, 120). Psychoanalytic support for this view is offered by Schafer 1973, who argues that "empirically self-sameness is usually a rather inconstant idea in that it can change markedly in content with a significant change in mood and circumstance" and that in part it changes because one views oneself and one's identity at different times, for different reasons, and from different vantage points (52); see also Lacan 1982, who restores to prominence the Freud who discovered the bisexuality and polymorphous perversity of children, emphasizing that repressed versions remain in the unconscious and constantly destabilize the ego's wish to keep these lost possibilities at bay.

Appendix

1. Plummer 1983, 123.

2. Collins 1990, 205.

3. On the modernization of sex research, see Robinson 1976. On the limitations of sexual science, see Weeks 1985; Irvine 1990.

4. Brake 1982, 23.

5. Plummer 1983, 136.

6. See, for example, Klein 1983; DuBois 1983; Reinharz 1983.

7. Klein 1983, 95. For a similar argument, see Oakley 1981; Edwards 1990; Ribbens 1989.

8. Krieger 1985.

9. Krieger 1985, 316.

10. On the method of "separating out," see Krieger 1985.

11. Ruth Frankenberg's book on the social construction of "whiteness" makes this argument (1993).

12. Riessman 1987. Just as consciously thinking about the interview as an interaction helped me situate myself in that process, it also helped me understand how at least in part my subjects constructed their narratives in relation to me, the interviewer. What my interviewees knew about me—about my lesbianism, my class background, my status as a graduate student and aspiring academic—undoubtedly influenced what they told me.

13. Whisman 1996.

14. Herman 1992.

15. Taylor and Rupp 1993, 41.

Bibliography

Abbott, Sidney. 1978. "Lesbians and the Women's Movement." In *Our Right to Love,* ed. Ginny Vida. Englewood Cliffs, N.J.: Prentice Hall.

Abbott, Sidney, and Barbara Love. 1972. *Sappho Was a Right-On Woman.* New York: Stein & Day.

Abelove, Henry. 1993. "Freud, Male Homosexuality, and the Americans." In *The Lesbian and Gay Studies Reader,* ed. Henry Abelove, Michele Barale, and David Halperin. New York: Routledge.

Abelove, Henry, Michele Barale, and David Halperin, eds. 1993. *The Lesbian and Gay Studies Reader.* New York: Routledge.

Adam, Barry D. 1987. *The Rise of a Gay and Lesbian Movement.* Boston: Twayne.

Bart, Pauline. 1993. "Protean Woman: The Liquidity of Female Sexuality and the Tenaciousness of Lesbian Identity." In *Heterosexuality: A Feminism and Psychology Reader,* ed. Sue Wilkinson and Celia Kitzinger. Newbury Park, Calif.: Sage.

Bauman, Zygmunt. 1991. *Modernity and Ambivalence.* Oxford: Polity.

Beck, Evelyn Torton, ed. 1982. *Nice Jewish Girls: A Lesbian Anthology.* Watertown, Mass.: Persephone.

Bell, Alan, and Martin Weinberg. 1978. *Homosexualities: A Study of Diversity among Men and Women.* New York: Simon & Schuster.

Bellah, Robert, et al. 1985. *Habits of the Heart: Individualism and Commitment in American Life.* Berkeley: University of California Press.

Berger, Peter, and Hansfried Kellner. 1964. "Marriage and the Social Construction of Reality: An Exercise in the Microsociology of Knowledge." *Diogenes* 46: 1–23.

Berger, Peter, and Thomas Luckmann. 1966. *The Social Construction of Reality: A Treatise in the Sociology of Knowledge.* New York: Anchor Books.

Berman, Marshall. 1974. *The Politics of Authenticity: Radical Individualism and the Emergence of Modern Society.* New York: Atheneum.

Bérubé, Allan. 1990. *Coming Out under Fire: A History of Gay Men and Women in World War II.* New York: Free Press.

Blumstein, Philip, and Pepper Schwartz. 1983. *American Couples: Money, Work, Sex.* New York: Morrow.

Boston Lesbian Psychologies Collective. 1987. *Lesbian Psychologies: Explorations and Challenges.* Urbana: University of Illinois Press.

Bourdieu, Pierre. 1987. "What Makes a Social Class? On the Theoretical and Practical Existence of Groups." *Berkeley Journal of Sociology* 43: 1–17.

Bourdieu, Pierre. 1991. *Language and Symbolic Power,* ed. John B. Thompson, trans. Gino Raymond and Matthew Adamson. Cambridge: Harvard University Press.

Brake, Mike, ed. 1982. *Human Sexual Relations.* New York: Pantheon.

Breines, Wini. 1992. *Young, White, and Miserable: Growing Up Female in the 1950s.* Boston: Beacon.

Brody, Michal. 1985. *Are We There Yet? A Continuing History of* Lavender Woman, *a Chicago Lesbian Newspaper, 1971–1976.* Iowa City: Aunt Lute.

Brown, Rita Mae. [1973] 1988. *Rubyfruit Jungle.* New York: Bantam.

Brown, Rita Mae. 1976. *A Plain Brown Rapper.* Oakland: Diana.

Burch, Beverly. 1987. "Barriers to Intimacy: Conflicts over Power, Dependency, and Nurturing in Lesbian Relationships." In *Lesbian Psychologies: Explorations and Challenges,* ed. Boston Lesbian Psychologies Collective. Urbana: University of Illinois Press.

Burch, Beverly. 1993. *On Intimate Terms.* Urbana: University of Illinois Press.

Burke, Phyllis. 1993. *Family Values: Two Moms and Their Son.* New York: Random House.

Butler, Judith. 1990. *Gender Trouble: Feminism and the Subversion of Identity.* New York: Routledge.

Butler, Judith. 1991. "Imitation and Gender Insubordination." In *Inside/Out: Lesbian Theories, Gay Theories,* ed. Diana Fuss. New York: Routledge.

Butler, Judith. 1993. *Bodies That Matter.* New York: Routledge.

Caprio, Frank. 1954. *Female Homosexuality: A Psychodynamic Study of Lesbianism.* New York: Citadel.

Cass, Vivienne. 1984. "Homosexual Identity Formation: Using a Theoretical Model." *Journal of Social Research* 20: 143–67.

Cerullo, Margaret. 1987. "Night Visions: Toward a Lesbian/Gay Politics for the Present." *Radical America* 21 (March–April): 67–71.

Chauncey, George. 1982. "From Sexual Inversion to Homosexuality: Medicine and the Changing Conceptualization of Female Deviance." *Salmagundi*, nos. 58–59: 114–46.

Chodorow, Nancy. 1978. *The Reproduction of Mothering: Psychoanalysis and the Sociology of Gender.* Berkeley: University of California Press.

Chodorow, Nancy. 1989. *Feminism and Psychoanalytic Theory.* New Haven: Yale University Press.

Chodorow, Nancy. 1994. *Femininities, Masculinities, Sexualities: Freud and Beyond.* Lexington: University Press of Kentucky.

Clark, Danae. 1993. "Commodity Lesbianism." In *The Lesbian and Gay Studies Reader,* ed. Henry Abelove, Michele Barale, and David Halperin. New York: Routledge.

Clausen, Jan. 1990. "My Interesting Condition." *Out/Look,* Winter, pp. 11–22.

Cluster, Dick, ed. 1979. *They Should Have Served That Cup of Coffee.* Boston: South End.

Coleman, Eli. 1981–82. "Developmental Stages of the Coming Out Process." *Journal of Homosexuality* 7(2–3): 31–43.

Collins, Patricia Hill. 1990. *Black Feminist Thought.* Boston: Unwin Hyman.

"The Combahee River Collective Statement." [1974] 1994. In *Theorizing Feminism: Parallel Trends in the Humanities and Social Sciences,* ed. Anne Herrmann and Abigail Stewart. Boulder: Westview.

Connell, R. W. 1987. *Gender and Power.* Stanford: Stanford University Press.

Coser, Rose. 1991. *In Defense of Modernity: Role Complexity and Individual Autonomy.* Stanford: Stanford University Press.

Creet, Julia. 1991. "Daughter of the Movement: The Psychodynamics of Lesbian S/M Fantasy." *differences* 3(2): 135–59.

DellaPergola, Sergio. 1994. "An Overview of the Demographic Trends of European Jewry." In *Jewish Identities in the New Europe,* ed. Jonathan Webber. London: Littman Library of Jewish Civilization.

de Lauretis, Teresa. 1990. "Eccentric Subjects: Feminist Theory and Historical Consciousness." *Feminist Studies* 16: 115–50.

de Lauretis, Teresa. 1991. "Queer Theory: Lesbian and Gay Sexualities." *differences* 3(2): iii–xviii.

D'Emilio, John. 1983. *Sexual Politics, Sexual Communities: The Making of a Homosexual Minority in the United States, 1940–70.* Chicago: University of Chicago Press.

Denzin, Norman. 1989. *Interpretive Biography.* Newbury Park, Calif.: Sage.

Devault, Marjorie. 1990. "Talking and Listening from a Woman's Standpoint: Feminist Strategies for Interviewing and Analysis." *Social Problems* 37(1): 96–117.

Duberman, Martin. 1993. *Stonewall.* New York: Dutton.

Duberman, Martin, Martha Vicinus, and George Chauncey, eds. 1989. *Hidden from History: Reclaiming the Lesbian and Gay Past.* New York: New American Library.

DuBois, Barbara. 1983. "Passionate Scholarship: Notes on Values, Knowing, and Method in Feminist Social Science." In *Theories of Women's Studies,* ed. Gloria Bowles and Renate Duelli Klein. London: Routledge & Kegan Paul.

Duggan, Lisa. 1992. "Making It Perfectly Queer." *Socialist Review* 22(1): 11–31.

Ebaugh, Helen Rose Fuchs. 1988. *Becoming an Ex: The Process of Role Exit.* Chicago: University of Chicago Press.

Echols, Alice. 1984. "The Taming of the ID: Feminist Sexual Politics, 1968–83." In *Pleasure and Danger,* ed. Carole Vance. Boston: Routledge.

Echols, Alice. 1989. *Daring to Be BAD: Radical Feminism in America.* Minneapolis: University of Minnesota Press.

Edwards, Rosalind. 1990. "Connecting Method and Epistemology: A White Woman Interviewing Black Women." *Women's Studies International Forum* 13: 477–90.

Ehrenreich, Barbara, and Deirdre English. 1978. *For Her Own Good: Experts' Advice to Women.* Garden City, N.Y.: Anchor.

Ellis, Carolyn. 1991. "Sociological Introspection and Emotional Experience." *Symbolic Interaction* 14(1): 23–50.

English, Deirdre, Amber Hollibaugh, and Gayle Rubin. 1981. "Talking Sex." *Socialist Review* 11(4): 43–62.

Epstein, Steven. 1987. "Gay Politics, Ethnic Identity: The Limits of Social Constructionism." *Socialist Review* 17(3–4): 9–50.

Epstein, Steven. 1991. "Sexuality and Identity: The Contribution of Object Relations Theory to a Constructionist Sociology." *Theory and Society* 20: 825–73.

Erikson, Erik. 1959. "Identity and the Life-cycle." *Psychological Issues* 1: 1–171.

Erikson, Kai. 1964. "Notes on the Sociology of Deviance." In *The Other Side: Perspectives on Deviance,* ed. Howard Becker. New York: Free Press.

Escoffier, Jeffrey. 1985. "Sexual Revolution and the Politics of Gay Identity." *Socialist Review* 15(4–5): 119–53.

Esterberg, Kristin. 1990. "From Illness to Action: Conceptions of Homosexuality in *The Ladder,* 1956–1965." *Journal of Sex Research* 27(1): 65–80.

Evans, Sara. 1979. *Personal Politics: The Roots of Women's Liberation in the Civil Rights Movement and the New Left.* New York: Vintage.

Faderman, Lillian. 1981. *Surpassing the Love of Men: Romantic Friendship and Love between Women from the Renaissance to the Present.* New York: Morrow.

Faderman, Lillian. 1991. *Odd Girls and Twilight Lovers: A History of Lesbian Life in Twentieth-Century America.* New York: Columbia University Press.

Feinberg, Leslie. 1993. *Stone Butch Blues.* Ithaca, N.Y.: Firebrand.

Ferguson, Kathy E. 1993. *The Man Question: Visions of Subjectivity in Feminist Theory.* Berkeley: University of California Press.

Fitzgerald, Frances. 1986. *Cities on a Hill: A Journey through Contemporary American Cultures.* New York: Simon & Schuster.

Flacks, Richard, and Jack Whalen. 1989. *Beyond the Barricades: The Sixties Generation Grows Up.* Philadelphia: Temple University Press.

Foucault, Michel. 1978. *The History of Sexuality,* vol. 1. New York: Random House.

Frankenberg, Ruth. 1993. *White Women, Race Matters.* Minneapolis: University of Minnesota Press.

Freedman, Estelle. 1979. "Separatism as Strategy: Female Institution Building and American Feminism, 1870–1930." *Feminist Studies* 5: 512–29.

Freedman, Estelle. 1987. " 'Uncontrolled Desires': The Response to the Sexual Psychopath, 1920–1960." *Journal of American History* 74: 83–106.

Freedman, Estelle, and John D'Emilio. 1988. *Intimate Matters: A History of Sexuality in America.* New York: Harper & Row.

Freeman, Jo. 1975. *The Politics of Women's Liberation.* New York: Longman.

Freud, Sigmund. [1922] 1949. *Group Psychology and the Analysis of the Ego,* trans. James Strachey. London: Hogarth.

Frye, Marilyn. [1978] 1993. "Some Reflections on Separatism and Power." In *The Lesbian and Gay Studies Reader,* ed. Henry Abelove, Michele Barale, and David Halperin. New York: Routledge.

Fuss, Diana. 1989. *Essentially Speaking: Feminism, Nature, and Difference.* New York: Routledge.

Fuss, Diana, ed. 1991. *Inside/Out: Lesbian Theories, Gay Theories.* New York: Routledge.

Gaar, Gillian. 1992. *She's a Rebel: The History of Women in Rock and Roll.* Seattle: Seal.

Gagnon, J. H., and William Simon. 1973. *Sexual Conduct: The Social Sources of Human Sexuality.* Chicago: Aldine.

Gamson, Joshua. 1995. "Must Identity Movements Self-Destruct? A Queer Dilemma." *Social Problems* 42: 390–407.

Garfinkel, Harold. 1967. "Passing and Managed Achievement of Sex Status in an 'Intersexed' Person, Part 1." In *Studies in Ethnomethodology.* Englewood Cliffs, N.J.: Prentice Hall.

Gay Revolutionary Party Women's Caucus. [1972] 1977. "Realesbians and Politicalesbians." In *Out of the Closets: Voices of Gay Liberation,* ed. Karla Jay and Allen Young. New York: Harcourt Brace Jovanovich.

Gerson, Deborah. 1995. "Speculums and Small Groups: New Visions of Women's Bodies." Department of Sociology, University of California, Berkeley. Photocopy.

Gerson, Judith M., and Kathy Peiss. 1985. "Boundaries, Negotiation, Consciousness: Reconceptualizing Gender Relations." *Social Problems* 32: 317–31.

Giddens, Anthony. 1984. *The Constitution of Society: Outline of the Theory of Structuration.* Berkeley: University of California Press.

Giddens, Anthony. 1991. *Modernity and Self-Identity: Self and Society in the Late Modern Age.* Stanford: Stanford University Press.

Giddens, Anthony. 1992. *The Transformation of Intimacy.* Stanford: Stanford University Press.

Gilligan, Carol. 1982. *In a Different Voice: Psychological Theory and Women's Development.* Cambridge: Harvard University Press.

Gilroy, Paul. 1993. *The Black Atlantic: Modernity and Double Consciousness.* Cambridge: Harvard University Press.

Glaser, Barney, and Anselm Strauss. 1967. *The Discovery of Grounded Theory.* Chicago: Aldine.

Goffman, Erving. 1959. *The Presentation of Self in Everyday Life.* Garden City, N.Y.: Doubleday.

Goffman, Erving. 1961. *Encounters: Two Studies in the Sociology of Interaction.* Indianapolis: Bobbs-Merrill.

Goffman, Erving. 1963. *Stigma: Notes on the Management of Spoiled Identity.* Englewood Cliffs, N.J.: Prentice Hall.

Golden, Carla. 1987. "Diversity and Variability in Women's Sexual Identities." In *Lesbian Psychologies: Explorations and Challenges,* ed. Boston Lesbian Psychologies Collective. Urbana: University of Illinois Press.

Gornick, Vivian. 1978. *Essays in Feminism.* New York: Harper & Row.

Grahn, Judy. 1970. "Lesbians as Bogeywomen." *Women: A Journal of Liberation* 1(4): 36–38.

Gramick, Jeanine. 1984. "Developing a Lesbian Identity." In *Women-*

Identified Women, ed. Trudy Darty and Sandee Potter. Palo Alto: Mayfield.

Grier, Barbara, and Coletta Reid, eds. 1976. *The Lavender Herring: Lesbian Essays from "The Ladder."* Baltimore: Diana.

Habermas, Jurgen. 1979. *Communication and the Evolution of Society.* Boston: Beacon.

Hall, Lisa Kahaleole Chang. 1993. "Bitches in Solitude." In *Sisters, Sexperts, Queers: Beyond the Lesbian Nation,* ed. Arlene Stein. New York: Plume.

Hall, Radclyffe. [1928] 1982. *The Well of Loneliness.* London: Virago.

Hall, Stuart. 1989. "Cultural Identity and Cinematic Representation." *Framework,* no. 36: 65–72.

Haraway, Donna. [1985] 1991. "Manifesto for Cyborgs: Science, Technology, and Socialist Feminism in the 1980s." In *Simians, Cyborgs, and Women.* New York: Routledge.

Harding, Sandra. 1990. "Feminism, Science, and the Anti-Enlightenment Critiques." In *Feminism/Postmodernism,* ed. Linda Nicholson. New York: Routledge.

Hebdige, Dick. 1988. *Subculture: The Meaning of Style.* New York: Routledge.

Herdt, Gilbert. 1992. "Coming Out as a Rite of Passage." In *Gay Culture in America,* ed. Herdt and Andrew Boxer. Boston: Beacon.

Herdt, Gilbert, and Andrew Boxer. 1993. *Children of Horizons: How Gay and Lesbian Youth Are Leading a New Way out of the Closet.* Boston: Beacon.

Herman, Ellen. 1988. "Getting to Serenity: Do Addiction Programs Sap Our Political Vitality?" *Out/Look,* Summer, pp. 10–21.

Herman, Ellen. 1992. "Lesbian Motherhood Meets Popular Psychology in a Dysfunctional Era." Photocopy.

Herrmann, Anne, and Abigail Stewart. 1994. *Theorizing Feminism: Parallel Trends in the Humanities and Social Sciences.* Boulder: Westview.

Hewitt, John P. 1989. *Dilemmas of the American Self.* Philadelphia: Temple University Press.

Hoagland, Sarah L., and Julia Penelope, eds. 1988. *For Lesbians Only: A Separatist Anthology.* London: Onlywomen.

Hochschild, Arlie. 1979. "Emotion Work, Feeling Rules, and Social Structure." *American Journal of Sociology* 85: 551–75.

Hochschild, Arlie. 1983. *The Managed Heart: Commercialization of Human Feeling.* Berkeley: University of California Press.

Hochschild, Arlie, with Anne Machung. 1989. *The Second Shift: Working Parents and the Revolution at Home.* New York: Viking Penguin.

Hochschild, Arlie. 1992. "Gender Strategies in Women's Advice Books."

Paper presented at the annual meeting of the American Sociological Association, Atlanta, Georgia.

Hollibaugh, Amber, and Cherríe Moraga. [1981] 1983. "What We're Rollin' Around in Bed With: Sexual Silences in Feminism: A Conversation toward Ending Them." In *Powers of Desire*, ed. Ann Snitow, Christine, Stansell, and Sharon Thompson. New York: Monthly Review.

hooks, bell. 1984. *Feminist Theory: From Margin to Center.* Boston: South End.

hooks, bell. 1989. *Talking Back: Thinking Feminist, Thinking Black.* Boston: South End.

Hughes, Everett C. 1971. *The Sociological Eye: Selected Papers.* Chicago: Aldine Atherton.

Hull, Gloria, Patricia Bell Scott, and Barbara Smith, eds. 1982. *All the Women Are White, All the Blacks Are Men, But Some of Us Are Brave.* New York: Feminist.

Hutchins, Loraine, and Lani Kaahumanu, eds. 1990. *Bi Any Other Name: Bisexual People Speak Out.* Boston: Alyson.

Irvine, Janice. 1990. *Disorders of Desire: Sex and Gender in American Sexology.* Philadelphia: Temple University Press.

Jay, Karla, and Joanne Glasgow, eds. 1990. *Lesbian Texts and Contexts: Radical Revisions.* New York: New York University Press.

Jay, Karla, and Allen Young, eds. [1972] 1977. *Out of the Closets: Voices of Gay Liberation.* New York: Harcourt Brace Jovanovich.

Jay, Karla, and Allen Young. 1979. *The Gay Report: Lesbians and Gay Men Speak Out about Sexual Experiences and Lifestyles.* New York: Summit Books.

Jeffreys, Sheila. 1994. *The Lesbian Heresy: A Feminist Perspective on the Lesbian Sexual Revolution.* London: Women's Press.

Johnston, Jill. 1973. *Lesbian Nation: The Feminist Solution.* New York: Simon & Schuster.

Johnston, Susan. 1994. "On the Fire Brigade: Why Liberalism Can't Stop the Anti-Gay Campaigns of the Right." *Critical Sociology* 20(4): 3–19.

Kaminer, Wendy. 1992. *I'm Dysfunctional, You're Dysfunctional: The Recovery Movement and Other Self-Help Fashions.* Reading, Mass.: Addison-Wesley.

Kanter, Rosabeth Moss. 1972. *Commitment and Community.* Cambridge: Harvard University Press.

Katz, Jonathan. 1976. *Gay American History: Lesbians and Gay Men in the U.S.A.* New York: Avon.

Katz, Jonathan. 1990. "The Invention of Heterosexuality," *Socialist Review* 20(1): 7–34.

Kennedy, Elizabeth, and Madeline Davis. 1993. *Boots of Leather, Slippers of Gold: The History of a Lesbian Community.* New York: Routledge.

King, Katie. 1994. *Theory in Its Feminist Travels: Conversations in U.S. Women's Movements.* Bloomington: Indiana University Press.

Kinsey, Alfred, Wardell Pomeroy, and Clyde Martin. 1948. *Sexual Behavior in the Human Male.* Philadelphia: Saunders.

Kinsey, Alfred, et al. 1953. *Sexual Behavior in the Human Female.* Philadelphia: Saunders.

Kitzinger, Celia. 1987. *The Social Construction of Lesbianism.* Newbury Park, Calif.: Sage.

Klein, Renate Duelli. 1983. "How to Do What We Want to Do: Thoughts about Feminist Methodology." In *Theories of Women's Studies,* ed. Gloria Bowles and Klein. London: Routledge & Kegan Paul.

Kraus, Natasha Kirsten. 1990. "Butch/Fem Relations of the 1940s and 1950s: Desire Work and the Structuring of a Community." Department of Sociology, University of California, Berkeley. Photocopy.

Krieger, Susan. 1985. "Beyond 'Subjectivity': The Use of the Self in Social Science." *Qualitative Sociology* 8: 309–24.

Krieger, Susan. 1982. "Lesbian Identity and Community: Recent Social Science Literature." *Signs* 8: 91–108.

Krieger, Susan. 1983. *The Mirror Dance: Identity in a Women's Community.* Philadelphia: Temple University Press.

Lacan, Jacques. 1982. *Feminine Sexuality: Jacques Lacan and the "école freudienne,"* ed. Juliet Mitchell and Jacqueline Rose, trans. Jacqueline Rose. New York: Norton.

Lancaster, Roger. 1992. *Life Is Hard: Machismo, Danger, and the Intimacy of Power in Nicaragua.* Berkeley: University of California Press.

Laporte, Rita. 1976. "Sex and Sexuality." In *The Lavender Herring: Lesbian Essays from "The Ladder,"* ed. Barbara Grier and Coletta Reid. Baltimore: Diana.

Lasch, Christopher. 1978. *The Culture of Narcissism: American Life in an Age of Diminishing Expectations.* New York: Norton.

Lash, Scott, and Jonathan Friedman. 1992. *Modernity and Identity.* Oxford: Blackwell.

LeVay, Simon. 1993. *The Sexual Brain.* Cambridge: MIT Press.

Lewin, Ellen. 1993. *Lesbian Mothers: Accounts of Gender in American Culture.* Ithaca, N.Y.: Cornell University Press.

Lewin, M. A. 1976 "Psychological Aspects of Minority Group Membership: The Concepts of Kurt Lewin." In *Contemporary Social Psychology: Representative Readings,* ed. Thomas Blass. Itasca, Ill.: Peacock.

Lindenbaum, Joyce. 1985. "The Shattering of an Illusion: The Problem of

Competition in Lesbian Relationships." *Feminist Studies* 11: 85–103.

Lockard, Denyse. 1985. "The Lesbian Community: An Anthropological Approach." *Journal of Homosexuality* 11(3–4): 83–95.

Lorde, Audre. 1982. *Zami, a New Spelling of My Name.* Watertown, Mass.: Persephone.

Lorde, Audre. 1984. *Sister Outsider.* Trumansburg, N.Y.: Crossing.

Loulan, JoAnn. 1987. *Lesbian Passion.* San Francisco: Spinsters/Aunt Lute.

Lugones, Maria. 1994. "Purity, Impurity, and Separation." *Signs* 19: 458–79.

MacCowan, Lyndall. 1984. Review of "The New Gay Lesbians." *Journal of Homosexuality* 10(3–4): 85–95.

Mann, Bonnie. 1987. "Validation or Liberation? A Critical Look at Therapy and the Women's Movement." *Trivia* 10: 45–62.

Mannheim, Karl. [1928] 1952. "The Problem of Generations." In *Essays on the Sociology of Knowledge,* ed. Paul Kecskemeti. New York: Oxford University Press.

Marcus, George. 1992. "Past, Present, and Emergent Identities: Requirements for Ethnographies of Late Twentieth Century Modernity Worldwide." In *Modernity and Identity,* ed. Scott Lash and Jonathan Friedman. Oxford: Blackwell.

Marias, Julian. 1968. "Generations: The Concept." In *The International Encyclopedia of the Social Sciences.* New York: Macmillan.

Martin, Biddy. 1992. "Sexual Practice and Changing Lesbian Identities." In *Destabilizing Theory: Contemporary Feminist Debates,* ed. Michèle Barrett and Anne Philips. Palo Alto: Stanford University Press.

Martin, Biddy. 1993. "Lesbian Identity and Autobiographical Difference(s)." In *The Lesbian and Gay Studies Reader,* ed. Henry Abelove, Michele Barale, and David Halperin. New York: Routledge.

May, Elaine Tyler. 1988. *Homeward Bound: American Families in the Cold War Era.* New York: Basic Books.

McAdam, Doug. 1994. "Culture and Social Movements." In *New Social Movements: From Ideology to Identity,* ed. Enrique Larana, Hank Johnston, and Joseph Gusfield. Philadelphia: Temple University Press.

McIntosh, Mary. 1968. "The Homosexual Role." *Social Problems* 16: 262–70.

Mead, George Herbert. 1934. *Mind, Self, and Society.* Chicago: University of Chicago Press.

Melucci, Alberto. 1989. *Nomads of the Present: Social Movements and Individual Needs in Contemporary Society.* London: Century Hutchinson.

Miller, Neil. 1989. *In Search of Gay America.* New York: Atlantic Monthly.

Moraga, Cherríe, and Gloria Anzaldúa, eds. 1981. *This Bridge Called My*

Back: Writings by Radical Women of Color. Watertown, Mass.: Persephone.

Morgan, Robin, ed. 1970. *Sisterhood Is Powerful: An Anthology of Writings from Women's Liberation.* New York: Random House.

Morgan, Robin. 1973. "Lesbianism and Feminism: Synonyms or Contradictions?" *Amazon Quarterly* 1(3): 9–20.

Myron, Nancy, and Charlotte Bunch, eds. 1975. *Lesbianism and the Women's Movement.* Baltimore: Diana.

Nagel, Joanne. 1994. "Constructing Ethnicity: Creating and Recreating Ethnic Identity and Culture." *Social Problems* 41(1): 152–76.

Near, Holly. 1990. *Fire in the Rain—Singer in the Storm: An Autobiography.* New York: Morrow.

Nestle, Joan. 1981. "Butch-Fem Relationships: Sexual Courage in the 1950s." *Heresies* 3(4): 21–24.

Nestle, Joan. 1987. *A Restricted Country.* Ithaca, N.Y.: Firebrand.

Nestle, Joan, ed. 1992. *The Persistent Desire: A Femme-Butch Reader.* Boston: Alyson.

Newton, Esther. 1984. "The Mythic Mannish Lesbian: Radclyffe Hall and the New Woman." *Signs* 9: 557–75.

Newton, Esther. 1993. *Cherry Grove, Fire Island: Sixty Years in America's First Gay and Lesbian Town.* Boston: Beacon.

Nichols, Margaret. 1987. "Lesbian Sexuality: Issues and Developing Theory." In *Lesbian Psychologies,* ed. Boston Lesbian Psychologies Collective. Urbana: University of Illinois Press.

Oakley, Ann. 1981. "Interviewing Women: A Contradiction in Terms." In *Doing Feminist Research,* ed. Helen Roberts. Boston: Routledge.

Omi, Michael, and Howard Winant. 1986. *Racial Formation in the United States.* New York: Routledge.

Parker, Richard, and John Gagnon, eds. 1995. *Conceiving Sexuality: Approaches to Sex Research in a Postmodern World.* New York: Routledge.

Patton, Cindy. 1993. "Tremble, Hetero Swine." In *Fear of a Queer Planet: Queer Politics and Social Theory,* ed. Michael Warner. Minneapolis: University of Minnesota Press.

Penelope, Julia. 1988. "The Mystery of Lesbians." In *For Lesbians Only: A Separatist Anthology,* ed. Sarah L. Hoagland and Julia Penelope. London: Onlywomen.

Penelope, Julia, and Susan Wolfe, eds. 1993. *Lesbian Culture: An Anthology.* Freedom, Calif.: Crossing.

Penn, Donna. 1994. "The Sexualized Woman: The Lesbian, the Prostitute, and the Containment of Female Sexuality in Postwar America." In *Not June Cleaver: Women and Gender in Postwar America*, ed. Joanne Meyrowitz. Philadelphia: Temple University Press.

Person, Ethel Spector. 1987. "A Psychodynamic Approach." In *Theories of Human Sexuality*, ed. James Geer and William O'Donohue. New York: Plenum.

Person, Ethel Spector. 1988. *Dreams of Love and Fateful Encounters: The Power of Romantic Passion*. New York: Viking Penguin.

Phelan, Shane. 1989. *Identity Politics: Lesbian Feminism and the Limits of Community*. Philadelphia: Temple University Press.

Phelan, Shane. 1993. "(Be)Coming Out: Lesbian Identity and Politics." *Signs* 18: 765–90.

Phelan, Shane. 1994. *Getting Specific: Postmodern Lesbian Politics*. Minneapolis: University of Minnesota Press.

Phelps, Linda. 1976. "Female Sexual Alienation." In *The Lavender Herring: Lesbian Essays from "The Ladder,"* ed. Barbara Grier and Coletta Reid. Baltimore: Diana.

Plath, David. 1980. *Long Engagements: Maturity in Modern Japan*. Stanford: Stanford University Press.

Plummer, Ken. 1975. *Sexual Stigma: An Interactionist Approach*. London: Routledge & Kegan Paul.

Plummer, Ken. 1981. "Homosexual Categories." In *The Making of the Modern Homosexual*, ed. Plummer. Totowa, N.J.: Barnes & Noble.

Plummer, Ken. 1982. "Symbolic Interactionism and Sexual Conduct: An Emergent Perspective." In *Human Sexual Relations*, ed. Mike Brake. New York: Pantheon.

Plummer, Ken. 1983. *Documents of Life*. London: Allen & Unwin.

Plummer, Ken. 1995. *Telling Sexual Stories: Power, Change, and Social Worlds*. New York: Routledge.

Pollack, Sandra, and Jeanne Vaughn, eds. 1987. *Politics of the Heart: A Lesbian Parenting Anthology*. Ithaca, N.Y.: Firebrand.

Ponse, Barbara. 1978. *Identities in the Lesbian World: The Social Construction of Self*. Westport, Conn.: Greenwood.

Popkin, Ann Hunter. 1979. "The Personal Is Political." In *They Should Have Served That Cup of Coffee*, ed. Dick Cluster. Boston: South End.

Radicalesbians. [1970] 1988. "The Woman Identified Woman." In *For Lesbians Only: A Separatist Anthology*, ed. Sarah Hoagland and Julia Penelope. London: Onlywomen.

Raymond, Janice. 1989. "Putting the Politics Back into Lesbianism," *Women's Studies International Forum* 12: 149–56.

Reback, Cathy, and JoAnn Loulan. 1988. "Out of the Closet and into Her

Arms: Constructions of Romantic Love for the Novice Lesbian." Paper presented at the annual meeting of the American Sociological Association, Atlanta, Georgia.

Reinharz, Shulamith. 1983. "Experiential Analysis: A Contribution to Feminist Research." In *Theories of Women's Studies,* ed. Gloria Bowles and Renate Duelli Klein. London: Routledge & Kegan Paul.

Ribbens, Jane. 1989. "Interviewing—An 'Unnatural Situation'?" *Women's Studies International Forum* 12: 579–92.

Rich, Adrienne. 1976. *Of Woman Born: Motherhood as Experience and Institution.* New York: Norton.

Rich, Adrienne. 1980. "Compulsory Heterosexuality and Lesbian Existence." *Signs* 5: 631–61.

Rich, Adrienne. 1986. "Notes toward a Politics of Location." In *Blood, Bread, and Poetry: Selected Prose, 1979–1985.* New York: Norton.

Rich, Ruby. 1986. "Feminism and Sexuality in the 1980s." *Feminist Studies* 12: 525–61.

Richardson, Diane. 1984. "The Dilemma of Essentiality in Homosexual Theory." *Journal of Homosexuality* 9(2–3): 79–89.

Riessman, Catherine Kohler. 1987. "When Gender Is Not Enough: Women Interviewing Women." *Gender and Society* 1(2): 172–207.

Risman, Barbara, and Pepper Schwartz. 1988. "Sociological Research on Male and Female Homosexuality." *Annual Review of Sociology* 14: 125–47.

Robinson, Paul. 1976. *The Modernization of Sex.* New York: Harper & Row.

Rossi, Alice. 1980. "Life Span Theory and Women's Times." *Signs* 6: 4–32.

Rothblum, Esther, and Kathleen Brehony. 1993. *Boston Marriages: Romantic But Asexual Relationships among Contemporary Lesbians.* Amherst: University of Massachusetts Press.

Rubin, Gayle. 1975. "The Traffic in Women: Notes on the 'Political Economy' of Sex." In *Toward an Anthropology of Women,* ed. Rayna Reiter. New York: Monthly Review.

Rubin, Gayle. 1984. "Thinking Sex: Notes for a Radical Theory of the Politics of Sexuality." In *Pleasure and Danger: Exploring Female Sexuality,* ed. Carole Vance. Boston: Routledge.

Rubin, Gayle. 1992. "Of Catamites and Kings: Reflections on Butch, Gender, and Boundaries." In *The Persistent Desire: A Femme-Butch Reader,* ed. Joan Nestle. Boston: Alyson.

Rupp, Leila. 1989. " 'Imagine My Surprise': Women's Relationships in Mid-Twentieth Century America." In *Hidden from History: Reclaiming the Lesbian and Gay Past,* ed. Martin Duberman, Martha Vicinus, and George Chauncey. New York: New American Library.

Rust, Paula. 1993. "Coming Out in an Age of Social Constructionism," *Gender and Society* 7(1): 50–77.

Sahli, Nancy. 1979. "Smashing: Women's Relationships before the Fall." *Chrysalis* 8: 17–27.

Schafer, Roy. 1973. "Concepts of the Self and Identity and the Experience of Separation-Individuation in Adolescence." *Psychoanalytic Quarterly* 42: 42–59.

Schneider, Beth. 1988. "Political Generations and the Contemporary Women's Movement." *Sociological Inquiry* 58(1): 4–21.

Schneider, Beth, and Nancy Stoller, eds. 1995. *Women Resisting AIDS: Feminist Strategies of Empowerment.* Philadelphia: Temple University Press.

Schulman, Sarah. 1990. *People in Trouble.* New York: Dutton.

Scott, Joan. 1989. *Gender and the Politics of History.* New York: Columbia University Press.

Sedgwick, Eve Kosofsky. 1990. *Epistemology of the Closet.* Berkeley: University of California Press.

Segal, Lynne. 1983. "Sensual Uncertainty or Why the Clitoris Is Not Enough." In *Sex and Love,* ed. Sue Cartledge and Joanna Ryan. London: Women's Press.

Segal, Lynne. 1994. *Straight Sex: Rethinking the Politics of Pleasure.* Berkeley: University of California Press.

Seidman, Steven. 1993. "Identity and Politics in a Postmodern Gay Culture." In *Fear of a Queer Planet: Queer Politics and Social Theory,* ed. Michael Warner. Minneapolis: University of Minnesota Press.

Shelley, Martha. [1969] 1970. "Notes of a Radical Lesbian." In *Sisterhood Is Powerful: An Anthology of Writings from Women's Liberation,* ed. Robin Morgan. New York: Random House.

Simon, William, and John Gagnon. 1967. "Femininity in the Lesbian Community." *Social Problems* 15: 212–21.

Simon, William, and John Gagnon. 1987. "A Sexual Scripts Approach." In *Theories of Human Sexuality,* ed. James Geer and William O'Donahue. New York: Plenum.

Simonds, Wendy. 1992. *Women and Self-Help Culture: Reading between the Lines.* New Brunswick: Rutgers University Press.

Smith, Barbara, ed. 1983. *Home Girls: A Black Feminist Anthology.* New York: Kitchen Table/Women of Color.

Smith-Rosenberg, Carroll. 1975. "The Female World of Love and Ritual." *Signs* 1: 1–29.

Snitow, Ann. [1989] 1990. "Pages from a Gender Diary: Basic Divisions in

Feminism." In *Conflicts in Feminism,* ed. Marianne Hirsch and Evelyn Fox Keller. New York: Routledge.

Snitow, Ann, Christine Stansell, and Sharon Thompson, eds. 1983. *Powers of Desire: The Politics of Sexuality.* New York: Monthly Review.

Snow, David, and Leon Anderson. 1987. "Identity Work among the Homeless." *American Journal of Sociology* 92: 1336–71.

Snow, David, and Robert Benford. 1988. "Ideology, Frame Resonance, and Participant Mobilization." In *From Structure to Action,* ed. Bert Klandermans, Hanspeter Kriesi, and Sidney Tarrow. Vol. 1 of *International Social Movement Research.* Greenwich, Conn.: JAI Press.

Stacey, Judith. 1990. *Brave New Families.* New York: Basic Books.

Stanley, Julia Penelope, and Susan J. Wolfe. 1980. *The Coming Out Stories.* Watertown, Mass.: Persephone.

Stein, Arlene. 1989. "Three Models of Sexuality: Drives, Identities, and Practices." *Sociological Theory* 7(1): 1–13.

Stein, Arlene. 1992a. "All Dressed Up, But No Place to Go? Style Wars and the New Lesbianism." In *The Persistent Desire: A Femme-Butch Reader,* ed. Joan Nestle. Boston: Alyson.

Stein, Arlene. 1992b. "Sisters and Queers: The Decentering of Lesbian Feminism." *Socialist Review* 22(1): 33–55.

Stein, Arlene, ed. 1993a. *Sisters, Sexperts, Queers: Beyond the Lesbian Nation.* New York: Plume.

Stein, Arlene. 1993b. "The Year of the Lustful Lesbian." In *Sisters, Sexperts, Queers: Beyond the Lesbian Nation,* ed. Stein. New York: Plume.

Stein, Arlene. 1994. "Crossover Dreams: Lesbians and Popular Music since the 1970s." In *The Good, the Bad, and the Gorgeous: Popular Culture's Romance with Lesbianism,* ed. Diane Hamer and Belinda Budge. London: Pandora.

Stein, Arlene, and Ken Plummer. 1994. "I Can't Even Think Straight: Queer Theory and the Missing Sexual Revolution in Sociology." *Sociological Theory* 12(2): 178–87.

Stevens, Patricia E., and Joanne M. Hall. 1991. "A Critical Historical Analysis of the Medical Construction of Lesbianism." *International Journal of Health Services* 21: 291–307.

Stewart, Abigail J. 1994. "The Women's Movement and Women's Lives." In *Exploring Identity and Gender,* ed. Amia Lieblich and Ruthellen Josselson. Vol. 2 of *The Narrative Study of Lives.* Thousand Oaks, Calif.: Sage.

Stryker, Sheldon. 1987. "Identity Theory: Developments and Extensions." In *Self and Identity: Psychosocial Perspectives,* ed. Krysia Yardley and Terry Honess. Chichester: Wiley.

Swidler, Ann. 1986. "Culture in Action: Symbols and Strategies." *American Sociological Review* 51: 273–86.

Taylor, Verta, and Leila Rupp. 1993. "Women's Culture and Lesbian Feminist Activism: A Reconsideration of Cultural Feminism." *Signs* 19: 32–61.

Taylor, Verta, and Nancy Whittier. 1992. "Collective Identity in Social Movement Communities: Lesbian Feminist Mobilization." *Frontiers of Social Movement Theory*, ed. Aldon Morris and Carol Mueller. New Haven: Yale University Press.

Terry, Jennifer. 1991. "Theorizing Deviant Historiography." *differences* 1(2): 55–74.

Toder, Nancy. 1978. "Sexual Problems of Lesbians." In *Our Right to Love*, ed. Ginny Vida. Englewood Cliffs, N.J.: Prentice Hall.

Tolman, Deborah L. 1991. "Adolescent Girls, Women, and Sexuality: Discerning Dilemmas of Desire," *Women & Therapy* 11(3–4): 55–69.

Turner, Ralph. 1970. *Family Interaction*. New York: Wiley.

Turner, Victor. 1969. *The Ritual Process*. Chicago: Aldine.

Udis-Kessler, Amanda. 1990. "Culture and Community: Thoughts on Lesbian-Bisexual Relations." Department of Sociology, Boston College. Photocopy.

Vance, Brenda, and Vicki Green. 1984. "Lesbian Identities: An Examination of Sexual Behavior and Sex Role Attribution as Related to Age of Initial Same-Sex Sexual Encounter." *Psychology of Women Quarterly* 8(3): 293–307.

Vance, Carole, ed. 1984. *Pleasure and Danger: Exploring Female Sexuality*. Boston: Routledge.

Vance, Carole. 1989. "Social Construction Theory: Problems in the History of Sexuality." In *Homosexuality, Which Homosexuality? Essays from the International Scientific Conference on Gay and Lesbian Studies*, ed. Dennis Altman et al. London: GMP Publishing.

Varenne, Herve. 1977. *Americans Together*. New York: Teachers College Press.

Vargo, Sue. 1987. "The Effects of Women's Socialization on Lesbian Couples." In *Lesbian Psychologies: Explorations and Challenges*, ed. Boston Lesbian Psychologies Collective. Urbana: University of Illinois.

Vicinus, Martha. 1989. "Distance and Desire: English Boarding School Friendships, 1870–1920." In *Hidden from History: Reclaiming the Lesbian and Gay Past*, ed. Martin Duberman, Vicinus, and George Chauncey. 1989. New York: New American Library.

Vida, Ginny, ed. 1978. *Our Right to Love*. Englewood Cliffs, N.J.: Prentice Hall.

Warner, Michael. 1991. "Fear of a Queer Planet." *Social Text* 29: 3–17.

Warner, Michael, ed. 1993. *Fear of a Queer Planet: Queer Politics and Social Theory.* Minneapolis: University of Minnesota Press.

Warren, Carol. 1974. *Identity and Community in a Gay World.* New York: Wiley.

Webber, Jonathan, ed. 1994. *Jewish Identities in the New Europe.* London: Littman Library of Jewish Civilization.

Weeks, Jeffrey. 1985. *Sexuality and Its Discontents.* London: Routledge.

Weigert, Andrew, J. Smith Teitge, and Dennis W. Teitge. 1986. *Society and Identity: Toward a Sociological Psychology.* New York: Cambridge University Press.

Weise, Elizabeth Reba, ed. 1992. *Closer to Home.* Seattle: Seal.

Weitz, Rose. 1984. "From Accommodation to Rebellion: The Politicization of Lesbianism." In *Women-Identified Women,* ed. Trudy Darty and Sandee Potter. Palo Alto: Mayfield.

Weston, Kath. 1991. *Families We Choose: Lesbians, Gays, Kinship.* New York: Columbia University Press.

Weston, Kath. 1993a. "Do Clothes Make the Woman?: Gender, Performance Theory, and Lesbian Eroticism." *Genders,* no. 17: 1–21.

Weston, Kath. 1993b. "Lesbian/Gay Studies in the House of Anthropology." *Annual Review of Anthropology* 22: 339–67.

Whisman, Vera. 1996. *Queer by Choice: Lesbians, Gay Men, and the Politics of Identity.* New York: Routledge.

Wilkinson, Sue, and Celia Kitzinger, eds. 1993. *Heterosexuality: A Feminism and Psychology Reader.* Newbury Park, Calif.: Sage.

Williams, Raymond. [1980] 1991. "Base and Superstructure in Marxist Cultural Theory." In *Rethinking Popular Culture: Contemporary Perspectives in Cultural Studies,* ed. Chandra Mukerji and Michael Schudson. Berkeley: University of California Press.

Wittman, Carl. [1970] 1972. "Refugees from America: A Gay Manifesto." In *The Homosexual Dialectic,* ed. Joseph McCaffrey. Englewood Cliffs, N.J.: Prentice Hall.

Wolf, Deborah Goleman. 1980. *The Lesbian Community.* Berkeley: University of California Press.

Wolfe, Alan. 1991. "Introduction: Change from the Bottom Up." In *America at Century's End,* ed. Wolfe. Berkeley: University of California Press.

Wrong, Dennis. 1961. "The Oversocialized Conception of Man in Modern Sociology." *American Sociological Review* 26: 183–93.

Young, Iris. 1990. *Throwing Like a Girl and Other Essays in Feminist Philosophy and Social Theory.* Bloomington: Indiana University Press.

Young, Iris. 1990. "The Ideal of Community and the Politics of Difference."

In *Feminism/Postmodernism,* ed. Linda Nicholson. New York: Routledge.

Zemsky, Beth. 1991. "Coming Out against All Odds: Resistance in the Life of a Young Lesbian." *Women & Therapy* 11(3–4): 185–200.

Zimmerman, Bonnie. 1990. *The Safe Sea of Women: Lesbian Fiction, 1969–1989.* Boston: Beacon.

Index

women, 16; of color, 3, 6, 7; heterosexual,
    17–18, 104; "mannish," 25, 47; passionate
    friendships between, 26, 39, 58, 94;
    woman-identified, 41; working-class, 6, 7
Women against Violence in Pornography,
    124
Women's Liberation, 35, 36, 42
women's music, 132–33, 188

work, 126, 135–36, 137, 138. *See also* manual
    labor; professionals
working class: and lesbian culture, 16; lesbi-
    ans in, 17, 29, 30, 41, 57–60, 78–79, 82,
    101, 103–4, 124, 136; women in, 6, 7
World War II, 14, 27

Zimmerman, Bonnie, 91, 201

Compositor:	Maple-Vail Book Mfg. Group
Text:	11/13.5 Caledonia
Display:	Caledonia
Printer:	Maple-Vail Book Mfg. Group
Binder:	Maple-Vail Book Mfg. Group